Life in Mexico under
Santa Anna, 1822–1855

Life in Mexico
under Santa Anna,
1822–1855

By Ruth R. Olivera and Liliane Crété

University of Oklahoma Press : Norman and London

By Ruth R. Olivera

A Bibliography of Latin American Theses and Dissertations, Tulane University, 1912–1978 (New Orleans, 1979)
Life in Mexico under Santa Anna, 1822–1855 (Norman, 1991)

By Liliane Crété

La Vie quotidienne en Louisiana, 1815–1830 (Paris, 1978, 1990)
La Vie quotidienne à La Rochelle au temps du grand siège, 1627–1628 (Paris, 1987)
La Vie quotidienne en Californie au temps de la ruée vers l'or (Paris, 1982)
Coligny (Paris, 1985)
La Traité des nègres sous l'Ancien Régime (Paris, 1989)
Daily Life in Louisiana, 1815–1830 trans. Patrick Gregory (Baton Rouge, La., 1981)
La Femme au temps de Scarlett: Les Américaines au 19e siécle (Paris, 1990)
Life in Mexico under Santa Anna, 1822–1855 (Norman, 1991)

LC: 90-50693; ISBN: 0-8061-2320-6.

The paper in this book meets the guidelines for permanence and durability of the committee on Production Guidelines for Book Longevity of the Council on Library Resources, Inc.♾

CONTENTS

ILLUSTRATIONS

Except for the portrait of Don Antonio Eugenio Gordoa from Federico Sescosse, all illustrations are courtesy of the Latin American Library, Tulane University.

MAPS

PREFACE

The genesis of this book has been our desire to present a picture of daily life in Mexico at the time of Santa Anna.

The reasons for our interest in Santa Anna's time are two-fold. First was our interest in the period itself, which spanned the beginning of the republic and many military *pronunciamientos* or rebellions that leave an imprint on the history of Mexico to this day. The years from 1822 to 1855 mark the rise and fall of one man, Antonio López de Santa Anna, who was the product and the personification of the period, a figure who returned again and again to power, in one guise or another, rising renewed from his ashes like the mythical Phoenix of the Arabian desert. Our second reason was the abundance of material documenting those calamitous years. We have had access to many books written by contemporary chroniclers, as well as the valuable papers of the wealthy Mexican Gordoa family.

It was a time of unrest: economic stagnation, political chaos, profiteering, lack of production, industrial indolence, maladministration, revolutions, and wars. The new republic became a staging ground for the rebellion of generals. Fifty-six different governments came and went between 1821 and 1861, and Santa Anna became president of Mexico on eleven occasions between 1830 and 1855. Four wars were fought: the Texas conflict, the so-called "Pastry War" against the French, the Mexican-American War, and the beginning of the Caste War in Yucatán.

Meanwhile, in the northern part of the country people faced constant Indian raids.

Mexico was—and still is—a multifaceted world. We have endeavored to study aspects of both urban and rural society, Mexican habits, customs, and ways of living, working, playing, and dying. The republic was a mixture of heterogeneous races geographically isolated by large expanses of land. The population comprised the educated Creole minority, who were totally unprepared for self-government and wanted to enjoy independence while keeping all their advantages from the past; a native majority, unacculturated, passive, and indifferent; and in between, a population of mestizos who were passionate, aggressive, and eager to climb the social ladder.

Scholars will probably deplore the fact that we have dedicated more time to examining contemporary chronicles, travelers' accounts, and correspondence than to analyzing marriage contracts, succession sales, statistics, and sundry court and council records. Our aim has been to resurrect the social, religious, cultural, and political events as they were perceived at the time, in a vivid, colorful way so that the reader may have the feeling of zooming in on a real event, in a real place, at a real time. We have sought to assemble carefully the psychological profiles of the various populations and to enter genuinely into their mental and emotional values. The papers of the Gordoa family in the Latin American Library of Tulane University have been a resource for many details in the lives of the wealthy Creole class. Their far-flung interests, recorded in personal letters, business correspondence, hacienda inventories, and mining records, reflect diverse elements of Mexican life. And we have devoted as much attention to the Indians as to the Creoles.

Contradictions are a part of life, and probably no other country shows more crosscurrents than Mexico: extravagance and splendor alongside disaster and wretchedness, cruelty and brigandage alongside chivalry and gallantry, buffoonery alongside tragedy. The behavior of the Mexicans inspires a discussion of their antecedents, and therefore we often have gone back to colonial times, and even to pre-Hispanic times, to give a clearer picture of nineteenth-century Mexico. Indeed, the past inevitably affects the present. Although the Indians were seldom more than silent witnesses to the Mexican drama, their social and spiritual influence was felt, not only because their blood mixed with that of the whites but also by their very presence. The face of Mexico, like that of the Virgin of Guadalupe, patroness of the whole nation, is dark.

The Mexican setting is of prime importance to comprehend the people. Consequently, the book begins with a geographical description of Mexico, then traces briefly the political and economic developments of the period before examining minutely the many particular aspects of Mexican society. We have chosen to study daily life in Mexico proper, and not to include the northernmost provinces of Texas, Alta California, and New Mexico.

Unless otherwise noted, all translations from Spanish or French into English are those of the authors.

RUTH R. OLIVERA

New Orleans, Louisiana

LILIANE CRÉTÉ

Paris, France

ACKNOWLEDGMENTS

We wish to express our deep appreciation to those people in the United States, Mexico, and France who have helped bring this work to completion by their steadfast encouragement and valuable assistance. For carefully and patiently reading the manuscript our grateful thanks go to Dr. Guillermo Náñez, Helen Burkes, Deborah Deaton, Becky Olivera, and especially to Mary Le Blanc and Professor Otto Olivera, who was always an available authority when needed. His never-failing interest and support have been indispensable.

Sincere thanks too go to Martha Robertson, Pamela Murray, and Dr. Thomas Niehaus of the Latin American Library of Tulane University. To Dr. Xavier Noguez, Donald Caldwell, Robert Ryal Miller, and the staff of the Bibliothèque Nationale of Paris we are grateful as well.

Credit for the initial inspiration for the book can be traced to Sr. Federico Sescosse of Zacatecas, Mexico, who so graciously supplied important data about the Gordoa family, to his sister-in-law María Herlinda Pesquera de Sánchez of Guadalajara, who provided even more details, and most of all to Elizabeth Ramos de la Torre of Zacatecas, who entered into the spirit of adventure with us in setting out to find the modern-day hacienda Maguey.

Life in Mexico under
Santa Anna, 1822–1855

INTRODUCTION

Mountains physically dominate Mexico. Common to plateaus, valleys, deserts, and coasts is a horizon of mountain ranges. The Sierra Madre Occidental, at altitudes of 10,000 to 12,000 feet, forms a formidable barrier along the Pacific Ocean, pierced only in three or four places. This fortress is prolonged on the southeast by the Sierra Madre del Sur, which comes down to the edge of the Atlantic Ocean. The Eastern Sierra, the Sierra Madre Oriental, runs for a thousand miles, rising on the south to a green wall 9,000 feet high. Between the two sierras lies the Plateau of Mexico, at an altitude of 7,000 to 8,000 feet, which covers about two-thirds of the total area of the country. On this Mesa del Norte, which extends from the United States border to 22° north (the latitude of San Luis Potosí), vast areas of the country are among the driest in the world. In the early nineteenth century whole plains were carpeted with grass, but, in the words of a nineteenth-century traveler, John Russell Bartlett, they were "entirely destitute even of the smallest bushes. An occasional cactus or yucca rose now and then to break the monotony of the broad plains. Sometimes they appeared in groups, and at distance resembled men on horse-back or on foot" (Bartlett [1854] 1965, 2:469).

Wherever water could be found, the Spanish had settled. Towns were embosomed among gardens and orchards, or surrounded by vineyards: large haciendas were buried in groves of trees; fields of maize, wheat, and maguey extended far and wide over the plains; immense herds of

3

cattle, sheep, and horses roamed the steppelands. Rich mines also were exploited in the mountains near Chihuahua, Parral, San Luis Potosí, Aguascalientes, Fresnillo, Zacatecas, and Catorce.

Farther south lies the Mesa Central, higher, more violently uplifted, more humid and wooded than its northern counterpart. This is the country of the ancient Mexicans, the Aztecs. There, encompassed by a towering rampart of porphyritic rock, is situated the Valley of Mexico. A line of volcanoes of incomparable beauty stretches across the altiplano. Nineteenth-century visitors left gorgeous word pictures of the impressions made on their senses by these volcanoes. Bayard Taylor, a journalist who traveled through Mexico on his way back to New York from California in 1850, wrote: "No peak among mountains can be more sublime than Orizaba. Rising from the level of the sea and the perpetual summer of the tropics with an unbroken line to the height of eighteen thousand feet, it stands single above the other ranges, with its spotless crown of snow" (Taylor [1850] 1949, 324).

South of the Mesa Central, a rough, broken, mountainous country extends to the Isthmus of Tehuantepec. The highlands of Oaxaca are covered with dense pine and oak forests; the valley is broad and beautiful. Here was the land of the Mixtecs and Zapotec Indians. The former lived on the west, the latter on the east. The Isthmus of Tehuantepec, a bottleneck of jungle and arid brush that separates the country of Oaxaca from the mountains and plains of Chiapas, is likewise populated by Zapotec Indians. The Pacific lowlands are arid, desperately lacking in rainfall. On the Atlantic side, on the contrary, it rains constantly, and broad rivers meander across the low plains. The southern end of the isthmus contains low ranges inland from the coastal area, which is fringed with lagoons.

Quite different is Chiapas. Geographically, historically, and culturally, it belongs to Guatemala. Extinct volcanoes carpeted with dense forests dominate the rough limestone plateau, which drops off northward into the high coastal plain along the Gulf of Mexico. In the nineteenth century the country had not changed much since the conquest. It remained a wilderness populated by Maya tribes who lived in small hamlets on the slopes of the high mountains. John L. Stephens described a view of the Rio Lagartero as "a scene of wild and surpassing beauty with banks shaded by some of the noblest trees of the tropical forests, water as clear as crystal, and fish a foot long" (Stephens [1841] 1969, 2:243). Although a *camino real* wound its way southward to Guatemala, the difficulty of the terrain made communication northward with the peninsula of Yucatán almost impossible. A great plain, broken by a range of hills, the Puuc, comprises northern Yucatán. On the east and the south, the bush gives way to dry forests, and then to a rain forest. The eastern forests, as well as the region south of the Puuc, were virtually uninhabited in the nineteenth century. The bulk of the population clustered in the northwest, where the economy was based on the cultivation of henequen and sugarcane, combined with cattle raising. Water was a major problem. A dependable supply of water could be found only in caves or where the roof of a cave had collapsed to form a *cenote*, or well, around which the people settled. The peninsula of Yucatán was a world unto itself, an isolated state where the whites and the Ladinos[1] considered themselves Yucatecans rather than Mexicans, and where the Mayas preserved the social structure, agricultural methods, and religion of their ancestors. In spite of its separatist tendencies, Yucatán entered into the Mexican confederation as one of the states of the new republic, but it was not long before a revolt would break out against the government of Mexico.

Mexico, at the time of Santa Anna, was no more a political entity than a geographical one.

THE TRIALS OF THE YOUNG NATION

It is not easy to follow the tangled course of events after the old authoritarian system of Spain collapsed in 1821 leaving no group of citizens trained to assume the responsibility of government. The Mexicans tried every form of government: an empire with a self-made emperor, a federal republic, a centralist republic, a dictatorship. The results were always disastrous. Two institutions, in particular, which were legacies of Spanish rule, made democracy impossible: the church and the army. The situation required a national consensus, but personal ambition prevailed among the leaders. The dominant features in the history of early Mexico were the rebellions of generals who pronounced themselves against the government and proclaimed a "plan" denouncing existing abuses and promising reforms. As historian Robert Ryal Miller said: "After independence, the members of the educated elite in Mexico soon were divided into liberal and conservative camps. For the next half-

---

[1] Ladinos were persons of Spanish or mestizo descent who considered themselves white and lived, dressed, and thought according to a European heritage.

century, control of the government changed back and forth between representatives of these factions. Upon taking power, the next group not only changed key government personnel, it also rewrote laws and even the constitution to reflect its philosophy" (Miller 1985, 203).

The liberals drew support from the middle-class intellectuals, journalists, teachers, lawyers, and small entrepreneurs, who considered themselves heirs to the ideals of the French and American revolutions and favored federalism, freedom of the press, and public education. The conservatives supported a centralized state, preservation of the *fueros* or privileges, and the monopoly of the Roman Catholic Church. They found their strength among the church hierarchy, the army officers, the *hacendados* (rural landlords), mine owners, and great merchants. This ideological cleavage between liberals and conservatives also manifested itself in a unique manner. Both political factions identified themselves with a branch of freemasonry: conservatives attached themselves to the Scottish Rite masons, the Escoceses, and liberals to the York Rite, or Yorkinos (Meyer and Sherman [1979] 1987, 317).

The leading actor in this tragicomedy was Antonio López de Santa Anna Pérez de Lebrón. Born in Jalapa on February 21, 1794, to a family of indifferent social standing, he had a gift for concocting plans and instigating *pronunciamientos* that remains unmatched to this day. A talented commander, revered as a hero for his battle victories, and a clever politician who was able to shift his allegiance when public opinion changed, he was in turn the champion of the liberals, the defender of the conservatives, and the promoter of dictatorship. True were the words of his contemporary, historian Lucas Alamán, when he wrote that the history of Mexico in that period "could rightly be called the history of the revolutions of Santa Ana" (Alamán [1849–52] 1942, 5:637).

Santa Anna at age fourteen was an infantry cadet fighting for the Spanish against the insurgents. He first appeared on the political scene at Veracruz in 1821 when he switched his allegiance away from Spain and pronounced for "El Libertador," Agustín de Iturbide. Iturbide, a staunch conservative, had published a plan for independence, the Plan of Iguala, after ultraliberal forces in Spain threatened the privileges of the clergy and the military. As Santa Anna said in his autobiography, "[When] the *Plan de Iguala* was made public, by proclamation of Colonel Agustín Iturbide, on February 24, 1821, I hurried to sponsor it, wishing to contribute my own little grain of sand to our great political rebirth" (Crawford 1967, 9).

On May 19, 1822, Iturbide was named emperor of Mexico amidst cheers and flowers. But the self-made emperor indulged in festivities and extravaganzas. The treasury was empty; the government subsisted on forced loans and confiscations from the Spaniards. Iturbide was soon driven to desperate expedients. He began to print paper money. Prices rose. The rich were disgusted, the poor indignant, and the army unpaid. Within ten months the empire collapsed. The rebellion against Iturbide took a definite form in December, 1822, when Santa Anna, from Veracruz, pronounced against the empire and proclaimed a republic, starting a stampede. Province after province fell away. Iturbide abdicated and embarked with his family for exile in Europe. But badly advised by friends, he returned to Mexico the next summer and was arrested in Tamaulipas, where the state congress had him shot on July 19, 1824.

After the fall of the First Empire, a three-man junta governed Mexico provisionally. A new congress met on November 27, 1823, and a constitution was promulgated the following October. In it the United Mexican States were divided into nineteen states and five territories (Miller 1985, 202). The Constitution of 1824 was a close copy of that of the United States, with the omission of religious tolerance and trial by jury. In addition, it gave the president of the republic dictatorial powers in time of emergency and guaranteed to members of the clergy and the military their special *fueros* (Miller 1985, 202; Meyer and Sherman [1979] 1987, 316). The state legislatures chose as president Guadalupe Victoria, a federalist, and as vice-president Nicolás Bravo, a centralist. Both were better soldiers than statesmen (González 1981, 110).

The young republic was marked by political instability, financial problems, and humiliations in dealing with foreign powers. Eleven years of guerrilla warfare with Spain had left the economy of Mexico in ruins, and as the economic pressure mounted, the centralist-federalist struggle intensified. By 1827 the two political factions were at loggerheads, and the first breach in the constitution occurred. Bravo organized a rebellion which drew upon the Scottish Rite masons for support. The movement was ultimately suppressed by the old mestizo insurgent Vicente Guerrero, grand master of the Yorkinos. The precedent of the military coup was now set in the young nation.

A year later, another coup shook the country. It was organized this time by the liberals, who opposed presidential election results which showed that Manuel Gómez Pedraza, an accomplished scholar, had carried ten of the nineteen state legislatures. The liberals pronounced for Vicente Guerrero and issued an appeal to arms. Santa Anna heard the

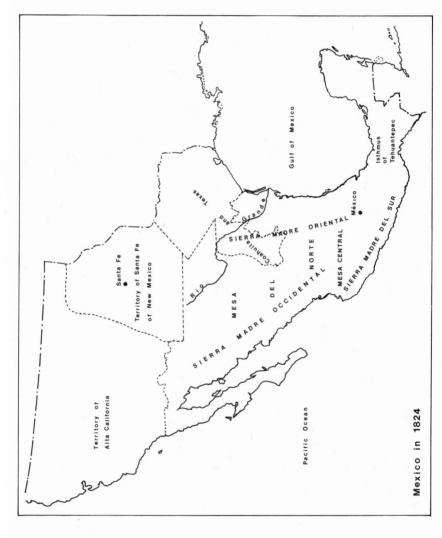

Mexico in 1824

Mexico in 1824. Map by Don Caldwell

call from Veracruz. He too pronounced himself against the election of Gómez Pedraza. As he himself explained it, he "adhered to the pleadings of the people that Vicente Guerrero be declared constitutional President of the republic" (Crawford 1967, 20). There was fighting and looting in the capital. Gómez Pedraza resigned and went into exile. As a reward for the role he played in the coup, Santa Anna was promoted to a division generalship, the highest rank in the army (Meyer and Sherman [1979] 1987, 320). Guerrero was installed as president. The new administration abolished slavery and enforced the decree of March, 1829, expelling almost all remaining Spaniards from Mexico (Meyer and Sherman [1979] 1987, 320).

The expulsion of the Spaniards and reports of internal dissension prompted Spain, which had never recognized Mexican independence, to send a small expedition to Mexico to reconquer her former colony. In July, 1829, three thousand soldiers from Cuba landed at Tampico. Guerrero placed the military operation in the hands of Santa Anna. The new general rushed to Tampico to beat off the Spaniards, who had already been defeated by heat and yellow fever. After a short but bloody action, the Spanish troops surrendered, and Santa Anna began to be known throughout Mexico as the "Savior of the Country," the "Victor of Tampico." The national congress later voted him the title of "Benefactor of the Fatherland" (Meyer and Sherman [1979] 1987, 321). Santa Anna himself retired to his hacienda, Manga de Clavo, in Veracruz, "pleading to heaven," he said, "that I would not have to answer another call to arms" (Crawford 1967, 25).

But more troubles were ahead. Vice-president Anastasio Bustamante pronounced against Guerrero, and early in 1830 he took over the president's office, while congress disqualified the president (Miller 1985, 206). Bustamante's administration improved government finances but ruled Mexico through terror, imprisonment, and assassination. One victim of the firing squad was Guerrero, who was treacherously seized by an Italian sea captain, who sold him for 50,000 pesos in gold (Simpson [1941] 1966, 238). The execution of the old *caudillo* angered many Mexicans and triggered another military revolt. Santa Anna was one of the first to pronounce against Bustamante. The news of the rebellion aroused the northern provinces as well as Acapulco. Santa Anna was joined by many federalists, and Bustamante was ousted in September, 1832. Gómez Pedraza was brought back from exile, and on January 3, 1833, installed as provisional president. In his inaugural address he referred to Santa Anna as "that singular and illustrious military genius of the people" (Callcott 1936, 95). On April 1, 1833, Santa Anna was elected president of the republic. The vice-president was Valentín Gómez Farías, an ardent liberal (Meyer and Sherman [1979] 1987, 325). When the day of his inauguration arrived, Santa Anna pleaded sickness and again retired to his extensive hacienda in the state of Veracruz. He left the executive power to Gómez Farías, probably so that his vice-president would make the badly needed reforms that were bound to prompt discontent among the conservatives and erode his popularity (Priestley [1923] 1926, 269).

THE ERA OF SANTA ANNA

Gómez Farías indeed cleaned house from attic to basement. He sponsored many good measures, though his reforms displeased the clergy and the army. Colonels and generals began to rebel, raising the cry of "Religion y fueros." Colonel Anthony Butler, the United States chargé d'affaires in Mexico between 1830 and 1836, wrote on June 3, 1833, that "three gritos or pro-nunciamentos have taken place within the last week" (United States Legation in Mexico Papers, Latin American Library, Tulane University, New Orleans).

During the second half of 1833, Santa Anna and Valentín Gómez Farías alternated in control of the executive power. Then, in 1834, Santa Anna ousted Gómez Farías, dissolved congress, discharged all officials suspected of liberalism, repealed the anticlerical legislation of his predecessor—"careless reforms," he called them (Crawford 1967, 49)—and repressed rebellions with merciless brutality. When he had completely undone Gómez Farías's work, he called a new congress. The federal system was abolished and replaced with a centralized government in which the states of the federal republic were transformed into military departments governed by *caudillos* appointed by the president himself (Miller 1985, 210). The conservatives were pleased, but liberal politicians in many parts of Mexico were dismayed and led rebellions against Santa Anna.

The strongest opposition to the new laws came from the northern province of Texas, where many Americans had settled. In 1835 there were about 30,000 Anglo-American immigrants in Texas, while the Mexican population there barely reached 7,800 (Meyer and Sherman [1979] 1987, 336). At the time of the establishment of the republic, the Mexican government had encouraged Americans to settle in Texas, but the Mexicans, finding that they were losing control of the province,

General Antonio López de Santa Anna. Engraving in Juan Suárez y Navarro, *Historia de México y del general Antonio López de Santa-Anna. Comprende los acontecimientos políticos que han tenido lugar en la nación, desde el año de 1821 hasta 1848* (1850).

abruptly changed their policy. Immigration was halted, duties were imposed on all foreign imports, and customs posts were set up on the borders. The colonists began to speak out about their grievances. One major grievance was that Texas was appended politically to Coahuila, which had nine times its population. By 1835 the Texans were convinced that there could be no compromise with the Mexicans. The only answer was war. And on October 2 they launched the first of a series of assaults on Mexican garrisons. In March, 1836, delegates to a convention at Washington-on-the-Brazos declared independence from Mexico (Miller 1985, 213). "With the fires of patriotism in my heart and dominated by a noble ambition to save my country, I took pride in being the first to strike in defense of the independence, honor, and rights of my nation," Santa Anna recalled years later (Crawford 1967, 50). And so, determined to crush the rebellion, he gathered an army of 6,000 men and started northward across the deserts of Coahuila. Six weeks of marching brought him to San Antonio, where the heroic stand of William Travis was made at the Alamo. Santa Anna demanded unconditional surrender. When Travis refused, Santa Anna signaled that the assault to follow would be to the death, with no quarter or clemency. The Mexicans won the battle, and there was no mercy for the defenders (Miller 1985, 213). Even his own officer, Lieutenant Colonel José Enrique de la Peña, in his diary could not justify Santa Anna's actions at the Alamo, declaring that "one would have to write nothing at all to avoid censuring his conduct" (Peña 1975, xxv). But a month later Sam Houston's Texans, with blood-curdling shouts of "Remember the Alamo," pounced on Santa Anna's unwary troops and defeated them in thirty minutes. Santa Anna fled for safety. Two days later he was captured by one of Houston's patrols.

In return for his release, the wily Santa Anna agreed to recognize the independence of Texas, although in his memoirs he claimed to have maintained that "to the Mexican Congress solely belongs the right to decide that question" (Crawford 1967, 57). Back in Mexico, he found himself in disgrace and retired to Manga de Clavo. In April, 1837, the congress named Bustamante president. His government repudiated the treaty that Santa Anna had signed.

A dispute between France and Mexico in 1838 allowed Santa Anna to regain his prestige. During the past few years claims amounting to 600,000 pesos had been filed by French citizens against the Mexicans for losses suffered during the disorders of 1828. Since one claimant was a baker, the Mexicans dubbed the incident the Pastry War. When the French admiral Charles Baudin landed 3,000 troops in Veracruz, the flamboyant Santa Anna hastened to the port. As the French forces were in retreat to their boats, a cannonball shattered his leg, and it was clumsily amputated the following day. The accident proved to be a blessing in disguise for Santa Anna. He would forever be the martyred hero bleeding for his beloved homeland.

In 1841, Santa Anna became the dictator of Mexico for three years. As such he proved to be remarkable in collecting money—taxes and more taxes. He imposed "voluntary" contributions on all householders of the capital, increased import duties by 20 percent, exacted forced loans from the church, and sold mining concessions to the British. But the money was spent for the glory and the pleasure of the dictator, not for the welfare of the general population or the good of the republic. Whenever he tired of life in the capital, he was off again to Manga de Clavo and his prized fighting cocks.

In December, 1844, Santa Anna was ousted from power and banished from the country "for life to reside in Venezuela with the half pay of a general" (Jones 1968, 95). He went instead to Cuba, and his exile lasted a year and a half. Before the end of 1846 he was to return to Mexico with the help of the American government, which hoped to utilize him in settling the war that had broken out between Mexico and the United States.

On March 1, 1845, the United States had announced the admission of Texas into the Union. A year later, a dispute over the southern border of Texas led to the long-expected military clash. No country in history, probably, was ever less prepared to fight a war than Mexico. The treasury was empty, the army counted a disproportionate number of officers, and anarchy reigned supreme. The struggle for power was not only between the centralists and the federalists. The federalists were divided in their opinions on both domestic and foreign policies. The Gómez Farías federalists, who were known as the *puros*, became the spearhead of the movement for war, while the *moderados* wanted to negotiate with the United States, rightly convinced that Mexico was bound to lose the war. As for the supporters of Santa Anna, they formed a fourth party, the Santanistas, who threatened to upset the government.

General Mariano Paredes, a federalist, overthrew the government and took over the presidency. On April 23, 1846, he said, "From this day defensive war begins." The official congressional declaration of war oc-

Mexico in 1853. Map by Don Caldwell.

curred in Mexico City on July 2 (Miller 1985, 220–21). By that time the American armies had already begun their victorious march toward Mexico. Early in May an American agent had gone to Cuba to confer with Santa Anna in Havana. The exiled dictator promised to make peace on favorable terms if the United States would let him slip through the blockade at Veracruz. The naïve Americans agreed, and in mid-August the former dictator landed at Veracruz. He rode into Mexico City in the government's state coach, dressed in "quite a democratic fashion" (Ramírez 1950, 77). At the end of the year Santa Anna reassumed the presidency, with a provisional president to fill the executive role. With his genius for creating armies out of nothing, he marched his troops northward, where he met General Zachary Taylor in battle at Buena Vista. The two armies fought one another to a standstill, then Santa Anna abruptly withdrew, "ordered," as he conveniently explained later, by a special messenger "to defend the capital and restore law and order" (Crawford 1967, 93). Shortly thereafter he took to the field to meet Winfield Scott's army, who had landed at Veracruz. Attacked from the front and flank and back, the Mexican army was cut to pieces at Cerro Gordo, and the survivors fled. The Americans pressed on to Puebla. By August they had reached the suburbs of Mexico City and were ready to attack, and on September 14 the city fell. Santa Anna retired once more into exile.

Mexico City could have been defended. As Lesley Byrd Simpson puts it, "The Mexicans were defeated in advance by hatreds, jealousies, poverty, despair, indifference and apathy" (Simpson [1941] 1966, 252). Some Mexicans, however, fought with great courage and obstinacy. On February 2, 1848, a peace treaty was signed between the United States and Mexico at Guadalupe Hidalgo, just outside the capital. The effects of the war in Mexico were to reduce its size considerably, because of the loss of what are now the states of California, Nevada, and Utah and parts of Texas, Arizona, New Mexico, Colorado, and Wyoming, but to fill up the Mexican treasury by $15 million.

The moderates remained in power a few years and the country enjoyed the most honest government it had ever had. But their reforms displeased the army. More *pronunciamientos* followed. The conservatives returned to power, and Santa Anna was called back from exile. Reluctantly he abandoned his happy retirement because he felt it was his duty "to heed the call of my country" (Crawford 1967, 120). At first his administration was mildly promising because the respected Lucas Alamán was named minister of foreign affairs. But Alamán died, and influence shifted to a corrupt group around Santa Anna. He adopted the title of "Most Serene Highness," and on December 16 was declared "Perpetual Dictator." To replenish his coffers he sold the Mesilla Valley, now part of southern Arizona and New Mexico, to the United States for $10 million, in what is known as the Gadsden Purchase.

A rebellion slowly gathered strength. In February, 1854, an old Indian insurgent, Juan Alvarez, revolted in Guerrero, and in March he published the Plan of Ayutla, which was ratified with a few amendments by the Creole Ignacio Comonfort and some moderates. The plan demanded the removal of Santa Anna and called for a constituent congress to frame a federal constitution. By the spring of 1855 most of northern Mexico had pronounced for the Plan of Ayutla. The "perpetual dictator" finally slipped out of Mexico City in August; he published his abdication in Perote, then reached Veracruz and sailed with his family into exile. A tumultuous chapter in Mexican history had ended. The former perpetual dictator was allowed to return to his homeland seventeen years later. He spent his last four years in solitude and died destitute and forgotten on June 1, 1876.

ECONOMIC WOES

Those long and chaotic years checked industry and commerce, forced the government to mortgage every resource at ruinous interest, and burdened the country with foreign debts. Agriculture and mining were disrupted, reduced, or abandoned. Commercial relations with Spain, which had been a monopoly for three centuries, were suspended, and relations with other countries were not yet established by treaties. Smuggling, a national institution, intensified. The new government assumed the national debt from the late colonial period, which amounted to over 76 million pesos (Meyer and Sherman [1979] 1987, 319). It unwisely expelled the Spaniards, which was a disaster for Mexico, as most of them were middle-class citizens engaged in useful productive work and, when they left, they took their capital with them. Finally, the new leaders spent recklessly, keeping, for example, an army of over 50,000 men under arms (Meyer and Sherman [1979] 1987, 319).

To meet the deficit, the government borrowed heavily. Two loans were contracted with the houses of Goldschmidt and Barclay in London, totaling 6.4 million pounds (32 million pesos), and British economic penetration began (Cué Cánovas 1947, 109). German and French capital also entered Mexico. In the struggle for commercial privileges, the United States was in an unfavorable position. Lucas Alamán, the young and able minister of state, had developed a violent suspicion of Americans, and did his best to put obstacles in the way of a commercial treaty between the two countries. The American minister to Mexico, Joel Poinsett, was a capable but tactless person with a passion for democracy, and he did nothing to dispel apprehension. Poinsett flung himself into Mexican politics on the side of the York Rite masons and made himself so disliked that he was ultimately recalled.

The new republic was caught in a vicious cycle: financial problems caused political turmoil, which in turn unsettled an already shaky economy. From 1825 onward, wrote Agustín Cué Cánovas, the public debt increased constantly (Cué Cánovas 1947, 110). The government borrowed money not only from the English but also from greedy speculators, the *agiotistas*, who lent money at a monthly rate of 3 percent, receiving in return a mortgage on government property or on customs duties. In 1828 a loan was authorized at 536 percent annual interest (*Historia general de México* 1976, 3:40). José Valadés wrote: "The *agiotistas* were the owners of the custom revenues that made up 90 percent of the income of the national treasury. . . . In ten years (1826–1836) the customhouse of Veracruz repaid these moneylenders 6 million pesos; that of Mazatlán, 2 million; that of San Blas, 1.8 million; that of Guaymas, 1 million" (Valadés 1979, 143).

By far the most important sources of revenue were the import and export duties, whether from the ports or the frontiers of the republic. Taxes on imported goods, for example, totaled slightly more than 6,350,000 pesos in 1844, which possibly would have been 8,000,000, had smuggling been prevented (Cué Cánovas 1947, 210). Mexico's chief exports were precious metals. The figures for 1842 were $20 million, of which $18.5 million were in gold and silver (Mayer 1844, 306). Other sources of revenue were from the monopolies of tobacco and gunpowder, the saltworks, the post office, the lottery, the territories of the federation, the produce from national properties (such as estates that formerly had belonged to the Inquisition or to convents suppressed while Mexico was under the dominion of Spain) and all buildings formerly considered property of the crown (Ward 1828, 1:368). To those were added revenues from taxes on items such as stamped paper, pulque, and turnpikes. The old *alcabala*, a general sales tax, was suspended on August 4, 1824, and replaced by a duty of 15 percent on all goods forwarded from the ports into the interior (Ward 1828, 1:458). The import taxes collected at the customhouses were set at 25 percent, then raised to 40 percent (Cué Cánovas 1947, 103).

When the economic situation was desperate, the government resorted to the abhored *préstamos forzosos*, or forced loans. Forced loans were not a creation of the republic; they had been a favorite of the viceroys. And they were not restricted to Mexican citizens. "Forced loans have been wrested from our merchants," complained American Brantz Mayer (Mayer 1844, 310). Among the French demands during the Pastry War was an exemption from forced contributions for their nationals.

To be sure, agricultural activities revived quickly. Joel Poinsett wrote in 1824, "The buildings are in ruins, yet the country appears to be cultivated as extensively and as carefully as ever" (Poinsett 1824, 106). Revenues increased in the course of time, but so did expenses, and in greater amounts, so that almost every budget presented a large deficit calling for more loans and more taxes. In 1838, for example, expenditures were disproportionate to revenues when 25 million pesos were collected and nearly 41 million were spent; and in 1853, 19 million pesos were collected and over 32 million pesos were spent (Salvat Editores de México, S.A., 1974, 7:204). At the outbreak of the war with Texas, the minister of the treasury informed the president that there were only 10,034 pesos in the special fund that had been established in 1830 for the defense of the country (Valadés [1936] 1979, 142). When the government pressed for a loan from the rich landowners of the capital, Gregorio Mier y Terán was the only one who lent money—50,000 pesos (Valadés [1936]1979, 142).

Pondering over the miseries of his country, Samuel Ramos, one hundred years later, wrote, "The calamities of Mexican history in the nineteenth century are not due to an internal deficiency of race, but to the excessive ambition of governing minorities, who, obsessed with fantastic plans for national administration, overlooked the real problem of the Mexican people (Ramos 1962, 42).

CHAPTER ONE

SOCIETY

*The Mexican population presents the most striking
contrasts. . . . On one side splendour and luxury,
elegant carriages, and Parisian toilette, on the other
dirt and indigence.*—Carl Sartorius

The census made in the year 1793 by Viceroy Re-
villa-Gigedo listed a population of 4,484,429 Mexicans exclusive of the
intendancies of Veracruz and Guadalajara. The population was further
broken down into 2,319,741 Indians; 7,904 Europeans; 677,458 white
Creoles, and 1,478,426 of different castes (quoted in Mayer 1844, 299).
According to the British minister H. G. Ward, "this was the *minimum* of
the population," for not only were censuses carelessly made but also "a
census was always regarded as the prelude to some new system of taxa-
tion, which the natives endeavored to elude, by diminishing the number
of those upon whom it was to operate" (Ward 1828, 1:26). Alexander
von Humboldt estimated the population of the "Kingdom of Mexico" at
the end of 1803 to be 5,800,000 (Humboldt 1822, 1:199). A later es-
timate by the Mexican government in 1842 listed 7,015,509 inhabitants
(Mayer 1844, 300).

In the struggle for independence caste distinctions were abolished.
Henceforth all citizens were to be known as "Americans," but, though
they lived in the same land and breathed the same air, the inhabitants
of the young republic had a long way to go before melting into a new
breed, the Mexican. Very few, at that time, were conscious of their *mexi-
canidad*, even among the insurgents of Spanish ancestry who loudly
claimed themselves to be the heirs of Moctezuma. In the territory of
Mexico coexisted two different and scarcely related worlds: one was regarded as primitive, that of the Indians; the other was supposedly civi-

lized, that of the whites. Before the Mexicans leaped out of the caldron in which the various ethnic, cultural, and racial ingredients had been bubbling since the days of the conquest, Mexico would need more than one revolution. Although the rebels raised their banner with the cry "Death to the gachupins!"[1] they had not freed themselves from Spanish society, nor from the colonial methods of rule and the colonial way of life. Mexican life still tended to conform to the cultural molds imported from Europe.

Customs do not die easily. The rebels indeed had tried to abolish caste distinctions: many heroes of the revolutionary wars were mestizos and even full-blooded Indians, and under the new system every citizen was capable of holding the highest offices of the state. Yet the mention of whites, Indians, and *castas* was still found on official documents and in statistical tables, and the social hierarchy, according to foreign visitors, remained roughly the same as always. It was divided into six general groups: whites or Creoles (those who prided themselves on their descent from the Spanish, yet might be of mixed blood), mestizos, mulattoes, zambos (descendants of Negroes and Indians), Indians, and Negroes.

The various social strata formed a huge pyramid. At the summit were the Hispanic whites and mestizos—a minority made up of the Creole landed class and town bourgeois, the higher order of the clergy, and military parvenus. Military officers constituted new class that had risen during the wars of independence and was looked down upon by the first families of Mexico. Next on the social pyramid were the mestizos who were not affiliated with the Creole upper class, a heterogeneous population of mixed white and Indian blood that included politicians and peasants, artisans and priests, small landowners and beggars, lawyers, and house servants. Although they had inherited the vices and virtues of both the Spaniard and the Indian, they had developed a non-Indian way of life, adopting the customs, religion, and language of the conquerors. More numerous than the Creoles, they were also more energetic. Their favorite passion was politics, and they later became the middle class that was to make up the hard core of Mexican society.

Below them, forming the base of the great pyramid, were the Indians, by far the most numerous racial group. There were probably 4 million in 1842 (Mayer 1844, 301). Nominally converted to Catholicism, they retained the social structure, the customs, and living skills of their an-

---

[1] *Gachupin* was a term of opprobrium applied to Spaniards in Mexico.

cestors, and sometimes even their former religion, in spite of the zeal with which the Spanish friars had destroyed their gods. Even before the conquest the Indians had been set against all forms of change, and the slow rhythms of their village lives persisted. They stuck to their routines and, unlike the mestizos, generally kept aloof from the political evolution of Mexico.

Lowest of all were the blacks. Slavery, suppressed by the insurgent leader José María Morelos in his message to the congress of Chilpancingo in November, 1813, was officially abolished on July 13, 1824. Many slaves had already been emancipated, as Spanish laws regarding manumission were quite liberal. Most of them, as well as most mulattoes and zambos, were found on the coasts in the ports of Veracruz and Acapulco, on sugar plantations, and in the mines, where they maintained their status as an "ignominious minority" (González 1981, 86). Blacks had numbered about 20,000 in the middle of the sixteenth century, but the census of 1842 listed only 6,000 (Mayer 1844, 301). The sharp decrease in the black population was compensated for by an increase in the number of zambos.

H. G. Ward noted the zambo presence on the coast: "They have multiplied there in an extraordinary manner, by intermarriages with the Indian race, and now form a mixed breed, admirably adapted to the *Tierra Caliente*" (Ward 1828, 1:29). Whether they were slaves or freemen, Negroes and their descendants generally worked harder and more efficiently than did Indians, and they dominated the sugar industry. Of their place in Mexican society, Waddy Thompson, minister plenipotentiary of the United States in Mexico, wrote: "It is a very great mistake to suppose that they enjoy anything like social equality even with the Indian population. . . . The negro in Mexico, as everywhere else, is looked upon as belonging to a class a little lower than the lowest" (Thompson 1846, 5). Although those of pure African descent had the lowest status in Mexican society, zambos did succeed in climbing the social ladder. Blacks often melted into the mestizo population. Still, on the coasts they retained a few traits of their African heritage. Twentieth-century writer Miguel Covarrubias noted their "characteristic clipped accent" and their "devil-may-care sense of humour" (Covarrubias 1946, 11).

D. A. Brading's study on haciendas and ranchos in the Mexican Bajío northwest of Mexico City provides us with interesting information on mulattoes in the lowlands. "By the close of the eighteenth century," he wrote, "the Indian and mulatto groups of the Bajío were on the point of coalescence. Already many individuals could not accurately describe their own ethnic status." Not infrequently, for example, a man declared his future spouse to be a mulatto "only to hear her describe herself as an Indian" (Brading 1978, 47).

THE RULING CLASS

"The most important distinction, civil and political, was founded on the colour of the skin," wrote Joel Poinsett. "Here, to be white was to be noble; and the rank of the different casts [sic] is determined by their nearer or more distant relation to the whites" (Poinsett 1824, 119). One might also say that to be noble was to be white. Race barriers had never been insurmountable in New Spain. Kings and viceroys favored the Indian nobles who cooperated; they assured them of their privileges, confirmed their titles, approved their possession of lands and vassals. These nobles were allowed to bear arms, to wear Spanish clothing, and to ride saddled horses. They married into leading Spanish families and in time became thoroughly Spanish in their culture and thought. They were called Creoles, and some of them occupied the upper stratum of Mexican society. To be sure, Agustín de Iturbide had Indian blood; some historians even mentioned him as a mestizo. Yet, because he was handsome, well educated, and had good manners, he passed for a Creole and became a favorite of society (Bancroft 1885, 12:702).

Now that the gachupines were gone, the Creoles were preeminent in Mexico, and none occupied a higher position in the hierarchy than the landed class. The desire to possess a coat of arms and land was a legacy of the Spanish conquistadors. European traditions of nobility had a profound effect on Creole social habits: the more land they had, the greater their perceived nobility. In the century following the conquest, Spaniards had received huge land grants and had set themselves up as semi-independent feudal lords, enjoying on their fiefs the traditional privileges of the noble class.

The raison d'être of a noble, in feudal times, was to make war and defend the king. Land was the reward of the lord, battles his pleasure. But the noble had to live according to certain codes. Even the poorest knight, for example, could not go into trade without losing his noble status. In the northern provinces of New Spain the *hacendado* incessantly had to fight the ferocious Chichimecas; he did it "with his arms, servants, and horses," and generally without any financial help from the viceroy (Chevalier 1952, 224), thus providing a service to the crown that fit perfectly into the medieval social structure. In other provinces, however, he had no war to fight, nor king nor vassal to defend. Yet he still clung to his sword—the emblem of nobility—and to his horse. The word "knight" in Spanish is *caballero*, which means "man on horseback." Without a horse the knight was the "son of nobody." In the tradition of the *hidalgo*,[2] these descendants of the conquistadors often saw themselves as too noble to work.

There were indeed very few occupations that the Creole could pursue without loss of social status. Apart from entering the church or the army (traditional European upper-class professions), he could be a government official, physician, lawyer, or mining proprietor. For the *hidalgo*, nothing could be lower than trade. Yet the commercial age began in Mexico with independence, and some Creoles transformed their aristocratic town houses to accommodate shops and offices; others opened coach lines, ran paper and cotton mills or gunpowder factories, even associated with foreign businessmen. A few *hacendados*, like the Sánchez Navarros of Coahuila, ran their estates with yankeelike efficiency. As Nelson Reed wrote in *The Caste War of Yucatan*, "The sons of the patriots of 1821 accepted their fathers' victories over the past and made their own revolution, the creation of a mercantile society" (Reed 1964, 7). What was true for Yucatán was true for the rest of Mexico, but most notably for the northern states.

The rich and prominent Gordoa family of Zacatecas, Guadalajara, and other cities in Mexico, serves well as a prototype of the best of the Creole tradition. The Gordoa interests ranged from mines to haciendas and from church to government, as we shall see.[3] And yet such enterprising Creoles were a minority. As a group the Creoles were passionate and volatile, but indolent.

For three hundred long years the Creoles had been excluded from the affairs of the colony by the Spaniards on the grounds that they were frivolous and irresponsible. From time to time they had raised their voices in protest, but in vain: Spanish authorities allowed no criticism. If, after independence, they behaved with the fecklessness of spoiled

---

[2] *Hidalgo* was a contraction of *hijo de algo*, meaning son of something. The hidalgo was a nobleman of secondary rank.

[3] Information about the Gordoas is available from a variety of sources, principally the Gordoa Family Papers, 1822–46, but also letters and a newspaper genealogy from Gordoa descendants in Guadalajara and Zacatecas in the posssession of Ruth Olivera; Cross 1976; *Diccionario Porrúa* [1964], 1970; Lyon 1828; and Ward 1828.

An *hacendado*, his daughter, and foreman. Engraving by Carl Nebel, *Voyage pittoresque et archéologique dans la partie la plus intéressante du Mexique* (1836).

children, we must seek the explanation in the old authoritarian system of Spain.

The failure of the Mexicans to establish a working government can be linked to other factors: an unconscious sense of inferiority, which led them to pattern their political life along French and American lines without taking into consideration their environment, and perhaps more important, their Hispanic heritage.

Passion and individualism are two Spanish character traits. The conquest of America was the work of individual adventurers, not of Spain as a nation, and rebellion had long been a habit among the conquistadors. Although Indian blood sometimes altered appearance and soul, and the routine life of New Spain sapped vitality, the Creole showed an individualism that was indeed antagonistic to all order and discipline.

PORTRAITS OF CREOLES

"I think the Mexican character is never seen to such advantage as in the country, amongst these great landed proprietors of old family, who live on their own estates, engaged in agricultural pursuits, and entirely removed from all the party feeling and petty interests of a city life" (Calderón de la Barca [1843] 1931, 475). So wrote Frances Calderón de la Barca, the Scottish wife of the first minister of Spain to Mexico. She was not speaking of any member of the Gordoa family, but she might well have been. Their paths could easily have crossed in the early 1840s. Luis Gonzaga Gordoa, lawyer, deputy, and senator, had lived in Mexico City for many years. His career was illustrious: he signed the Constitution of 1824, then served for five years as the secretary of the Mexican legation in Rome, returning to Mexico in 1830 to become later the rector of the Colegio de Abogados (*Diccionario Porrúa* [1964] 1970, 908). In the 1840s he was named administrator of the government-supervised mines at Fresnillo. Of his private life we know that in 1840, at the age of forty-three, he married the nineteen year-old Mariana Rubio of Querétaro. No heir was produced from this union, yet the marriage seems to have been one of domestic contentment and mutual affection, if one may read between the lines of Mariana's letters (Gordoa Family Papers).

Although Luis Gonzaga had left his native Catorce and his early home in Zacatecas, his older brother Antonio Eugenio, the Conde de Santa Rosa, remained on the family estate, where he pursued his agricultural interests and held high posts in the legislature of Zacatecas (Cross 1976, 298). To their father, Antonio María Gordoa, they and their several brothers and sisters owed the advantages of affluence and prestige. Antonio had discovered, or more correctly, had rediscovered, the rich silver mines at Catorce, and through perseverance and sheer good luck he had accumulated a considerable fortune. Wisely, he had invested in numerous haciendas in Zacatecas and San Luis Potosí, among them one known as Malpaso. G. F. Lyon passed through Malpaso in his travels and left a cameo portrait of Antonio María. He was then an old man of seventy, his head tied with a kerchief, and was attended on his balcony by a young wife of twenty-five (Lyon 1828, 1:244–45).

All observers agree that the *hacendado* who lived on his estate was a model of refinement and gentleness. Unfortunately, *hacendados* did not all live on their estates; many got into the habit of going off to the capital, or even to Paris or London to live, leaving the hacienda to an overseer.

Whether he was a man from the city or a country squire, the Creole generally was extremely courteous, kind, and benevolent, hospitable to strangers, moderate in the use of liquor, and, according to Carl Sartorius (a German who settled in the state of Veracruz in 1830), "liberal and tolerant even in religious matters" (Sartorius [1858] 1961, 61), which seems doubtful. Yet, although he loved luxury, showy equipages, and beautiful horses, there was no comfort in a Creole's house—a point stressed by every foreign visitor.

The Creole was easily moved—anger, love, and jealousy could drive him to "inconsiderate action"—but we learn that treachery was "foreign to him" (Sartorius [1858] 1961, 53). Some commentators found the Creole haughty, thoughtless, and excitable; all pointed out his addiction to gambling, his passion for festivities and amusements, his love for the fair sex. "No difficulties, no barriers are insurmountable to him," remarked Sartorius. "If the electric spark ignites, and his passion is returned, opportunity will soon be found" (Sartorius [1858] 1961, 55).

Creoles were superstitious in the extreme and zealous in the performance of religious obligations, but they often had no moral rigor in their daily lives. Their intellectual resources generally were good. Among the landed class were individuals of scholarly achievement and general education; many of them had been educated abroad and were well acquainted with Europe or the United States. Creoles in general, said Joel Poinsett, "possess good natural talents, and great facility of acquiring knowledge" (Poinsett 1824, 119).

When Francisco Javier Gordoa went abroad to study in the 1830s, older brothers Francisco Ignacio and Luis Gonzaga sent what might well be called concerned parental advice in letters which reflected the level of culture of this Creole family. On December 12, 1836, Francisco Ignacio urged Javier to make good use of his opportunity—to study drawing and music as well as languages and not to come home having seen Europe only superficially. And if he went to Paris, as he planned to do, he was to remember that there are more distractions there than in London. Francisco Ignacio would be pleased if Francisco Javier does not forget the music of the *"vaudevilles"* he requested, the most modern and pretty and well received in the theaters; also the newest comedies. And if Javier's money holds out, Ignacio would be most grateful for a good ebony flute and music by Rossini for one and two flutes. But, he cautions, buy intelligently and do not be deceived in the prices.

In the following year a letter of June 28 from Luis Gonzaga contains even more pointed admonitions. Javier is warned not to waste his time in dissipation, but to amuse himself moderately. Be careful with women, he is told. Do not let them entrap you or, even worse, infect you and ruin your health for life, which would be the greatest misfortune (Gordoa Family Papers). How well did Javier listen? We know only that he was not destined for long life and by 1844 was dead.

Ladies, according to Sartorius, savored a life "somewhat oriental" (Sartorius [1858] 1961, 59). It is interesting to compare his comments on Creole ladies with those made by Frances Calderón de la Barca, who moved in the best Mexican circles. Apparently, Sartorius met people with whom the Calderóns would never have associated. The summit of the pyramid undoubtedly comprised several strata.

On the lack of intellectual faculties among the ladies, and on their ability at sewing, all observers agree. It is really "painful to see so many young ladies, of excellent abilities, anxious to learn, but without any means of improvement, receiving little or no encouragement from their seniors, and the very reverse of encouragement from the priests," said Captain Basil Hall (Hall 1824, 2:230). And Frances Calderón reports: "Generally speaking . . . the Mexican Señoras and Señoritas write, read, and play a little, sew, and take care of their houses and children. . . . When I say they write, I do not mean that they can always spell; and when I say they play, I do not assert that they have generally a knowledge of music" (Calderón de la Barca [1843] 1931, 221).

Sad to say, Frances Calderón's critical words on the spelling ability of Mexican ladies could have been written about Mariana Gordoa and her sisters. Their letters fairly flew between Mexico City and Querétaro and San Luis Potosí, filled with family concerns expressed in phonetic Spanish. "No boi hoi a verte," wrote Mariana in an undated letter, and "asme favor." Literate they were, but literary they were not. And as to Mariana's playing or musical knowledge, there is not a hint; instead there are frequent comments by all of the sisters about the latest play or opera they have seen (Gordoa Family Papers).

Carl Sartorius, for his part, wrote of Mexican women that "they work beautifully with the needle, weave and embroider, play and sing; the intellectual element, however, is wanting." And he adds, "the understanding and the heart are uncultivated, and sensuality therefore easily obtains the upper hand" (Sartorius [1858] 1961, 59). According to this observer, women were "sadly in want of a good moral education," and mothers did not consider their daughters safe unless they were under their very eyes (Sartorius [1858] 1961, 55). On the morality of the Creole ladies, Frances Calderón, or Fanny as she was familiarly known, disagrees. Says she, "The young men when they do meet with young ladies in society, appear devoted to and very much afraid of them. . . . As for flirtation, the name is unknown, and the thing" (Calderón de la Barca [1843] 1931, 164). Was that because of virtue or lack or opportunity? Waddy Thompson, in his memoirs, notes, "Every house in Mexico has but one outside door, and a porter always at that. The old system of the duenna, and a constant espionage, are observed by every one" (Thompson 1846, 162).

The portrait of the Creole ladies would be incomplete if we did not speak of their manners, which were extremely warm and kind; of the Spanish etiquette observed by the better class, which Frances Calderón found "beyond measure tiresome"; of their habit of smoking cigars and *cigaritos*, even in the street and theater halls; and of the general carelessness of their dress at home, contrasting to the full dress that they adopted for visits. Even to go to church, ladies would sprinkle their dresses and mantillas with diamonds and pearls. For example, Frances Calderón described the panoply displayed by the wife of an "extremely rich" general who visited with her one morning: "A mantilla of black blonde, fastened by three diamond aigrettes. Diamond earrings of extraordinary size. A diamond necklace of immense value, and beautifully set. . . . On every finger two diamond rings, like little watches" (Calderón de la Barca [1843] 1931, 84–85).

The aristocratic ladies of old were on the wane. In their place a new race had arisen whose manners and appearance had "little of the *vieille cour* about them" (Calderón de la Barca [1843] 1931, 84). Revolutions are great social levelers, and at the balls given by Santa Anna, reported the distinguished Waddy Thompson, the company was far from select: "In fact, I saw there very few of the ladies belonging to the aristocracy; but very many others who had no business there" (Thompson 1846, 161).

A NEW ARISTOCRACY

The army and the church dominated Mexican life. "You are warned of this double dominion by the constant sound of the drum and the bell, which ring in your ears from morn to midnight and drown the sounds of industry and labor," noted Brantz Mayer (Mayer 1844, 346).

By 1840 the army had become very unpopular with the upper class as a profession, and its command was now "intrusted to men who have arisen immediately from the people" (Mayer 1844, 330). Mexican officers as a whole showed more talent for horsemanship and parade than ability to command under fire. This probably was a result of the speed with which a man might climb the ranks. Officers were often taken right from private life and put at the head of troops. Ascensions of four ranks were common. Santa Anna issued no less than 12,000 commissions (Gruening 1928, 297), and in March, 1821, he himself made three grades in twenty-four hours (Roeder 1947, 1:52).

Most of the officers had no experience in leadership, nor knowledge of obedience and discipline. The army seemed trained only to rebel. Indeed, Lucas Alamán observed that whatever was spent to arm troops served only to enable them to fight each other and give the illusion that there was an army for defense (Alamán [1849–52] 1942, 5:831).

The new aristocracy controlled the nation by authority and force, meddling in the government's affairs, turning the country into a battle-field. Instead of guarding the nation against invading enemies, the military protected the government against the people. The officers were the tools of the president, but they generally remained faithful to him just as long as he could pay them. Generals who commanded a division received 6,000 pesos annually, those who commanded a brigade, 4,000; while the salary of a governor was only 2,000 (*Historia general de México* 1976, 3:57). Those who entered the army were motivated more by ambition than patriotism; it was a sinecure, a stepping-stone to power. Like the clergy, they enjoyed the *fuero*, or privilege, of being tried only in their own law courts.

Most observers said that the army was the greatest nuisance and the most insurmountable barrier to the prosperity and progress of the country. Military parasites bled Mexico. Wrote Waddy Thompson: "They have more than two hundred generals, most of them without commands. Every officer who commands a regiment has the title of general, and is distinguished from generals who have no commands by the addition of 'general effectivo' " (Thompson 1846, 169). Santa Anna had his own favorite troops, newly made officers in new and bright uniforms. On all public occasions the Benemérito de la Patria himself wore the full uniform—blue and red and heavily embroidered with gold—of the chief of the army, and his chest was covered with richly gemmed decorations.

Brantz Mayer reports that the reception room of the palace was always filled with "a brilliant cortege of officers." Santa Anna ruled amid military pomp and music, and the etiquette at the palace was that of a

European court. It is obvious that he took Napoleon as a model: the walls of the reception room, noted Mayer, "are hung with ordinary oil pictures of the history of Napoleon" (Mayer 1844, 71). Did he look the part? By no means. Mayer saw Santa Anna in his coach, surrounded with his praetorian guard; at church, praying; in the ballroom, the cockpit, and the audience room; at the banquet and "in private interviews of delicate diplomacy"; and he wrote: "In perfect repose, you would think him looking on a dying friend, with whose sufferings he was deeply but helplessly sympathizing. His head and face are those of an attentive, thoughtful, melancholy but determined character. There is no ferocity, vindictiveness or ill-temper in his expression" (Mayer 1844, 73).

Frances Calderón de la Barca, after visiting with Santa Anna at his estate, Manga de Clavo, wrote that one would have thought him "a philosopher, living in dignified retirement—one who had tried the world, and found that all was vanity—one who had suffered ingratitude, and who, if he were ever persuaded to emerge from his retreat, would only do so, Cincinnatus-like, to benefit his country" (Calderón de la Barca [1843] 1931, 32).

Such is the portrait of the man who played the leading role in the political drama of his time. Santa Anna was very much the product of Mexican militarism, the portent and personification of his period, as buoyant, ambitious, and self-confident as he was inconsistent.

RELIGIÓN Y FUERO

The other plague of Mexico was the church. The early missionaries had been filled with apostolic zeal, and it would be unfair not to mention that they made every effort to check the cruelties of the *encomienda* system.[4] Yet, instead of teaching Christian morality to their flocks, they inculcated the more superficial aspects of the Catholic religion. The ceremonies, the processions, the cult of the saints, the penance, and the offerings—these were elements that the Indians adopted readily, since similar rites existed in the Aztec religion.

Dominicans, Franciscans, and Jesuits competed in erecting churches whose sumptuousness testified to motives more worldly than the desire to propagate the faith. Without compunction they used the Indians to build these edifices, as they used the Indians' service in the monasteries.

---

[4]An *encomienda* was an allotment of tribute-paying Indians given in trust to a Spaniard who had the duty of looking after their spiritual and material welfare.

Indians were gardeners, doorkeepers, cleaners, cooks, sacristans, messengers—"all without a penny of wages," complained Archbishop Montúfar to the Council of the Indies in 1556 (quoted in Simpson [1941] 1966, 87).

A second wave deposited secular priests on the shores of Mexico, and the long struggle of the crown to secularize convent towns began. The secular clergy was the arm of the crown—as opposed to the regular clergy in the various orders. Their interests were intricately interwoven. In 1571 the dreadful Inquisition was established in Mexico to castigate Jews and heretics. Indians fortunately were exempted from its ministrations by a decree of Carlos V, but the officers of the Holy Office infested every other community.

Through bigotry and superstition, the clergy worked on the people's conscience and the population of New Spain was brought into line. The crown was not ungrateful. Service in the church was made an attractive career for men, and it became the ambition of every family to have a son in the priesthood. The Spanish rulers, however, saw to it that only Spaniards had the opportunity to occupy the higher dignities of the church. By 1808 all but one bishopric of New Spain, and most of the rich benefices, were held by Europeans; parish priests were usually Creoles; and village *curas* were drawn from the lower-class mestizos.

During the course of the centuries, great riches were accumulated by the church. Priests were often landowners and enjoyed all the privileges of the *hacendados*; they also had huge properties in towns and cities. Yet in remote villages kind and generous priests, who did not want to squeeze money out of their poor flocks, lived in abject poverty.

During the wars of independence the clergy split. As Ernest Gruening observed, "the Mexican clergy were the brain and spirit of the struggle for and against Mexican national liberty" (Gruening 1928, 184). The dark Virgin of Guadalupe became the standard of the nationalists, brandished against the white Spanish Virgin of los Remedios, emblem of the royalist forces.

To be sure, the Mexicans did not fight for the love of religious liberty. The Inquisition was indeed abolished, but freedom of thought and religion was still strictly forbidden. Even the revolutionary priest José María Morelos proclaimed that only the Roman Catholic religion should be permitted in independent Mexico. The church, in fact, emerged from the war with increased power and larger estates.

But the popularity of the church waned as more and more attention was given to its great wealth and the small benefits the nation derived from it. Brantz Mayer estimated the riches of the clergy at $90 million, and he added, "The value of their churches, the extent of their city property, the power they possess as *lenders*, and the quantity of jewels, precious vessels and golden ornaments will raise the above statement, I am confident, to nearer $100,000,000 than ninety" (Mayer 1844, 329).

The revenues of the archbishop of Mexico in 1827 amounted to 130,000 pesos a year, while many village priests vegetated on an annual income of 100 to 120 pesos. Wrote Frances Calderón: "Were I to choose a situation here, it would undoubtedly be that of Archbishop of Mexico, the most enviable in the world, to those who would enjoy a life of tranquility, ease and universal adoration. . . . His palace in town, his well-cushioned carriage, well-conditioned horses, and sleek mules, seem the very perfection of comfort" (Calderón de la Barca [1843] 1931, 218–19).

All foreign observers were struck by the riches displayed by the Mexican prelates. Fanny attended the ceremony of the consecration of the new archbishop. She wrote that "the ceremony . . . was very superb, the music fine, the quantity of jewels on the dresses of the bishops and priests, and on the holy vessels, etc., enormous" (Calderón de la Barca [1843] 1931, 180). And Brantz Mayer, in his memoirs, speaks of a dignitary of the church he met at a diplomatic dinner who had "a cross of large diamonds and topazes hung round his priestly throat by a collar of gems" and displayed, when taking snuff, "a finger which almost blinded by the flash of its diamonds" (Mayer 1844, 74).

High dignitaries were by no means equally wealthy. The revenues of the bishop of Yucatán, for example, totaled $20,000 in 1827, while those of the bishop of Sonora were only $6,000. Still, they lived in luxury. John L. Stephens, who met the bishop of Yucatán in 1840, reports that he "was the greatest man in Merida," lived in the "greatest style," and was "handsomely dressed." Stephens was impressed by the man: "He was a Centralist, and a great politician, and spoke of letters from generals, sieges, blockades, and battles, in tones which brought up a vivid picture of some priestly warrior or grand master of the Temple" (Stephens [1841] 1969, 2:400–401).

The social status of the priests influenced their political views: the haves were found among the conservatives and the monarchical party; the have-nots among the liberals. According to contemporaries, corruption spread through the hierarchy, from bishops down to village priests. They sold salvation, taking advantage of the people's credulity. In some convents monks and nuns lived a life of frolic and luxury. Wrote Carl

Sartorius, "The Mexican monks are no ascetic dunces, who choose the desert for their dwelling-place, or allow themselves to be eaten up by the Apachas." He also remarked that in "most of the orders the restraint is not very great and the discipline tolerably lax" (Sartorius [1858] 1961, 105–6). The lower order was uneducated and generally licentious, according to some commentators.

Clerical celibacy was a joke, and in cities, towns, and villages alike lived illegitimate families born of concubinage. Albert M. Gilliam, an American who traveled through Mexico during the years 1843 and 1844, assured his readers that "nothing is more common than for the favourite unmarried wives to live with the holy fathers" (Gilliam 1847, 243), and John L. Stephens wrote that "except at Merida and Campeachy, where they are more immediately under the eyes of the bishop, the padres, throughout Yucatan, to relieve the tedium of convent life, have compagneras, or, as they are sometimes called, *hermanas politicas*, or sisters-in-law." The number of priests having concubines was indeed high. Stephens confessed that "the proportion of those who have to those who have not is about as the proportion in a well-regulated community of married to unmarried men." The erring priests were by no means banned from the society. Stephens said:

> Some look upon this arrangement as a little irregular, but in general it is regarded only as an amiable weakness, and I am safe in saying that it is considered a recommendation to a village padre, as it is supposed to give him settled habits, as marriage does with laymen. . . . Persons of what is considered respectable standing in a village do not shun left-hand marriage with a padre. (Stephens [1843] 1963, 2:73–74)

The clergy on the whole were probably no more greedy or immoral than other men, but because of their offices their practices seem distressing. A large number of priests actually were warm-hearted and devoted to their flocks. All foreign observers, even the bitterest adversaries of Roman Catholicism, praised the generosity and the unflagging hospitality of the *curas* they met while traveling through Mexico. "Whenever I have met with them I have found friends," wrote Stephens (Stephens [1843] 1963, 73). The same was true for virtually every foreign visitor. Brantz Mayer corroborates Stephens's opinion: "The village *curas* are the advisers, the friends and protectors, of their flocks. Their houses have been the hospitable retreats of every traveller. Upon all occasions they constituted themselves the defenders of the Indians" (Mayer 1844, 328).

To be fair, we should add that at times the church responded posi-

Submission to the clergy. Engraving in Claudio Linati, *Costumes civils, militaires el réligieux du Mexique; dessinés d'apres nature* (c. 1829).

tively to change. In Oaxaca the church cooperated with Benito Juárez after he assumed office in 1847, and this collaboration greatly facilitated establishment of the reform program of the Zapotec governor (Roeder 1947, 1:80–81).

THE MESTIZOS

Whether educated or illiterate, mestizos generally lived in the white world, and their social structure and way of life, as we have seen, were those of the Spaniards. Yet they were in the uncomfortable position of half-castes, despised by the Indians and scorned by the Creole elite, although the wealthier mestizos had the same manners as the whites.

They were found in every part of the country, and, though as a group they represented an intermediate class between whites and Indians, they actually occupied every position on the social scale. In some situations the mestizo was nearly the equal of the Creole; in others he stood below the poorest Indian. As Carl Sartorius observed, "the nearer the Mestizo approaches the Creole in colour, the more easy becomes the amalgamation with him" (Sartorius [1858] 1961, 88). While the Indian generally sought to marry his own, the mestizo, or at least the ambitious mestizo, endeavored to marry a wife fairer of skin than himself.

Sartorius praises mestizo kindness, hospitality, energy, and intelligence, and confides in his journal that the commoner mixed-blood often has "more decision and elasticity, and is less effeminate" than the Creole. "He adapts himself easily to every situation, and overcomes difficulties from which the Creole shrinks" (Sartorius [1858] 1961, 88–89). Many lacked education, but they were eager to learn and improve. Bayard Taylor, one of the most reliable observers of this period, relates that the population of El Ingenio, a village situated near Tepic, "were curious to know about our Free School System of which they had heard by some means. None of them knew how to read, and they lamented most bitterly that education in Mexico was so difficult for their class" (Taylor [1850] 1949, 264).

Given solid education, mestizos climbed the rungs of the social ladder without effort. The law and the church attracted them, but were often used simply as stepping-stones to a public office, whether national or local. Many mestizos entered public life or took up legal practice. Men of progress, along with liberal Creoles, they sowed the seeds of a movement destined to bring freedom from colonial rule. H. G. Ward wrote that mestizos were found among the lawyers, *curas*, artisans, small landed proprietors, and soldiers—what he called the "middling classes" (Ward 1828, 1:29); and Sartorius said, "They have access to the chamber of deputies, as well as to the benches of the courts of justice, and appear in the monk's cowl, as well as in the officer's uniform" (Sartorius [1858] 1961, 88).

Mestizos often occupied the position of *alcalde*, or mayor, in Indian villages, and that of *mayordomo*, or foreman, on haciendas. The *arrieros*, or muleteers, whose role in the economy was of prime importance because they were responsible for virtually the whole transit business of the country, were of mixed blood to a man, and so were the *rancheros*, the yeomen of Mexico.

In towns and cities a lower class of mestizos were market vendors, peddlers, *evangelistas* (public scribes), street porters, house servants, and beggars. About house servants Carl Sartorius and Frances Calderón, once again, make conflicting statements. Sartorius found them apt and skillful (Sartorius [1858] 1961, 87), while the wife of the Spanish minister wrote, "The badness of the servants, is an unfailing source of complaint even amongst Mexicans. . . . We hear of their addiction to stealing, their laziness, drunkenness, dirtiness, with a host of other vices" (Calderón de la Barca [1843] 1931, 183).

On the wickedness of *léperos*, all commentators agree: the beggars were the plague of every large city. "Go where you will in this city [Mexico City] you are haunted by beggars," complains Brantz Mayer. "Beggary is a *profession* . . . the capital employed in this business is blindness, a sore leg, a decrepit father or mother, or a helpless child. . . . With such a stock in trade, and a good sunny corner, or wall of a church door, the petitioner is set up for life" (Mayer 1844, 55).

Many wore a rosary or a scapulary around the neck and displayed excessive devotion. Yet "nothing escapes their lynx eyes, although they seem to be exclusively occupied with the prayer-book in their hands," said Sartorius. "But the arm is false, the hand holding the prayer-book is made of wax so as to defy detection whilst beneath the cloak they operate freely with both hands, like the most practised jugglers" (Sartorius [1858] 1961, 141). Their deformities, like their piety, were usually faked.

The *rancheros*, who also often were mestizos, were a happy contrast to city beggars. They were highly praised by all commentators. "It is impossible to see anywhere a finer race of men than these rancheros—tall, strong, and well made, with their embroidered shirts, coarse sarapes, and dark blue pantaloons embroidered in gold," wrote Frances Calderón (Calderón de la Barca [1843] 1931, 508). And B. M. Norman, an American ethnologist who toured Mexico in 1844, remarked: "They are brave, and full of life and vivacity. . . . Sallying forth on his sinewy horse, encased in leather, with the ready lasso at his saddle bow, he [the ranchero] seems, though in course attire, the embodiment of health, strength, and agility" (Norman 1845, 110–11).

Arrieros are equally praised by all. Contemporary witnesses seemed to compete in the choice of flattering expressions to describe them—"honest," "polite," and "skillful" are words found in everyone's

Arrieros in an engraving by Carl Nebel, *Voyage pittoresque et archéologique dans la partie la plus intéressante du Mexique* (1836).

memoirs. And when Captain Lyon writes, "I confess that of all the natives of Mexico, the Arrieros are my favourites" (Lyon 1828, 2:237), he reflects the general opinion.

Denied Spanish dress in colonial times, mestizos developed their own fashions. The men's costume consisted of a pleated shirt and embroidered short jacket ornamented with silver buttons; trousers of white cotton, brown buckskin, or dark velvet, enhanced with silver buttons on the side, opened from the knee down, and fastened with a bright silk *banda* around the waist; a colored silk handkerchief loosely tied about the neck; and a gaudy serape flung over the shoulder. When they rode, they wrapped their legs in a huge skin tied around the waist, richly embroidered, and always wore a broad-brimmed hat.

The dress of the women consisted of a lace-trimmed chemise with short sleeves and a low décolletage, worn with one or more petticoats shorter than the chemise, usually of two colors; a bright satin vest; white satin shoes; and a colorful rebozo gracefully thrown over the head and shoulders. This typical dress became known with the passage of time as the *china poblana*. Popular legend claims that it was inspired by the garb of a seventeeth-century princess of India whose misfortune it was to be kidnapped and sold as a slave to a merchant of Puebla. There she lived out her life as a servant, was married to a Chinese, and became known for her good works. In truth, the costume evolved from the fusion of native and Spanish cultures (Alvarez y Alvarez de la Cadena [1945] 1970, 415).

The typical mestizo man had inherited a passionate temper from his Spanish father, but love, that is sensual love, did not hold for him the smell of fear and death as it did for the Spaniard. He was more pagan than Christian in his concept of love, and therefore more free. "He does not coo like a sentimental dove, nor sigh in the moonshine," noted the shrewd Sartorius, "possession alone will satisfy him" (Sartorius [1858] 1961, 90). When a woman impressed his fancy, whether she was single or married, he would not rest until he had succeeded in conveying his passion to her and in satisfying it.

From both their Spanish and their Indian ancestors, mestizos inherited a love for music, dance, and song, an enthusiasm for fiestas, a deep perception of the sacred, an exalted religiosity, and a fascination with death.

Love of flowers, a taste for magic, and an inherent sadness were Indian legacies. But unlike the Indians, who accepted existing conditions with fatalism because they seemed inalterable, mestizos showed a vigorous unwillingness to let things take their course.

As a group mestizos were susceptible, emotional, restless, and unpredictable.

THE INDIANS

To be sure, the pure-blooded Indians did not share in the dualism that at times agitated the souls of the mestizos, but, as Samuel Ramos observed, their presence created the dualism of Mexican civilization (Ramos 1962, 36). Although in the first half of the nineteenth century the aborigenes were twice as numerous as the whites and mestizos, their role in the drama of Mexican history was that of the spectator. There were of course a few exceptions. A man like Benito Juárez, born in 1806, rose from a barefoot peasant childhood to a brilliant career as a lawyer, local congressman, governor of the state of Oaxaca, secretary of justice, president of the supreme court, and president of the republic.

Juarez's first twelve years of life had been spent like the youth of many a poor Indian. He was hardly three when his parents died, leaving him and his two older sisters in the care of their paternal grandparents. A few years later his grandparents died, and he went to live with an uncle, who taught him his first few words of Spanish. He minded a flock of sheep and every morning, before leaving for the fields, attended the village school, which was taught by an Indian. The boy longed for a good education, and he was aware that only by going to the city could he learn. So, at the age of twelve, he fled to Oaxaca, where he found a place in the home of a pious and honorable man who secured him an education in return for domestic services (Roeder 1947, 1:5–8).

On that day, December 17, 1818, when he left his village of San Pablo Guelatao for the city of Oaxaca, he crossed over the line dividing the two worlds of the natives and the whites. Benito Juárez was a Zapotec Indian. In former times the Zapotecs had been a powerful nation who occupied the uplands of Oaxaca. They were a fine race. The men and women were known to be clean, handsome, kind-hearted, bold, and independent, and to exhibit many intellectual qualities (Bancroft 1886, 1:668). Some of them took easily to Spanish art. The most popular Mexican painter of the eighteenth century, Miguel Cabrera, was a Zapotec Indian. He covered the Jesuit churches with pink-cheeked madonnas (Covarrubias 1946, 292–93).

One of the great wonders of Mexico was the variety of her native peoples. Although presenting some general characteristics in common, they differed entirely in language, custom, and dress. Of medium size, they all had straight, black, glossy hair, which they usually divided into two large, long braids, often decorated with ribbon, and they had small feet, good limbs, prominent cheekbones, and white teeth. The Mayas, as well as the Comanches, had large faces and mouths, while the inhabitants of the tableland had oval faces, long black eyes set wide apart, narrow foreheads, and small, rather flat noses. The skin of different tribes was of various hues, from a light olive to a red copper color.

Captain Lyon reports that the dress for the Indian men of central Mexico commonly was "a short tunic, of dark brown or blue woolen, confined round the waist, with breeches of the same material" (Lyon 1828, 2:238–39). Women's clothing consisted of a two-piece outfit barely covering the knees. Both sexes either went barefoot or wore a coarse kind of sandal. In the *tierra caliente* they all wore a straw hat. In remote parts of Chiapas, Indians were naked save for a cotton loincloth, while the Comanches of northern Mexico wore the buckskin dress and the moccasins of the Plains Indians.

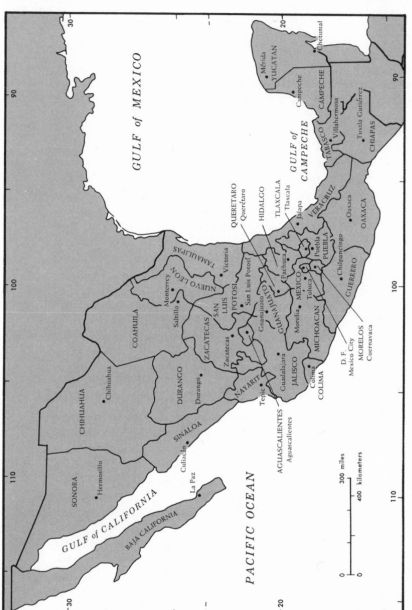

States and capitals of modern Mexico. Reproduced from Robert Ryal Miller, *Mexico: A History* (1985).

About twenty major languages, divided into ninety or more dialects, were spoken in the territory of Mexico proper, and only one of these languages lacked relatives in other parts of the Americas. That one was the Tarascan, which was confined to the state of Michoacán. The Aztec-Tanoan language group, in which Nahuatl, the Aztec language, is classified, and the Maya and its subdivisions were the most widely spoken of all the native tongues (Spencer et al. 1965, 438).

The Nahuatl speakers occupied central Mexico, and the Maya groups the whole peninsula of Yucatán. The Yaquis, the Mayos, the Pimas, the Coras, the Huichols, and the Tarahumaras were among the tribes scattered in the north. The state of Veracruz was the homeland of the Totonacs. The Otomís inhabited Jalisco, and the Chontals, Tabasco. The Tarascans lived in their quiet villages in Michoacán. The Mixe, Zoque, and Mixtec populations shared Chiapas and the Isthmus of Tehuantepec with the Zapotecs. The Apaches and the Comanches roamed freely along the Texas and New Mexico borders. An Apache tribe, the Lipans, had settled in the Bolsón de Mapimí, from which they raided the livestock haciendas of Coahuila, Chihuahua, and Durango.

Both the Comanches and the Apaches were nomadic or seminomadic Plains tribes. They were not, however, of the same linguistic stock: the former were of the Shoshonean family, while the latter were Athabascans (Spencer et al. 1965, 108–9). Unlike the other Indian populations of Mexico, they were never dominated by missionaries and had maintained their own civilization. These untamed *indios bravos*, as the Spaniards called them, were proud, fiery, crafty in war, feared, and admired. None excelled the Comanches in bravery on the battlefield, or in the skillful handling of horses and weapons. None loved freedom more than they. According to American historian Hubert H. Bancroft, they were "dignified in their deportment, vain in respect to their personal appearance, ambitious of martial fame, unrelenting in their feuds, always exacting blood for blood, yet not sanguinary" (Bancroft 1886, 1:525). But they were indeed the plague of the *hacendados* and *rancheros* of the northern provinces.

The Indians of central Mexico, in contrast, had long ago ceased to live in independent tribal groups. At the time of the conquest powerful nations had inhabited towns whose splendor had matched and even surpassed those of Europe. In their arts and crafts, in the richness of their poetry, in the magnificence of their architecture, in their trade network, and in their forms of government and administration, the Aztecs rivaled the Spaniards.

In spite of the clash of the Indian and Spanish cultures, and the devastating social upheaval suffered by the native population, large numbers of Indians still lived undisturbed village lives and spoke their traditional languages. Neither their primitive agriculture nor their dwellings had been altered, and some of their pre-Spanish crafts, such as pottery making and weaving, survived. They simply had changed masters. Said Miguel Covarrubias: "Instead of being subjects of an Aztec emperor . . . the Indians became the vassals of Spanish adventurers, who enslaved them, destroyed their ways of life, and seized their lands" (Covarrubias 1946, 28).

Indeed, despite the protection afforded them by the crown, they became serfs and too often were stripped of everything, including their dignity. The Indian mentality was foreign to whites. All observers pointed out their passivity, their apparent indifference, their indolence, their "abject" submission to their masters, and their propensity for drinking (Mayer 1844, 201–2; Poinsett 1824, 120; Calderón de la Barca [1843] 1931, 119–21; Sartorius 1858, 66).

Aztec ethics forbade young people to drink intoxicating liquor, but mature men were allowed to drink, so long as it was in privacy and they did not get drunk (Madsen 1960, 124). Although the friars wisely endeavored to prevent their flocks from drinking, many Indians developed a passion for liquor, and when they drank too much they could be dangerous. "They are said to be a very peaceable inoffensive race when sober," British Captain G. F. Lyon wrote of the Huichol Indians, "but quite outrageous in their drunken fits, when their quarrels are very bloody" (Lyon 1828, 1:296–97). The Comanches alone are praised for their temperance. In fact, said American Captain Randolph Barnes Marcy, who frequently dealt with them, they positively refused to drink intoxicating liquor, as they considered "that it makes fools of them, and that they do not desire it" (Marcy 1853, 102).

At best, contemporary observers felt pity for the Indians and put the blame on the colonial system, which, they said, had depressed the spirit of the Indians. Because it seemed impossible to assimilate Indians into white civilization, Americans, Europeans, and Creoles alike judged them inferior, when in fact they were only different. Two passages by John L. Stephens show the peculiar character of the Indians and throw into relief the conflict between them and white civilization. Stephens had been visiting the hacienda of Uxmal, owned by Don Simón Peón, a rich Yucatecan from Mérida. He reports that "when one of them is whipped, and smarting under stripes, with tears in his eyes, he makes a bow to the majordomo and says 'buenos tarde, señor;' 'good evening, sir.'" And he further writes, "Don Simón brought out the common churn from the United States, and attempted to introduce the making of butter and cheese; but the Indians could not be taught the use of them, the churns were thrown aside, and hundreds of cows wander in the woods unmilked" (Stephens [1841] 1969, 2:416).

Were Indians "abjectly" obedient to their masters? Could these humble Maya peons be the descendants of the heroic people who had made such a fiery resistance to the conquerors? An examination of Indian psychology reveals that such behavior, unintelligible to Stephens and probably to Don Simón Peón as well, was a reaction typical of Middle American cultures. An array of deities presided over the Mexican universe and ruled human beings' fate. From time immemorial, it had been the preoccupation of the natives to try to interpret divine will and to satisfy their gods. Only by maintaining harmony with their deities could the corn grow, the tribe prosper, wars be won, and life carry on. All events were determined by fate or necessity and were therefore inevitable. By submitting quietly to the lash of the master, the Indian yielded to the will of his gods. In the nineteenth century, as in the sixteenth, religion and destiny regulated the lives of the Indians. Gods alone were free.

CHAPTER TWO

MEXICO CITY

From an eminence we came suddenly in sight of the great valley of Mexico, with its beautiful city appearing in the centre, surrounded by diverging shady Paséos, bright fields, and picturesque Haciendas—G. F. Lyon

The first view of the City of Mexico was always a source of admiration to beholders, from the handful of Spanish conquerors who dared to enter Moctezumas's domain, to the many travelers of the nineteenth century who visited the new republic. "Gazing on such wonderful sights, we did not know what to say, or whether what appeared before us was real," wrote conquistador Bernal Díaz del Castillo in his memoirs (Díaz del Castillo 1956, 192). Three hundred years later the new city that grew out of the rubble of the razed Tenochtitlán caused the Frenchman Louis de Bellemare to proclaim it "the most beautiful city ever built by the Spaniards in the New World" (Bellemare 1856, 5).

A BIRD'S-EYE VIEW

Bellemare had climbed the steps of one of the two towers of the cathedral, as did numerous visitors of the time, to survey the magnificent panorama of the valley of Anáhuac. The valley was surrounded by mountains, including smoking Popocatépetl and snow-covered Ixtaccíhuatl on the southeast. The fine view encompassed lakes and meadows, church spires and villages, fields and gardens. On the west rose the hill of Chapultepec, once the playground of Moctezuma and residence of viceroys; on the north lay the village and shrine of Guadalupe; and on the east the ever-receding shores of Lake Texcoco.

So clear was the sky and so pure the atmosphere that distances seemed not to exist; the lofty mountains in the background appeared very near. The transparent air enhanced the color of the houses and revealed the graceful proportions of the architecture.

The city that spread out below the cathedral was home to some 170,000 inhabitants at mid-century (Meyer and Sherman [1979] 1987, 362) and covered an area about two miles in length and one and one-half miles in width. Although much of the water that had caused flooding in colonial times had been drained away from the five lakes, large stretches of marshy land still remained around the city and were crossed by causeways. Many roads led out from the city gates to destinations in all parts of the republic.

To Bellemare the city at his feet seemed to be a "chess-board, formed by terraces of houses." Indeed, that was the effect created by the wide, straight streets, which intersected each other at right angles; the flat-roofed dwellings, many with hanging gardens of flowers or "balconies decorated with striped cloth" (Bellemare 1856, 6); and the square public buildings, accented by domes and towers, which included many fine churches and old convents. Across all, from separate points of origin, were extended two enormous aqueducts supported on arches of stone. And looking down, Bellemare could see the Plaza Mayor, the vast square that held the cathedral, the offices of the federal and city governments, and the shops, stalls, and markets of people of all levels. Here were concentrated in one place the powers of religion, politics, and the economy.

Hardly perceptible from the church tower were the suburbs, the *barrios* of the poor, which were on the outskirts of the city, especially on the north. There the regular flow of streets and houses disintegrated into trackless labyrinths of crossroads and alleyways. In low-lying hovels of sun-baked adobe the lowest elements of society eked out an existence amid dirt, filth, vermin, and crime. Travelers entering the city through those suburbs made haste to proceed to the center of town.

The capital of the Aztecs must have appeared very different to Bernal Díaz del Castillo. Tenochtitlán was an island fortress near the western shore of Lake Texcoco. It was surrounded by great expanses of open water and inhabited by as many as 500,000 people. The city was connected to the land by three causeways, which passed through areas that were being claimed from the lake in the watery gardens called *chinampas*, before converging at the center of the island. On the great plaza of Tenochtitlán stood the magnificent palace of Moctezuma and a cluster of temples, dominated by the famous Templo Mayor dedicated to the sanguinary god of war Huitzilopochtli. His insatiable hunger for human hearts was affirmed by the thousands of human skulls strung upon racks in public view.

The Spanish conquerors destroyed the fabulous Indian city, and the gruesome yet beautiful pagan shrines were demolished in the name of the True God. Over the ruins of Tenochtitlán, often with the same stones on nearly the same sites, the Spaniards rebuilt the City of Mexico and raised the Christian cross. The great plaza, the Plaza Mayor, was to be the heart of New Spain for three hundred years, and in independent Mexico the plaza would become the focal point of ambitious generals' striving for power. From it all activities radiated.

THE PLAZA MAYOR

Through the years, the appearance of the Plaza Mayor underwent constant evolution.

When Viceroy Revillagigedo arrived in New Spain in 1789, he found the plaza both unsightly and unsanitary. Within five years this good administrator had improved conditions greatly. The plaza was paved; fountains were built in the four corners; street lamps and drainage pipes were installed; and the whole area was cleared of stalls and sheds (Enciclopedia de México 1966–77, 8:1047).

The next viceroy, the Marqués de Branciforte, at his own expense commissioned the Spanish sculptor Manuel Tolsá to create a colossal bronze equestrian statue of the Spanish king Carlos IV to be erected in the center of the plaza. Joel Poinsett had much praise for the statue in 1822 (Poinsett 1824, 56). Yet soon afterwards it was removed from the square, as it was thought to be a reminder of the country's oppressors. For years it languished in a small courtyard of the University of Mexico, only to appear again at mid-century in the Paseo de Bucareli.

In 1843, Santa Anna, as president, decided to construct an elaborate monument to independence in the center of the Plaza Mayor. Only the base, or *zócalo*, was ever completed, but it gave the plaza the name by which it would later be known—the Zócalo—although the square had been officially named the Plaza de la Constitución in 1813.

Dominating the Plaza Mayor with its twin towers was the massive cathedral, which extended across the entire northern side of the square. Construction began in 1563, but it was not consecrated until 1667, with some work continuing into the nineteenth century. The conservative baroque style of the cathedral was complemented by the addition of the Sagrario in Mexican churrigueresque, and enhanced by high-soaring,

Sagrario of the cathedral of Mexico City. Engraving by L. Auda and Casimiro Castro in J. Decaen, ed., *México y sus alrededores; colección de monumentos, trajes y paisajes* (1864).

vaulted ceilings. Magnificence and squalor strangely mingled. Brantz Mayer, like most observers, was as disconcerted by the dilapidated condition of the floors, which consisted of "loose disjointed boards filled with dirt and filth," as he was impressed by the richness of the church jewels and ornaments, particularly the gold and silver railing which encircled the main altar. "Around this splendid mine of wealth are half-naked Indians, gaping with surprise, or kneeling to the figure of some favorite saint—the misery of the man a painful contrast with the splendor of the shrine!" (Mayer 1844, 41). A giant Aztec calendar stone, a reminder of ancient Mexico, had been attached to the western side of the cathedral since its discovery during the leveling of the plaza in 1790. In the time of Santa Anna the cathedral was encircled by a line of posts with chains strung from one to another, known as Las Cadenas, a popular locale for a promenade.

Under the shadow of the cathedral, the Palacio Nacional stretched across the eastern side of the plaza. It was an imposing building, with a huge balcony running along the second story, yet it lacked balance because of the uneven arrangement of its doors and windows. The Palacio at different times had been the property of Hernán Cortés, the home of the viceroys, the palace of an emperor, and ultimately, the seat of government of the republic, which utilized every corner. One roof, separated by courtyards and galleries, sheltered the apartment of the president (much embellished by Santa Anna), the Ministry of Justice, the Ministry of Finance, the Supreme Court of Justice, the prison Cárcel de la Corte, a caserne for cavalry and another for infantry, the mint, the Chamber of Deputies, and the Senate Chamber.

Bayard Taylor visited the Chamber of Deputies, or Hall of Congress, which fronted one of the inner courtyards. He wrote:

> It is semicircular in form, and lighted by windows of blue glass, near the top. As in the Senate, the members have no desks, but are ranged along two semicircular benches, the outer one raised a step from the floor. . . . Behind the Speaker's chair, and elevated above it, is a sort of throne with two seats, under a crimson canopy. Here the President of the Republic and the Speaker of Congress take their seats at the opening and close of each session. Above the canopy in a gilded frame, on a ground of the Mexican tricolor, hangs the sword of Iturbide. A picture of the Virgin of Guadalupe, with her blue mantle and silver stars, completes the decorations. (Taylor [1850] 1949, 305)

Taylor noted that the speeches were "short, though not, in consequence, always to the point," and added: "I am told that any definite action on any subject is as difficult to be had as in our own Congress. It is better, however, to do nothing decorously than after a riotous fashion" (Taylor [1850] 1949, 305).

The Casa Municipal, or Town Hall, with offices for the administration of city government, faced the plaza on the south. The first floor contained the Exchange of Merchants of Mexico, the Lonja, which provided readers with newspapers from not only the republic but also Europe and the United States. There was a room for billiards as well.

All around the southern and western edges of the square ran *portales*—the Portal de las Flores near the Casa Municipal and the Portal de Mercaderes across from it. These arcades were filled with cafés, flower markets, bookstalls, and every sort of shop. In the southwest corner was the famed bazaar of shops called the Parián. The variety and elegance of its merchandise were undisputed. Domestic products such as hats and woolens from Puebla or blankets and leather goods from Guadalajara, as well as foreign jewelry, clocks, liquor, and the latest in ladies' fashions, were all to be found. The building itself, however, was considered an eyesore, and most observers thought it marred the symmetry of the whole plaza. Although it provided much-needed revenue for the city coffers, the Parián was demolished in 1843, in one of the less-harmful acts of Santa Anna.

Another building farther along the western side of the plaza, across from the cathedral, housed the Monte Pío, more properly called the Monte de Piedad. Founded in 1775 by the Conde de Regla, the Monte Pío was a national pawnbroking establishment, "a beneficial institution," observed Brantz Mayer, which daily provided loans to more than two hundred people in need, of every class. A walk through the extensive facility would reveal "every species of garment, from the tattered reboso of the *lépera* to the lace mantilla of the noble dame . . . from the blanket of the beggar, to the military cloak and jewelled sword of the impoverished officer" (Mayer 1844, 267–68).

STREETS AND HOUSES

Although many a beautiful building had been, in the words of Frances Calderón, "touched by the finger of time, or crushed by the iron heel of revolution" (Calderón de la Barca [1843] 1931, 60), no European or American visitor could help but be impressed by the air of grandeur of Mexico City, the substantial quality of the houses, and the liveliness of the street scenes.

Departing from the Plaza Mayor were the important streets of the city: Santo Domingo, Tacuba, Monterilla, San Francisco. Certain streets were devoted to particular lines of business. As the inveterate British traveler and writer Charles Joseph Latrobe said, "The jewellers have their street; the sellers of *mangas* theirs, and so forth" (Latrobe 1836, 111).

Most contemporary observers agreed that streets were broad and well paved with narrow sidewalks on each side, but their comments on other aspects of city life were quite varied. Captain Lyon commented in 1828 that "through their centre, beneath a line of broad slabs, runs the common sewer," adding, "it is a far cleaner town than might be expected; well lighted, and now under a good police" (Lyon 1828, 2:126). The Mexican statesman Lucas Alamán complained, on the other hand, that the superb carriages with their beautiful horses could scarcely roll on the pavement of the streets of Mexico, and that the deposit of waste materials along the streets made a shocking and sad contrast with the beauty of the houses (Alamán [1849–52] 1942, 5:851). Frances Calderón noted that "streets are so ill kept, the pavements so narrow, the crowd so great, and the multitude of *léperos* in rags and blankets so annoying" that few ladies ventured forth on foot in the narrow streets of Mexico City except, occasionally, to go to an early mass or to do an early shopping (Calderón de la Barca [1843] 1931, 105). As for Bayard Taylor, he found the system of naming streets "very confusing to a stranger. A name extends," he wrote, "no farther than a single block, the same street having sometimes as many as twenty different names of streets in different places" (Taylor [1850] 1949, 298).

Thus the beautiful Calle de San Francisco, which ran from the Alameda, the fashionable wooded park near the western edge of the city, toward the Plaza Mayor, became for the last two blocks the Calle Plateros, known as the high spot of shopping. The Calle Plateros abounded with not only the silversmiths for which it was named but also "goldsmiths, watchmakers, French hairdressers, French cooks, French milliners, French carvers and gilders, and French print-sellers" (Mayer 1844, 45). Everything French was the fashion of the day.

Shops in Mexico were not impressive; they were generally open to the street and of small proportion. On the Calle Plateros flourished the famed French barbershop "Jouvel, Peluquero de Paris y del General-Presidente," and the Mexican "Benito y Carlos, flebotomianos." As was commonplace in those days, these barbers also practiced the fine art of phlebotomy and extracted teeth, but their living depended as much on their ability as men of the world as on their skill with the razor. Their shops, in fact, were constantly the center of love plots and political intrigues (Salvat Editores de México S.A. 1974, 7:188).

As the Calle de San Francisco, the street contained some of the most sumptuous mansions of the city: the Casa de los Azulejos, or "House of Tiles," of the Conde del Valle, so called for the polychromed tiles of yellow, white, and blue that covered the exterior walls; the costly Palace of Iturbide; and the house where "la Güera Rodríguez," the belle of Mexican society who had fascinated Humboldt, spent her last days (Vargas Martínez 1961, 111). Also in this fashionable area was the home of Luis Gonzaga and Mariana Gordoa, at 19 Calle San José el Real.

The houses of the wealthy were indeed handsome. Constructed of a thick but light-weight volcanic stone called *tezontl*, two or three stories high, with terrace rooftops and iron balconies, they were colorfully painted pink, yellow, crimson, orange, blue, or green. Many were over-laid with glazed and stained porcelain tiles. Few of the mansions did not have a patron saint sculpted in stone on the facade, and, according to Charles Latrobe, most of the houses at the intersection of streets were ornamented with arabesque shrines that rose above the level of the terraced roof (Latrobe 1836, 87).

Arched gateways large enough for carriages to pass through led to interior courtyards. A glimpse through these gateways might reveal "a sunny picture of a fountain, a cluster of orange trees, or the slender, graceful arches of the corridor" (Taylor [1850] 1949, 298). The ground floor usually contained the porter's lodge, offices, and a carriage house. At times space was rented out for shops. A staircase generally led to an entresol for domestics, while the upper floors were devoted to spacious rooms for the family, secluded from the street and neighbors. Furnishings in such homes could be very luxurious: sofas and chairs of rose-wood decorated with silk, mother-of-pearl, and gold; cabinets inlaid with gold; alabaster lamps; fine paintings; mirrors with golden frames (Payno [1845–46] 1967, 130). Yet many houses of the well-to-do Creoles displayed a certain austerity of taste, even a lack of comfort, that impressed the sophisticated visitor.

Frances Calderón described the house that she and her husband rented, somewhat removed from the heart of town, as being "square, like all Mexican houses." Built around a stone-paved courtyard with a fountain, it contained about twenty rooms in the principal living area on the second floor, including a coal room, a wood room, a bathroom, and even a room for making chocolate. And there was water every-where—in the court, in the garden, and on the *azotea*, or rooftop. The first floor, with the same number of rooms, was occupied by the ser-vants. The house also had outhouses, coach houses, stables, a pigeon house, and a large garden house. All in all it was, she said, "a cross-breed between a palace and a barn" (Calderón de la Barca [1843] 1931, 90–91).

Mexican women spent a lot of time in their houses. Waddy Thomp-son claimed that "the general routine of female life is to rise late, and spend the larger portion of the day standing in their open windows which extend to the floor. It would be a safe bet at any hour of the day between ten and five o'clock, that you would in walking the streets see one or more females standing thus at the windows of more than half the houses" (Thompson 1846, 162).

OF CHURCHES, CONVENTS, AND HOSPITALS

Next to the Calderón's house stood a vast building, impaired by time, with a church adjoining it and bounded on one side by an enclosed orchard. It was the old monastery of San Fernando, where only seven or eight monks still lingered.

Churches and convents abounded, as one might expect, in a country where the influence of the clergy was so strong that each upper-class family had its own confessor, who intervened in every aspect of life. Charles Latrobe counted fifty-six churches within the limits of the city, besides the cathedral (Latrobe 1836, 86). Most of them were large, with statuary, paintings, carvings, and showy ornaments of silver and gold. The number of clergy, according to Joel Poinsett, totaled 550 secular and 1,646 regular priests, and there were no less than twenty-three convents of monks and fifteen convents of nuns (Poinsett 1824, 84).

None perhaps was more lovely than the monastery of San Francisco on the street of the same name. With five churches enclosed in one enormous square, San Francisco attracted many friars and travelers to its confines for meditation. Jean Louis Berlandier, a French botanist who lived in Mexico in the 1820s and 1830s, recalled an unforgettable moment he experienced there one night in June. The moon, in its first quarter, "had risen some fifty degrees above the horizon and illuminated the entire courtyard of the convent. In the distance, below the galleries and among the cypresses, the friars could be seen in the most profound silence, half buried in the darkness, praying fervently. Suddenly, bells from everywhere caused the air to reverberate with the Angelus, proclaiming to the faithful the beginning of night" (Berlandier 1980, 1:116).

A secret and hidden realm of the church existed within the walls of the convents. The doors were opened to Frances Calderón, and she, not yet a Catholic, was allowed to talk with the cloistered nuns through iron gratings and to witness the poignant ceremonies by which young girls willingly shut themselves away from the world. For many a young girl, innocent in the ways of the world, and under the domination of a confessor from early childhood, the secluded life of the convent seemed the sure way to achieve happiness and salvation.

Some of the convents were in fact as luxurious as palaces. Such was the convent of the Encarnación, which Fanny visited by special invitation of the archbishop. She was led into a spacious hall lighted with cut-glass lamps and was received by several nuns wearing long robes of the finest white cassimere. Fanny had never seen any convent as magnificent as this. She visited the well-kept garden, with its stone walls and benches and a sparkling fountain that murmured joyously; the splendid halls inside the convent; the refectory; the *botica,* or pharmacy; and the immense kitchen, "which seems hallowed from the approach even of a particle of dust." That was no wonder: each nun had a servant, and some even had two. "The convent is rich; each novice at her entrance pays five thousand dollars into the common stock," recorded Fanny (Calderón de la Barca [1843] 1931, 142–43). There were at that time in the convent about thirty nuns and ten novices.

The convent of the Encarnación was not unique. Ernest H. Gruening reports that shortly before the reforms of the 1850s the number of servants in the ten most prosperous convents of the capital exceeded the number of nuns (Gruening 1928, 194).

Life inside those convents contrasted dramatically with that of the sisters of Santa Teresa, where each abbess added a stricter rule and a more severe penance than her predecessor (Calderón de la Barca [1843] 1931, 190), as we shall see in chapter 9. It should be noted too that many sisters also dedicated their lives to the poor, the orphans, and the sick.

Hospitals in Mexico City were few in number and lacking, for the most part, in the most elemental facilities for patient comfort. Yet both Frances Calderón and Berlandier expressed admiration for one hospital, the Hospital de Jesús. The oldest in Mexico, it was the successor of the Hospital de la Purísima Concepción de Nuestra Señora, founded by Hernán Cortés. In fact, the remains of the conquistador at one time rested next to the hospital. Although a private institution, it was considered far better than the public hospitals because of "its cleanliness and its well-ordered service," and from its doors free pharmaceutical medicine was dispensed nightly at eight o'clock (Berlandier 1980, 1:115). Fanny, whose unquenchable curiosity led her to investigate every facet of Mexican society, arranged to visit the Hospital de Jesús. The building itself seemed "infinitely handsomer" than that of another hospital she had seen, and after touring the physicians' apartments and a large hall given over to soldiers who had been wounded in the latest *pronunciamiento,* she reported: "Each one had a separate room, or at least a compartment divided by curtains from the rest, and in each was a bed, a chair, and a small table—this on one side of the long hall. The other was occupied by excellent hot and cold baths." After visiting the women's quarters, she made her way up to the *azotea*, where dead bodies were dissected, after which she pronounced the whole establishment "healthy, cleanly, and well-conducted" (Calderón de la Barca [1843] 1931, 446). She neglected to report the number of patients who were cured and went home and the number who journeyed instead to the *azotea*.

OF HOTELS, CAFÉS, *FONDAS*, AND *PULQUERÍAS*

Mexico City boasted a number of hotels and inns. It also had 132 cafés, *fondas*, and eating houses, plus 379 *pulquerías* (Wilson 1855, 264). Everyone reported that hotels in Mexico City were by no means what a visitor accustomed to traveling in Europe or the United States expected to find in the capital of the former kingdom of New Spain.

During the colonial period there had been little demand for hotels, as travel was limited and those few persons of the upper class who came to the city made arrangements to stay with friends. With independence and the opening of the country to foreigners, the situation changed and accommodations for visitors became necessary.

By all accounts, the principal hotel, the Gran Sociedad, left much to be desired in those early years. Lieutenant Robert William Hale Hardy, of the General Pearl and Coral Fishery Association of London, who arrived in Mexico City in 1825, penned a vivid picture of this hotel before it underwent improvements. Known by some as the "Gran Suciedad,"[1] the large two-story hotel was located on the Calle del Espíritu Santo just two blocks west of the Plaza Mayor. The wide main entrance would admit a carriage through an iron gateway to a large paved courtyard with columns on three sides and a balcony above. On the sides of the courtyard were a café, "in which, of an evening, the whole world of beauty and fashion assemble to take ice, etc."; a billiard room, where only the "best and deepest players" were allowed to play; and a room with painted tables for those who wished to drink chocolate or spend an hour in conversation before the theater. A brick staircase led to the second floor, where a guest might find a special *sala* for gamblers; a *comedor*, or dining room, with a long table covered with a greasy cloth, where appetites could be "appeased for a dollar and a quarter, wine extra"; and another billiard room where the rank and file played. The four sleeping rooms were furnished with only a painted-board bedstead, a chair, and a table. Hardy provided his own bed and had his servant

[1] A play on words: *sociedad* means "society," and *suciedad* means "dirt" or "filth."

sweep the floor, as the hotel did not provide that service. And this, he concluded, "was the best hotel in Mexico" (Hardy 1829, 2–7). One wonders about the comfort in the lesser hotels.

Brantz Mayer, some fifteen years later, also took up residence in the Gran Sociedad, which he called a French hotel. Improvements had not been made on a grand scale in the course of the years. For seventy dollars a month, Mayer was provided with a "flea-haunted bed—space enough for my books and papers—a broad balcony shielded from the sun by a fanciful curtain—and two Frenchified meals per day" (Mayer 1844, 48).

The café of the Gran Sociedad was not the only meeting place of the social set of Mexico City. A café in the Hotel de Bazar was later in competition with it. Bayard Taylor recalled his visit there in 1850: "The Café de Bazar is kept by M. Arago, a brother of the French astronomer and statesman. . . . At night the light Moorish corridors around his fountained courtyards are lighted with gay-colored lamps, and knots of writers, politicians, or stray tourists are gathered there until ten o'clock, when Mexican law obliges the place to be closed" (Taylor [1850] 1949, 313).

Most visitors found accommodations in the *mesones*, which were, in the words of Captain Lyon, "beyond description offensive and incommodious" (Lyon 1828, 2:126). Although some furnished water, the patrons of inns wishing to wash themselves usually had to resort to public baths. Captain Lyon noted that there were some warm and cold baths in the capital, but that they were rarely used (Lyon 1828, 2:127). The Frenchman Ernest Vigneaux's first action, when he arrived in Mexico City, was to look for an inn and take a bath. We are glad to hear that the public establishment he found was "far superior" to those in Europe and much cheaper. For two reales, he had "two perfectly virgin little soaps, one hard and one soft, brushes for friction, brushes of every kind, toilet instruments and articles, two teeny-weeny bottles on a tray, one containing a few drops of perfume, the other the same amount of scented oil, plenty of linen, a spitoon" (Vigneaux 1863, 493–94).

One of the best inns in town in 1826, according to Captain Lyon, was the *mesón* Balbañera, situated on the *calle* of the same name. As the hotel provided him "nothing but water, a chair, and a rickity table," Lyon sent a servant to an eating place nearby to procure dinner. "It came at length in the shape of two square bits of dry tough muttons fried in pig's fat, and placed in a large dish of coarse brown crockery . . . , about an ounce of mashed cabbage sprinkled with hard yellow pease, and a bowl of 'caldo' (literally hot greasy water called broth)." To this was added a green chili and a piece of bread (Lyon 1828, 2:108).

Mexico City was certainly a purgatory for the sophisticated traveler used to the delicacy of French cuisine. "Cook shops for others than Arrieros and *léperos* are very scarce," noted Captain Lyon in his journal (Lyon 1828, 2:127). The eating places called *fondas* were indeed the choice of the muleteer, the *ranchero*, and the soldier. A meal could be had, including a glass of pulque—the ever-popular intoxicating drink of the maguey plant—for a real, or about twelve and a half cents. Knives and forks were never used in these meals, as tortillas served very well instead. Sartorius, whose keen eye missed little, observed: "The diners of this quarter have a singular habit, *viz*: after a meal . . . they drink a large glass of water, cross themselves with the words "bendito y alabado sea Dios" (God be praised), and then with open mouth and much noise allow the stomachic gas to explode. . . . The common people deem the practice very wholesome, and even those occupying a higher position do not disdain it" (Sartorius [1858] 1961, 114).

The ragged *lépero* and the Indian market vendor were among the best customers of the *pulquerías*, where pulque was sold. These were scattered all over the city, particularly in the vicinity of the marketplace, where the men retreated early in the morning while the women carried on their business. An idea of the importance of these establishments is seen in a statement of the municipal revenue for 1851, provided by Judge Robert Anderson Wilson. It reveals that the city fathers collected the greatest single sum—$65,297—from licenses on *pulquerias*, with the combined taxes on canals, coaches, and markets yielding a total of $83,085. The largest single expense was $69,863 for public prisons, with lights and the city patrol second at $52,422 (Wilson 1855, 264–65).

OF CRIMES AND PUNISHMENT

No wonder the largest expenses of the municipality were for the public prisons: the city was far from being safe. Robbers, pickpockets, and other criminals were very active, and knife fights, in which women and men showed equal skill, were commonplace around *the pulquerías* in those days. The police force consisted of a military patrol who also performed the duties of lamplighters. Considering the limited means of the municipal government, Wilson praised the way its laws were enforced. The number of arrests for the year 1851, he said, was 3,918 men and 3,430 women. Furthermore, the police force "*freed the city from the plague of 6048 dogs!* Just as many dogs arrested as human beings" (Wilson 1855, 265).

In 1851 the following arrests were made: 320 men and 120 women for robbery, 120 men and 25 women for picking pockets, 15 men and 3 women for murder, 728 men and 246 women for "affrays" and wounds, 354 men and 403 women for incontinence and adultery, 311 men and 318 women for the violation of public decency, 1,256 men and 1,944 women for excessive drinking (Wilson 1855, 265). When we think that besides 379 pulque shops, there were in Mexico City, 533 retail groceries in which liquor was sold by the gill, and 8 breweries (Wilson 1855, 264), we are not surprised to learn that the principal activity of the police consisted of apprehending drunkards.

Robbers were bold: they did not hesitate to break into houses even when people were inside, and, in many instances, they killed their victims. Frances Calderón tells at length of burglaries and murders committed in Mexico City: "We have had in our house various reports of robbers and frights, some true, some exaggerated, and some wholly false. . . . When Calderón went out I waited in trembling for his return—and one evening, when all were in bed but me, an attempt to open the door of the room in which I sat nearly threw me into a fit" (Calderón de la Barca [1843] 1931, 173).

The Calderóns then decided to hire two old soldiers to live in the house. But armed soldiers were not sufficient to deter Mexican robbers. Two months later, two days in a row, burglars broke into the Calderóns' mansion and managed to escape under the very noses of the soldiers (Calderón de la Barca [1843] 1931, 145–46). In the light of the many contemporary accounts we have read, it seems that no one would dare go into the streets unarmed, and even at home people had their pistols close at hand.

While in Mexico City, Frances Calderón devoted a day to visiting the notorious prison La Acordada. The building, near the popular Alameda and the equally popular Paseo de Bucareli, presented an innocuous front to passersby with its high walls of dark red. Inside were crammed all sorts of inmates, from ferocious murderers to ruffians, prostitutes, debtors, and political prisoners.

Fanny went first to the women's quarters, which were familiar to the Creole ladies, because many of them joined a *junta* devoted to teaching reading and Christian doctrine to the "female malefactors." She was surprised, even shocked, by the intimacy shown between the ladies and the inmates. "It is painful and almost startling to see the first ladies in Mexico familiarly conversing with and embracing women who have been guilty of the most atrocious crimes" (Calderón de la Barca [1843] 1931, 448). The women prisoners of "decent family" were kept apart from other prisoners. They seemed to be of all sorts, both well dressed and slovenly, but many had this in common, that they had killed their husbands. Fanny was comforted to hear that the "brutes deserved little better." In the lower level of the prison, in a "great, damp, vaulted gallery," hundreds of women of the poorer classes, dirty, ragged, and miserable-looking, were engaged in forced labor—baking tortillas for the prisoners. In another room they were cleaning and sweeping. Meanwhile, the little children of the prisoners were running about in the courtyard (Calderón de la Barca [1843] 1931, 449).

As for the men, they were kept all together in a huge courtyard: those whose only offense was the theft of a handkerchief were confined with the "midnight murderer" (Calderón de la Barca [1843] 1931, 450). These were the same convicts seen daily in chains watering the Alameda or mending the streets. Frances Calderón also visited the row of cells where disorderly criminals were kept in solitary confinement and the little chapel "where the criminal condemned to die" spent the last three days of his or her life with a priest "chosen for that purpose" (Calderón de la Barca [1843] 1931, 451).

A more distressing scene at La Acordada was overlooked by the wife of the Spanish minister, but recorded by Bellemare: that of the city morgue. Promenaders on the Paseo had to turn their eyes to avoid noticing a certain stone slab beyond a set of iron bars. On the slab were the still-bleeding and half-naked bodies of men and women who had been thrown together in "one promiscuous heap" (Bellemare 1856, 24). These were the victims of the frequent quarrels in the *barrios*, on view for all to see and perhaps to identify.

MORNING IN MEXICO CITY

Charles Latrobe wrote: "There are certain thoroughfares and places of resort, in Mexico, which seem to pour one incessant stream of human beings, from sunrise to sunset. Such are the main streets leading to the causeways; the vicinity of Parian and Plaza Mayor, where the bulk of business of the capital is concentrated" (Latrobe 1836, 109).

Day began in the Plaza Mayor before sunrise. Even as the big clock on the cathedral struck the hour of four, the stagecoach for Veracruz with its limit of nine passengers was pulling away from the diligencia station on the Calle Dolores, with a loud clatter of hooves. Night watchmen woke up. Prisoners began to sweep the streets, or to redistribute the dirt, while servants slipped out of the great houses to seek the first provisions of the day.

By five o'clock the gates of the city were opened and lines of burros laden with charcoal and wood entered. On the Viga Canal the Indians from the *chinampas* of Xochimilco and Chalco came gliding into market in flower-adorned canoes, bringing their supplies of fruits, vegetables, and flowers to the city. A colorful sight they made, the women wearing garlands of poppies or roses as headdresses, singing as they propelled their crafts with long poles, with the old folks and children in the center of the canoe and the men playing guitars for the pleasure of all. "On some canoes are heaps of meat and game and fowl," said Alcide d'Orbigny, the French naturalist, "on others there are corn or butter or fruit or dead kids. These articles are decorated with red and white poppies thrown over them like a veil" (Orbigny 1836, 427).

The main market of Mexico City was located just off the Plaza Mayor, in what was known as the Plaza del Volador. In preconquest days it may have been a site where the Indians dressed as eagles and, tied with cords, jumped from the top of a tall pole, flying as they descended in thirteen precise circles. In this way they commemorated the periodic cycle of fifty-two years, the basis of their calendar. Thus the flyer, the *volador*, gave the plaza its name. In colonial times the square served as a location for bullfights, cockfights, and rabbit races, witnessed by the aristocracy from the balcony of the Palacio. It also served then as a market, and continued to do so in the beginning years of the republic, with 303 movable stalls and booths crisscrossed by nearly impassable aisles. It was protected from the elements by a roof of mere thatch; however, in 1841, under Santa Anna, the City Council constructed a more permanent stone building.

In this plaza the Indians displayed flowers, which were in great demand by everyone, and the onions, cauliflowers, tomatoes, chilis, squash, and cabbages from the *chinampas*. Their stalls were among the most prosperous of the market. Poorer vendors who could not afford to rent a stall simply spread out their wares upon the ground.

Despite dirt and refuse, Orbigny proclaimed the market "a lively and amusing spectacle" and recounted the vast array of products for sale: "Fish of every kind, turtles, frogs, and axolotls (a kind of salamander) are everywhere plentiful. At the meat market there are beef, mutton and pork in abundance; there are also plenty of kids but veal is forbidden. Meat, here, is not as good as in Europe, but vegetables and fruit are excellent and various. No one can imagine how beautiful the fruit are—bananas, lemons, avocados, zapotes, grenadillas, pineapples, dates, mangoes, guavas, tomatoes, etc." (Orbigny 1836, 427).

Indians also peddled the produce of their gardens from house to house, calling out the names of the fruit contained in their baskets.

Mexico City abounded in street vendors, whose discordant cries filled the air from sunup to sundown. The "Carbón, Señor?" of the coal man mingled with the grease seller's "Mantequilla [lard] at one real and a half!" only to be interrupted by the butcher's hoarse voice announcing "Salt beef! Good salt beef!" Then the inviting cry of the *dulce* vendor, the seller of candies, crying "Caramelos de esperma! Bocadillo de coco!" could be discerned (Calderón de la Barca [1843] 1931, 64–65). Through it all ran the insistent drone of the numberless beggars harassing the passersby with their prayers and long recitations.

STREET CHARACTERS AT MIDDAY

By midmorning the Plaza Mayor was a beehive of humanity—"a singular exhibition," said Joel Poinsett, ". . . of the busy, the idle, and the devout" (Poinsett 1824, 77). There passed an Indian with a coop of chickens, another with a crate of earthenware, and a *cargador* carrying a heavy load, while a woman with a basket of oranges vied for attention with the man selling lottery tickets. Ragged *léperos*; groups of *rancheros* wearing embroidered jackets and ornamented hats and serapes; priests in black cloaks and shovel hats, sometimes accompanying fashionable Spanish señoras; monks of every order; soldiers and dragoons in their colorful uniforms; countrywomen in short petticoats, trimmed chemises, and satin shoes; government officials in black coats; and dark-faced Indians with long, braided hair; all met and mingled in what was by far the liveliest and the noisiest part of the city. Meanwhile, the drivers of the many public carriages parked along the square, waiting for passengers, assailed one and all with invitations to ride.

Foreign visitors never seemed to tire of the exotic spectacle in the Plaza Mayor. Three street characters particularly attracted their attention: the *evangelista,* the *aguador,* and the *lépero,* whom we have met before. While the *lépero* and the *aguador* were present everywhere in the city, the indispensable and trusted *evangelista,* or public secretary, was seen mainly in the Plaza Mayor.

Perhaps a dozen of these servants of the illiterate occupied places in the Portal de Mercaderes or along the Parián. The *evangelista* could be found seated under a makeshift awning, wrapped snugly in his blanket, his glasses perched on his nose. With a big bottle of ink at his side, a board across his knees, and a basket full of colored paper close by, he was ready to provide letters in verse or prose at a moment's notice. His facility was surprising, claimed Joel Poinsett: "Memorials to ministers and judges, letters of condolence and congratulation, and epistles breathing love and friendship, succeed each other rapidly, and appear to cost but little effort" (Poinsett 1824, 78). The tender feelings of a young girl on the stool in front of the *evangelista* might be transferred to pink paper in a declaration of love. According to Brantz Mayer, one could have such a delicate missive for a mere real, a "*scolding letter*," for a *medio*, and an "*upbraiding epistle*, full of daggers, jealousy, love, and tenderness . . . done upon azure paper besprinkled with hearts and doves, for the ridiculous price of *twenty-five cents*." Probably more money was earned by scribes in Mexico than anywhere else in the world (Mayer 1844, 40).

The *aguador*, or water carrier, was also a familiar figure on Mexican streets. Barefoot, with his short leather apron, his leather backpiece, and his leather cap, he plied his trade all day through the streets, bent forward in a characteristic position, bearing two earthen jars. The larger one was suspended by a leather strap around his forehead and hung down his back, while the smaller jar, suspended from a strap around the back of his head, hung down in front. Brantz Mayer told an anecdote of an Englishman who met an *aguador* on the street and struck the jar on the man's back with his cane. It broke, and the sudden weight of the other jar brought the carrier down on his nose. The offender immediately calmed the outraged carrier with a couple of dollars, saying "I only wanted to see whether you were *exactly balanced*, my dear fellow, and *the experiment is worth the money!*" (Mayer 1844, 43).

Of two great aqueducts bringing water into the city, the one leading from the springs of Santa Fe discharged its water near the Alameda; the other conducted water from the springs of Chapultepec to a fountain called Salto de Agua, several blocks to the south. From either of these sources the *aguadores* supplied their customers on their daily rounds.

The nature of this occupation demanded that the *aguador* be a decent sort of fellow, for he was admitted into the customer's household, where he enjoyed the privileged position of a confidant. He chatted with the servants and made friends with the children. The mistress of the house even consulted him when she intended to hire a new maid or footman.

Aguador. From Désiré Charnay, *Les Anciennes Villes du Nouveau Monde; voyages d'explorations au Mexique et dans l'Amerique Centrale* (1885).

He knew all the gossip and, as Sartorius asserted, he could give information on what was "going on in the bosom of families" (Sartorius [1858] 1961, 144–45).

A decided contrast to the industrious *aguador* was the lounging *lépero*. Look where you would about the Plaza Mayor or the streets of the city, it was impossible to avoid the ubiquitous *lépero*, whether in the form of a beggar, pickpocket, or mere idler.

To Fanny Calderón *léperos* seemed to be "moving bundles of rags" (Calderón de la Barca 1843, 1931, 51). Indeed, their classic garb consisted of little but a tattered blanket and a pair of leather or cloth breeches blackened with time. Sometimes there was a worn straw hat, and often a rosary or a scapulary, but never a pair of shoes. Berlandier provided a graphic description of the woman *lépera*: "The women bear on themselves the imprint of the greatest filth. Like the man they commonly are possessed of only one garment, which it is necessary to take off to wash. Consequently they may be seen in the streets with the stains of the menstrual flow, which all females strive to conceal." Still, according to this observer, some of these women were seen "wearing quite expensive, fringed silk petticoats, which they do not change until they fall into rags" (Berlandier 1980, 1:144). For both men and women, a dagger, whose use might be inspired by drink or jealousy, was an indispensable possession.

Home for many *léperos* was wherever night happened to overtake them; however, a married *lépero* might have a place on the outskirts of town, in the *barrios*—a single room with walls of adobe, a straw roof, and a dirt floor, equipped with little more than a few jugs and a sleeping mat on which everyone stretched out among little statues and pictures of saints and virgins. Life in the *barrios* existed amid a maze of tenements, in the stench of ditches filled with filth, dead animals, and heaps of garbage. Work was all but unknown, and the only ones to attain even a low level of income were the prostitutes and thieves (Salvat Editores de México S.A. 1974, 7:178).

FROM SIESTA TO EVENING PROMENADE

A degree of quiet prevailed in the Plaza Mayor between the hours of two and four, as this was dinnertime for people of all classes. Most shops and businesses were closed. For many of the proletariat, home kitchens did not exist. They ate their food in the street where they worked—their beans, chilis, tortillas, and tacos were purchased from Indian women busy over their charcoal braziers. Others crowded into their *fondas*, while merchants and the well-to-do repaired to their homes. The siesta was part of the daily routine for every Mexican, rich or poor. And "even those who maintained their stands were dozing," said Latrobe (Latrobe 1836, 111).

Later in the afternoon the ladies of the upper class went to the Alameda, the Paseo de la Viga, or to the Paseo de Bucareli to see and to be seen. Their occupations during the day had consisted of little more than performing charities, going to mass, or visiting friends. Everyone who was anyone felt compelled to be seen in the promenade. It is certain that Mariana Gordoa, even in poor health, joined her husband, along with the whole of Mexican society, for the evening *paseo*.

The Alameda, a lovely enclosed public park of some forty acres of poplars, was the choice of many for outings. As Waddy Thompson recalled it, "the whole square is intersected with walks paved with flagstones; all these walks unite in the centre where there is a beautiful jet d'eau, and from this point they diverge in every direction. . . . There is a carriage-way inside of the wall entirely surrounding the square" (Thompson 1846, 126). To be sure, the ladies appeared only in carriages, as it was considered unfashionable, even vulgar, to walk.

Located a short distance beyond the Alameda was the even more popular Paseo de Bucareli—a broad tree-lined avenue which expanded at intervals into large circular areas. At the center were stone fountains, and at the edges stone benches. From four until six or seven in the evening the Paseo teemed with rows of carriages filled with ladies and with crowds of horsemen in their picturesque costumes.

Carriages of all descriptions appeared, from the heavy ornate Mexican carriages and imitation English carriages pulled by fine horses, to hackney coaches drawn by mules and rented by those who would otherwise walk. Most fashionable were the *carretelas* with glass windows which revealed ladies in full formal dresses of silk and satin only six months behind the latest Paris styles, their heads crowned with flowers or jewels. More frequently the carriages were closed, and then "nothing is seen but an indistinct vision and a passing greeting with the fingers or a fan," to quote Fanny Calderón. And she added: "The equestrians . . . apparently take no notice of the ladies as they pass. . . . But they are generally well aware to whom each carriage belongs, and consequently when it behoves them to make their horses caracole or curvet, and otherwise show off their horsemanship to advantage" (Calderón de la Barca [1843] 1931, 106–7). It was possible in this way for courtships of long dura-

Paseo de la Viga, Mexico City. Engraving by Carl Nebel, *Voyage pittoresque et archéologique dans la partie la plus intéressante du Mexique* (1836).

tion to be carried on without the couple ever exchanging a word (Thompson 1846, 126).

Of growing popularity for the promenade in the 1840s was the Paseo de la Viga, the roadway along the canal that led to the *chinampas* of Xochimilco and Chalco. Indians crowded the canal in flat-bottomed boats and canoes as they returned to their homes at the end of the day, and enlivened the scene with their singing and dancing.

When the Aztecs had first arrived in the Valley of Mexico and settled on the island in Lake Texcoco, surrounded by enemies, they had of necessity developed a system of floating fields and gardens. By weaving together the roots of aquatic plants along the shore and intertwining them with sticks and branches, they were able to form a foundation strong enough to support soil scraped up from the shallow lake bottom and, on this base, plant their corn and chili. Besides the plants needed for survival, they raised the flowers they loved and used in the worship of their gods. Even in colonial times the *chinampas* produced considerable quantities of vegetables.

Did these gardens actually float? According to P. Blanchard, the *chi-*

nampas situated on Lake Chalco were "absolutely floating, and the inhabitants drive them quickly from one edge of the lake to the other by means of long poles." However, those on the canal of Chalco were immobile (Blanchard and Dauzats 1839, 189). Small huts stood upon some of them where the gardeners lived with their families, and trees and shrubs were planted along the edge. Frances Calderón noted that though "they give but a faint idea of what they may have been . . . when the Indians, in their barks, wishing to remove their habitations, could tow along their little islands of roses, it is still a pretty and a pleasant scene" (Calderón de la Barca [1843] 1931, 119).

IN AND AROUND THE CAPITAL

Just as every foreign traveler of the time visited the *chinampas*, so too did one and all ride to the celebrated castle of Chapultepec and to the famous shrine of the Virgin of Guadalupe.

The castle of Chapultepec, isolated on a wooded hill a short league west of Mexico City, was, in the words of Frances Calderón, "the most haunted by recollections of all the traditionary sites of which Mexico can boast" (Calderón de la Barca [1843] 1931, 68). Its ancient and gigantic cypresses, draped in graceful Spanish moss, had witnessed centuries of history. Under their venerable branches the defeated Moctezuma had meditated, the victorious Cortés had schemed, and the young and talented viceroy Bernardo de Gálvez, builder of the present castle, had strolled.

At the time of Santa Anna the never-quite-finished castle was in a state of decay, although it housed the Military College. To Frances Calderón the apartments seemed "lonely and abandoned" with "walls falling to ruin" (Calderón de la Barca [1843] 1931, 69). But from the terrace that surrounded the castle the view was one of unparalleled beauty. On the south could be discerned the villages of San Agustín, San Angel, and Tacubaya, which served as country residences for many an aristocratic Mexican family, including the Gordoas; and on the north, the collegiate church of Our Lady of Guadalupe. All the views were magnificently framed by mountains.

For countless thousands of Mexicans the shrine of Guadalupe was the object of devotion and pilgrimage, especially on December 12, the Virgin's feast day, when multitudes came together at the holy place. The road to Guadalupe headed north from the city, crossing swamplands on a tree-lined causeway. The church was one of the richest in all Mexico, lavishly ornamented, with an altar and choir railing of gilded silver simi-

Village of Guadalupe. Engraving by Casimiro Castro in J. Decaen, ed., *México y sus alrededores; colección de monumentos, trajes y paisajes* (1864).

lar to that of the cathedral in the capital. Candles lighted the main altar. Above it, in a solid gold frame edged in precious jewels, was the object of their adoration—the miraculous painting of the Virgin standing on a crescent, supported by a cherub, and wearing a gown of crimson and gold and a cloak of star-studded blue. Fanny dared pronounce the painting "course, and only remarkable on account of the tradition attached to it" (Calderón de la Barca [1843] 1931, 73).

Near the main church was a smaller, dome-shaped chapel built over a spring of bubbling water, also reputed to have miraculous qualities. From this place a steep path led up the hill of Tepeyac to another, muchneglected, chapel, which was also a place of pilgrimage. It marked the site where, according to tradition, the Virgin had appeared to the young Indian convert Juan Diego in 1531. Visitors could not help noticing a tall, saillike monument part way up the hill. It had been erected in gratitude by a Spaniard saved from a shipwreck, or so he believed, through the intercession of the Virgin of Guadalupe.

At any time of day, kneeling women wrapped in *rebosos*, and *léperos* counting their beads, could be seen in and about the cathedral. At the time of the evening angelus the church would be crowded with people of the village and with more *léperos*. But the hour had come for all visitors to return to the city, even those accompanied by armed outriders like the Calderóns, to return to the city.

Likewise, the gentry in the capital who had been taking the fresh air of the evening in the *paseos* and in the Alameda returned to their homes. At nightfall the gates of the Alameda were closed, as there was no system of lighting in the park. In the center of the city, however, 750 turpentine lamps, attached to the walls with iron brackets, dispelled the darkness in the Plaza Mayor, while another thousand, dimmer oil lamps served more distant streets (García Cubas 1904, 154). These were attended by some 120 lamplighters, ladders in hand, each in charge of fourteen lamps (Arizpe 1900, 54).

Soon the streets would be deserted except for a few vendors, a *lépero*, or a passing carriage. Life in the city had moved indoors.

CHAPTER THREE

TRANSPORTATION AND COMMUNICATION

I know few sensations more pleasing in life than those which I have experienced when starting, thus accompanied, upon one of my expeditions, with all my party well-mounted, a few spare mules and horses driven before us.—H. G. Ward

Transportation had always been of vital importance in the economy of Mexico, and much money and time were expended on it during the colonial era. The main roads within the Valley of Mexico were the enlarged and modified trails used by the Aztecs.

In preconquest times military operations and the development of trade had led to the establishment of a network of paths which spread in all directions from the capital. A class of powerful traders, the *pochteca*, plied Mexico, exchanging local produce for foreign goods. The Aztecs had lacked pack animals, and their goods were transported on the backs of professional carriers, called *tamemes*. Trading was a perpetual adventure; the farther the *pochteca* went, the more dangerous the roads became. They had to face the hostility of unconquered tribes, and they were regularly attacked by fierce bands of robbers. These indefatigable travelers had to transform themselves into warriors to survive.

The Spaniards introduced pack animals and opened new roads. The transport of silver and other supplies was made by mule train, and the *arriero* became a famous character on Mexican roads as well as an indispensable element in the work force. By 1800 nine main roads linked the capital with the remote areas of New Spain. The Zacatecas and Pachuca roads on the north provided communication with the mining region, and the Toluca road linked Mexico City with Michoacán and the west. Two roads connected the capital with the *tierra caliente* and the Pacific port of Acapulco, one through Cuernavaca and the other by way of

Cuautla. Two roads led to Puebla and thence to Veracruz through Jalapa, and to Oaxaca via Atlixco and Izúcar de Matamoros; and two other routes on the east provided additional connections with Jalapa and Veracruz—one via Tepetlaoztoc, and the other through Otumba (Gibson 1964, 361). Paths were also blazed by Spanish explorers and missionaries through the Indian territory on the north to connect the capital with the far reaches of the viceroyalty. Cart roads were few, and in some places foot trails continued to be served by *tamemes*.

The busiest routes led to Veracruz and Acapulco; the longest to Santa Fe, the capital of New Mexico, by way of Durango. Every three years a caravan traveled from Mexico City to Santa Fe, carrying supplies; it took six months to go, six to unload and distribute the goods, and six to return. Later, an annual caravan from Chihuahua took manufactured goods to the colonists, returning south with hides, wool, and salt.

The routes to the coasts presented great difficulties. Even though the mountain ranges of the Western Sierra do not slope as sharply as those of the Eastern Sierra, the road to Acapulco was dangerous during the rainy season and sometimes impassable when the Papagayo and Mescala rivers rose so that they could not be forded. Humboldt had to cross the Mescala on a raft made of dried squashes on which reeds had been tied. Two Indians guided the raft, holding it with one hand and swimming with the other (Humboldt 1822, 4:45).

Far from improving the existing network, republican Mexico let it decay. People traveling through Mexico in the time of Santa Anna kept up a continual lament. Poinsett wrote in 1822: "The road to Acapulco . . . is in a ruinous state; no repairs having been made on it from the commencement of the war of independence: there are many places impassable even for mules. The deep and rapid river Papagayo . . . occasions every year distressing accidents to mules and travellers" (Poinsett 1824, 329).

Of the much-frequented Veracruz–Mexico City road, Brantz Mayer said in 1841: "Although it is the duty of the Government to keep this highway in order, yet, as the chief travelling is on horseback, and the principal part of merchandise is transported on mules, no one cares how these animals get along" (Mayer 1844, 13). From Plan del Río to Jalapa the road was so bad that the stagecoach on which Mayer had taken a seat was "heaving over the stones like a ship in a heavy sea"; at times the driver was compelled to leave his seat "and *feel* for the track" (Mayer 1844, 14).

Bayard Taylor, in 1850, used a canoe to cross the Santiago River, northwest of Guadalajara, taking with him his saddle, bridle, and blankets while his horse "swam bravely" behind him. On the riverbanks, he reports, "were scattered arrieros, mules and rows of pack saddles, while half a dozen large canoes were plying backwards and forwards with their loads" (Taylor [1850] 1949, 262).

Taylor ascended the tableland on a "stony trail, barely large enough for two mules to pass." But he mentions that "large numbers of workmen" were engaged in completing the trail for carriages, and that "over the deepest chasm" a bridge was being constructed by the state of Jalisco. "Five years, however, is the shortest period named for the completion of the work, up to which time the barranca will remain impassable, except for mules" (Taylor [1850] 1949, 270).

The routes north to the mining areas were comparative smooth because the tableland between Mexico City and El Paso del Norte slopes evenly; however, traveling with carts was slow and arduous. The broken wheels and broken axles were countless. Bullocks, which were sometimes wild, and drivers, who were often reckless, seem to have been as responsible as the roads for the breaking down of carriages. Yet, when heavy machines such as steam engines and boiling pans had to be carried to mines, sugar mills, or factories, wagons were preferred over mule trains.

Although in many areas one rode many hours, even a whole day, without meeting a human being or seeing a house, on much-frequented roads and, more specifically, around cities and mines, traffic jams were not unknown. Trains of several hundred mules, caravans of forty or fifty wagons, *rancheros* on horseback, elegant carriages, and herds of cattle, sheep, and horses crossed and mingled. When the path was too narrow for two parties to cross, said Albert M. Gilliam, "it is the rule in Mexico, for the weaker party always to give the way" (Gilliam 1847, 208). Likewise, on mountain trails the descending train gave way to the ascending one. But nothing would deter the *arriero* when he had merchandise to deliver. For example, on dangerous mountain roads long trains of mules conveying the ore from the mines to the haciendas boldly overtook trains of wagons heavily loaded with timber.

OF MULES AND MEN

Mules were indeed the most useful of all Mexican animals. Gilliam, who journeyed long distances in Mexico mounted on a "little mule," wrote: "It is not considered safe to travel on any other animal . . . as the mules are very sure-footed and sagacious" (Gilliam 1847, 229).

Excellent for long journeys, capable of enduring exhaustion and of carrying heavy loads, mules could travel in the most arid and hilly parts of the country where there were no roads at all. According to Mathieu de Fossey, a French gentleman who settled in Mexico in 1831, mules generally carried two loads of 200 pounds each, one on each side, and despite this burden, "they move along light-footed and free, grazing here and there without resting until they reach the halting place. A day's journey seldom exceeds seven leagues" (Fossey 1857, 349). A league was a common measure of distance, the equivalent of about three miles.

Mules also were used as draft animals, and many Mexicans preferred them to horses to pull carriages. Even in the capital, noted Brantz Mayer, one could see many "antique vehicles" to which were attached "a pair of mules almost hidden in a heavy harness studded with brass bosses and shining ornaments, while the tails of the luckless animals are invariably stuck into leathern bags by way of queue!" (Mayer 1844, 284). Mules were likewise used to pull stagecoaches on the roughest roads.

Arrieros were as tough as their mules. Both man and animal suffered hardship, withstanding extremes of heat and cold and excesses of moisture and dryness, as oblivious of the scorching sun as of the torrential rains, each depending on the other for their existence. Both expended their energies sparingly, and both possessed the same great vitality.

Morning and night the *arrieros* loaded and unloaded the heavy burdens of their mules, and during the day they incessantly rode up and down the caravan to encourage the beasts. In northern Mexico, where one could travel 1,500 miles or more without finding a single *mesón*, they always camped out, lying down among the mules' harnesses, after having cooked their frugal meal of tortillas and chili, while the animals pastured nearby under the care of their *mozos*. They slept on the ground, wrapped in the warm serape that each man carried behind his saddle. "Many of them," wrote B. M. Norman, "pride themselves much upon their vocation, which frequently passes down from father to son, through several generations" (Norman 1845, 111).

The honesty of *arrieros* was proverbial, and merchants placed in their care the most valuable merchandise. They transported gold and silver ingots, rich ores and coins, "giving no other security than a bill of lading" (Sartorius [1858] 1961, 87). Thousands, even millions, of pesos were entrusted to their charge and were defended against highwaymen under peril of death. The *arriero*, noted Brantz Mayer, "has a multitude of dangers and difficulties to contend with. He overcomes them all . . . and, at the appointed day, comes to your door with a respectful saluta-

tion, and tells you that your wares or monies have passed the city gates"
(Mayer 1844, 18).

In the midst of this hymn of praise two discordant notes sound: Sartorius writes that "their constant intercourse with asses does not improve their manners, nor make their language the most elegant" (Sartorius [1858] 1961, 87); and Albert M. Gilliam confides to his journal:
"Mexicans never wash when travelling, believing it to be injurious to
their health" (Gilliam 1847, 207)—an idea most English and American
travelers did not share.

Robbers, "untamed" Indians, bad food, bad lodgings or no lodgings
at all, vermin, mosquitoes, fleas, bugs, pigs, dirt, and fever were some
of the miseries the nineteenth-century traveler had to put up with. John
L. Stephens, who rode, walked, and canoed from Guatemala to Yucatán,
observed "it was not like travelling in England" (Stephens 1841, 2:143).

Besides the reliable and omnipresent mule, the voyager had at his
disposal stagecoaches, caleches, horses, and *literas*, to name the most
common means of transportation. Stagecoaches, called *diligencias*, were
to be found only on main routes such as those linking the capital with
Puebla, Veracruz, Guadalajara, and Zacatecas. According to Bayard Taylor, the style of stagecoach travel in Mexico was "preferable to that of
any other country. The passenger is waked at three o'clock in the morning, has a cup of chocolate brought him . . . takes his seat, and has
nearly reached the end of the second post by sunrise" (Taylor [1850]
1949, 287).

Waddy Thompson agreed that Mexico had a good line of stages,
"making three trips every week," said he, "between Vera Cruz and Mexico, which has nearly superseded all other modes of conveyance. Although the fare is enormously high, yet, it is cheaper than the litera,
more expeditious and on every account more pleasant." (Thompson
1846, 10).

The stagecoaches were built at Troy, New York; the drivers were all
Americans, though the horses, the mules, and the owners were Mexicans. A passenger paid fifty dollars for the Veracruz-Mexico City trip in
1841 (Mayer 1844, 284). Nearly ten years later Bayard Taylor paid
thirty-four dollars—but as "the seats in the diligence had all been engaged for ten days previous," he had to take a place "in the *pescante*, or
driver's box" (Taylor [1850] 1949, 314).

While Taylor praises the skillfulness of the drivers, as most Americans
did, P. Blanchard, Admiral Baudin's interpreter during the Pastry War,
criticizes their recklessness. His comments on the trip he made from

Veracruz to the capital are hilarious: "We do not go downhill," he laments, "we rush downhill. The coach jumps over the rocks until a big one obstructs the way." The passengers are then obliged to alight and to "carry the coach for a few fathoms." The descent to Paso de Ovejos was terrifying: "I never doubted that we would arrive, but I was afraid we would arrive head first; we whirled downward on this bumpy road as on an avalanche." At Jalapa the mules were replaced by "half-wild horses," and the coach galloped on at breakneck speed. As they were approaching Mexico City, the coach started a race with the official carriage that had been sent forward to escort the French delegation: "The driver refused to be overtaken by the official coach, and a chariot race such as those of ancient Rome ensued. We moved along at a frightening speed, now first, now second, and in no time reached Mexico" (Blanchard and Dauzats 1839, 98, 123, 151, 153).

One might think that Blanchard, with his Gallic temper, exaggerated the danger. By no means. Judge Wilson took the Veracruz-Mexico stagecoach three times, and he overturned twice.

In the 1820s, when coaches could be hired only from Mexico City, visitors arriving by sea at Veracruz had to rent mules for the journey, or depend on returning coaches, or hire a *litera*—which was Joel Poinsett's choice. "It is a very luxurious method of passing mountains, unless the mules prove unruly, for then the liter is tossed about in a strange manner, as I experienced more than once to-day" (Poinsett 1824, 29). Captain Lyon, who traveled in a *litera* from Jalapa to Veracruz in 1826—a trip he enjoyed very much—left a detailed description of this unusual means of transportation:

> The body is mounted on two strong poles, secured in thick leather straps to the peculiarly shaped saddles of a pair of strong mules; the one in front is led by a man, mounted on a third mule on the off side; and the animal in the rear, as well as having its halter fastened to the back of the litera, is kept to its work by the whip of a driver, who has also charge of two or three loose beasts, the carriers being changed every four or five leagues. The body of the vehicle is sufficiently long and broad for the traveller to stretch out on a small mattress, or to sit beneath the roof, which is supported on little pillars, and inclosed at pleasure by light curtains" (Lyon 1828, 2: 204–5).

Water also provided means of transportation. In the time of Santa Anna, as in the time of Moctezuma, the canals were used to bring food

Traveling by *litera*. From Robert Anderson Wilson, *Mexico: Its Peasants and Its Priests* (1855).

and goods into the capital. Moreover, the use of *tamemes* was not quite abandoned to carry goods, mail, or passengers.

From the first days of the republic the government recognized its responsibility to maintain regular mail service. The charges, which were very high, were determined by weight, and letters arriving or departing by sea could not be delivered without first passing through the post office. Travelers' baggage was searched, and it was prohibited for a captain or a consignee to receive a letter without the government stamp. Mail service, said B. M. Norman, was more regular than rapid, "being, for the most part, transported on the backs of the Indians" (Norman 1845, 101–2). Neither money nor valuable documents were entrusted to the mailman; "an armed *conducta* performs this service between the mines and the capital, and between the capital and the principal seaports" (Norman 1845, 102).

A great deal of correspondence flowed between absentee landlords and their administrators. In Coahuila, for example, we learn that, although postal service was something of a problem, mail was delivered to Patos, headquarters of the Sánchez Navarros' latifundio, "at least once a week" (Harris 1964, 49), and we find that a letter that Luis Gordoa mailed from Mexico City to his mine administrator, Fermín Mata, in Catorce on March 1, 1843, arrived by March 23 (Gordoa Family Papers).

ACCOMMODATIONS

Travelers had to be fed and housed for the night, and a system of "diligence hotels" was set up along the roads, whose comfort and cleanliness varied greatly from one establishment to the next. An advertisement appearing in the government newspaper, the Mexico City *Diario Oficial*, on July 6, 1836, announced new stagecoach service between Querétaro and San Luis Potosí—just a two-day trip instead of the usual five. It assured passengers of fine accommodations in the *posadas*, with no expense spared.

At such stopping places as Puebla, Jalapa, and Veracruz, accommodations were indeed good, even excellent. Elsewhere the ratings ran from poor to very bad.

P. Blanchard's journal of travel from Veracruz to the capital is an excellent tourist guide. The Diligence Hotel at Veracruz is described as a "real palace" with a courtyard "circled with pillars of white marble supporting a gallery also ornamentd with pillars." At Paso de Ovejas, Blanchard had the pleasure of eating "a delicious European meal" accompanied by Bordeaux wine. At Plan del Río (a third-rate place where the distinguished Frances Calderón de la Barca refused to stop when she arrived in Mexico) the cuisine was Spanish and the beds had no mattress; Blanchard and his companion, Commandant Leroy, were compelled to sleep directly on the straps. The next stop was Jalapa, where the hotel, Blanchard wrote, "is one of the best I have ever seen not only in Mexico but in Spain as well." At Perote, the *posada* had bleak rooms similar to those at Plan del Río, but on the beds were "very hard mattresses." At Puebla our Frenchmen spent the night in a "beautiful hotel" and enjoyed the comfort of a suite "furnished à la française," which prompted the reflexion that "the number of mattresses, as well as their comfort, increased in proportion with the wealth of the city, and with the altitude. In the tierra caliente, we had none; in the tierra templada, we had a small one; in the tierra fría, we had two rather comfortable mattresses" (Blanchard and Dauzats 1829, 87, 99, 110, 134).

Needless to say, as soon as one left the highway for side roads, there were no accommodations worthy of the name hotel. In colonial times a

system of *posadas* or *mesones* had been established along the more fre-
quented routes, offering accommodations for travelers and their animals. There mules found forage and a corral, and their drivers a roof for
the night. In an Indian village the *casa de comunidad*, or *casa real*,[1] was
also a stopping place for arrieros. Eventually, regular inns sprang up
here and there along the *camino real*.

The system of *mesones* continued in use throughout the era of Santa
Anna. In fact, in most of these native caravansaries travelers had to provide their own food and bed—a situation that greatly annoyed foreign
visitors. Trotting into Cuernavaca south of the capital, "after a ride of
fourteen leagues," Brantz Mayer and six companions looked for an inn
whose "flaming advertisement" he had read in the Mexico City papers.
The tired and hungry travelers dashed into the courtyard, where they
found the landlord, and "everything went to the tune of *'No hai!'* No hai
beds, rooms, meats, soups, supper—nada!. They had nothing!" (Mayer
1844, 171).

The secretary of the United States legation and his friends were finally
served a soup, a fragment of stewed mutton, a dish of lima beans, another of turkey and peppers, and finally an "enormous head of lettuce"
garnished with "outposts of oranges on either side, while two enormous
pine-apples reared their prickly leaves in front and rear" (Mayer 1844,
171). A luxurious meal for a Mexican inn. Travelers were usually fed on
tortillas, *frijoles*, and chili with an occasional cup of chocolate.

Brantz Mayer had worse experiences elsewhere. At the *mesón* of Cuautla, a charming southern town, the walls of one of the rooms were "literally black with fleas"; and in the second room, a "full grown ass" had
made himself at home (Mayer 1844, 200).

Most places swarmed with mosquitoes, fleas, and other bugs, which
greedily feasted on travelers. Pigs and hens were frequent visitors. Judge
Robert Wilson left a humorous account of his experience traveling from
Acapulco to Mexico. At the *venta* of Lemones, where he passed the night
"sleeping upon a table on the veranda," he made his first acquaintance
with the "*venta* pig, who considers himself the peculiar friend of the
traveling public. All the advances made by my new acquaintance at this
first interview were occasional tugs at the blanket during the night, and
divers unsuccessful attempts to turn the table over. At Alta, two stages

[1]A *casa real*, or *casa de comunidad*, was a public building in every village, provided
by the royal government's Audiencia, which was supposed to contain apartments for
travelers.

farther on, the pig . . . gave me no farther annoyance than an occasional visit, and thrusting of his nose into the hammock where I slept" (Wilson 1855, 137–38).

Captain Lyon's traveling adventures were no less amusing. He reports that in the Indian village of Tanjuco, situated along the river Pánuco at Tampico, he had to share a hut not only with the owner, his wife, his children, dogs, and pigs but also with "four hens with broods of chickens, and three others which were sitting on their eggs, [and] occupied various snug corners" (Lyon 1828, 1:73–74). The houses of Indian peasants, as well as those of many *rancheros*, seldom had more than one room, into which parents, children, various animals, and an occasional visitor were crammed for the night.

Joel Poinsett, who stopped overnight with an old couple at the village of Las Vigas, was quite surprised to see "three decent looking beds, besides our own. The old couple had retired before us, and I must confess that I was curious to see how the young ladies (the couple had four daughters) would go to bed in our presence. . . . They came in soon after, and paired off to the two vacant beds, where they contrived to undress under the clothes with great decency" (Poinsett 1824, 31–32).

Bayard Taylor had a similar experience at the *mesón* at Escuinapa on the Pacific coast south of Mazatlán. The only room was already occupied by Mexican travelers; when he asked the landlady where he would sleep, she answered with a charming smile "Conmigo," meaning "With me." "I was horror-struck and must have looked so," Taylor said. The lady took him to a windowless closet in the rear of the house, in which were two frames "covered with matting and some bags of maize and barley. 'This is your bed,' said she, pointing to one of them 'and this is ours'" (Taylor [1850] 1949, 257).

In the backcountry travelers had either to camp in the open or to spend the night with friendly village *curas*, *hacendados*, *rancheros*, or Indian families. In the latter case they had first to see the village leaders, who generally procured them shelter and food when they had money to pay for it. There were, however, a few places where the *alcalde* refused even access of the village to strangers. We are told by Brantz Mayer that the inhabitants of an Indian village situated in the vicinity of Cuernavaca did not permit the visits of white people. "If their settlement is ever entered by a *white, the transgressor is immediately seized, put under guard in a large hut, and he and his animal are fed and carefully attended to until the following day, when he is dispatched from the village under an escort of Indians*" (Mayer 1844, 175–76).

STEPHENS'S VOYAGES

John L. Stephens and his artist friend Frederick Catherwood were "Yu-catán's first tourists," as Nelson Reed calls them. Searching for ruined cities, they wandered through the wilderness of the peninsula, as well as in the silent forests of Chiapas. They spent nights in the *casa de co-munidad* of Indian villages, at the houses of congenial *padres*, in con-vents, and at the haciendas of friends; or they camped in the ghost cities of the defunct Maya confederation. They went to isolated villages where full-blooded Indians had never before seen any foreigner, where no lan-guage other than Maya was spoken, where cacao beans were still used as money. Stephens was astonished that, "while the manners and cus-toms of the Indians have undergone an immense change, while their cities have been destroyed, their religion dishonoured, their princes swept away, and their whole government modified by foreign laws, no experiment has yet been made upon their currency" (Stephens [1843] 1963, 1:114–15).

In most Indian villages the *casa de comunidad* was a large hut with mud walls and a thatched roof, and an open place in front shaded by an arbor of leaves. These huts, "when swept out, and comparatively clear of fleas," wrote Stephens, "made a large and comfortable apartment, and furnished ample swinging room for six hammocks, being the number requisite for our whole retinue" (Stephens [1843] 1963, 2:3). In some places, however, the *casa de comunidad* was a mere shed.

Curas and *hacendados* offered shelter that was hardly more comfort-able. At the hacienda of Uxmal, which belonged to the rich Don Simón Peón, furniture was so scarce that there were not enough chairs for them all to sit for breakfast. Don Simón "went into the church and brought out the great confessional chair." There was no bed either. Nobody ever used a bed at Uxmal. "The Indians "were all born in hammocks, and expected to die in them," said Stephens [1843] 1963, 1:139–40).

In the course of his trips through Chiapas and Yucatán in 1840 and 1841, Stephens used various conveyances, including *carricoches, coches, sillas de cabeza,* and *bongos.* The *carricoche*, widely used in Yucatán, was "a long wagon, on two large wheels, covered with cotton cloth as a protection against the sun." On the bottom was stretched a mattress broad enough to accommodate two persons. The vehicle was drawn by a horse "with a driver riding as postillion," while another horse followed to change (Stephens [1843] 1963, 1:123). The *coche* was a native sedan chair made out of a hammock tied to two poles that Indian carriers placed on their shoulders. The *silla de cabeza*, used in Chiapas to cross very steep mountains, was an armchair that an Indian carried on his back by means of a bark strap around his forehead.

One might think that *coches* and *sillas de cabeza* were safe means of transportation. They were not. Sick with fever, Stephens and his friend had to use *coches* to go from Nohcacab to Ticul in Yucatán. Alas, "two fete days in succession were rather too much for the Indians of Nohcacab," lamented Stephens. Their carriers staggered on their feet. Although the *alcaldes* told them that they would sober up before the first league passed, our travelers left with apprehensions, particularly because their carriers "set off on a full run." On top of the *sierra* rain came on as the night closed in. The Indians hurried down, and Stephens, all of a sudden, felt the *coche* going over, and, "with a frightful crash, it came down on its side." His shoulder and side were bruised, but fortunately "none of the Indians were missing" (Stephens [1843] 1963, 1:207–8).

Traveling in the forests of Chiapas in a *silla de cabeza*, even with sober Indian carriers, was for Stephens no less an adventure. He was in fact opposed from the start to using one, assuming that where an Indian could climb with someone on his back, he could climb alone. But the steep ascent, together with the heat, proved too much for him, and he reluctantly resorted to it. His carrier, a rather small and "very thin" Indian, was progressing slowly, with one man on each side. "It was a great relief," wrote Stephens, "but I could feel every movement even to the heaving of his chest." Stephens faced backwards, and he could not see where he was going, but he noticed that the Indian on his left "fell back." A few minutes later, looking over his shoulder he saw that they were approaching the edge of a chasm "more than a thousand feet deep." Alarmed, Stephens wanted to dismount, but he could not make himself understood.

Wrote Stephens: "I rose and fell with every breath, felt his body trembling under me, and his knees seemed giving way. The precipice was awful, and the slightest irregular movement on my part might bring us both down together." Descending was much worse than ascending; "if he fell, nothing could keep me from going over his head; but I remained till he put me down of his own accord" (Stephens [1841] 1969, 2:274–76).

At night they camped near a shallow river. But there were so many mosquitoes that Stephens could not get any sleep, and he finally spent the rest of the night in the river: "It was the first comfortable moment I had had," he said (Stephens [1841] 1969, 2:279).

Porter using a *silla de cabeza*. Engraving by Claudio Linati, *Costumes civils, militaires el réligieux du Mexique; dessinés d'apres nature* (c. 1829)

When Stephens and Catherwood left Palenque for Yucatán, they rode on a muddy road to Las Playas, "head of navigation of the waters that empty in this direction into the Gulf of Mexico." There the justice, a mulatto "well dressed, and very civil," and owner of a canoe, promised to procure two rowers in the morning (Stephens [1841] 1969, 2:369). The task proved difficult; two days later our travelers embarked, and one of the boatmen was the justice himself. "The canoe," wrote Stephens, "was about forty feet long, with a toldo or awning of about twelve feet at the stern, and covered with matting." At half past twelve they started ascending the sluggish Río Chico and at six entered the "great Usumacinta" (Stephens [1841] 1969, 2:374–75).

At two o'clock the day after, they reached La Palisada, their first stop in the state of Yucatán. After two days, furnished with provisions by the wife of a generous and hospitable Yucatecan, Don Francisco Hebreu, whose hacienda stretched out along the river, they embarked on a *bongo* for Laguna. The *bongo* "was about fifteen tons, flat bottomed, with two masts and sails, and loaded with logwood." The deck was so cluttered with mangoes, plantains, and other fruit and vegetables, that it was impossible for them to move (Stephens [1841] 1969, 2:380–81).

They spent a terrible night, surrounded by alligators and much bitten by mosquitoes. At ten o'clock they entered the lake of Terminados and saw at last the town of Laguna, on the island of Carmen, their port of destination. "The passage into the lake was shoal and narrow, with reefs and sandbars, and our boatmen did not let slip the chance of running her ashore." They finally landed and walked to the house of the American consul, with whom they had dinner that night. "We could hardly believe ourselves the same miserable beings who had been a few hours before tossing on the lake, in dread alike of the bottom and of another night on board the bungo [sic]" (Stephens [1841] 1969, 2:386–90).

RIDING IN STYLE

Traveling in Mexico also had its bright side. H. G. Ward was the English chargé d'affaires, and he enjoyed every minute of it. His organization was faultless. He wrote:

> My luggage generally consisted of a canteen, which contained cooking utensils, as well as a small breakfast and dinner set for four people, and formed a light load for one mule; one of Thompson's small brass camp beds, with a porte-manteau to balance it, was alloted to a second mule; the third carried two boxes for wine, provisions, and other necessaries . . . and

the fourth, the beds of Dr. Wilson and Mr. Carrington, a young friend by whom I was generally accompanied. (Ward 1828, 2:311–12)

An *arriero* took charge of the party. In addition, there were two Mexican servants and an English groom. All were armed to the teeth. Ward left a flattering portrait of Mexican servants: "They are a fine manly race, excellent horsemen, adept in the use of the indispensable instrument the lasso, and capable of enduring every sort of fatigue. They eat anything . . . sleep upon the ground . . . round your bed if you bivouac, or stretched across your room door at the Ventas" (Ward 1828, 2:312).

They usually rode from daybreak to one o'clock, then had time to bathe and dress before dinner, and, afterwards, to stroll until bedtime. "It is then that the luxuries of mosquito curtains and portable bedsteads are really felt, particularly if the length of the legs is calculated, (as it always should be) so as just to raise you beyond the maximum of a flea's leap" (Ward 1828, 2:317).

Mathieu de Fossey also traveled in style. Riding to Acapulco with friends and servants, he camped near the Indian village of Tacahuamilpa. The servants put up the beds and prepared dinner: "As veteran travelers, we had done our best to make our journey pleasant. We brought with us soup, chicken stuffed with truffles, Bordeaux lamprey, and peas which were accompanied by Madeira, Chateau Latour, Cognac and cafe of Velasco" (Fossey 1857, 305).

When Frances Calderón and her husband traveled, they usually stopped for the night at the haciendas of friends where they were lavishly entertained. However, when they journeyed through Michoacán, they had, like ordinary people, to pass the night in a village which consisted of "a few miserable huts filled with Indians." Finally, an old barn was discovered, "and there the beds of the whole party were put up!" The servants brought them tea, which they drank by the dim light of a candle, seated upon their trunks. Frances Calderón spent a most uncomfortable night, confronted with the usual miseries plaguing Mexican travels. "The pigs grunted, the mosquitoes sung, a cold air blew in from every corner, and, fortunately we were not until morning aware of the horrid fact that a whole nest of scorpions with their tails twisted together, were reposing above our heads in the log wall" (Calderón de la Barca [1843] 1931, 487–88).

For long journeys rich Mexicans generally rode in their *avío*, a heavy ornate coach drawn by teams of mules. Charles H. Harris, in his remarkable study of the Sánchez Navarro empire in Coahuila, provides many details on the traveling organization of the family. As we may see from the following account, trips to and from Mexico City were carefully planned and organized.

At the beginning of April, 1851, Jacobo Sánchez Navarro, who had gone to Mexico City on business, decided to return home with the family coach. He accordingly wrote to Juan de Arizpe, the lawyer who was in charge of the latifundio during his absence, that he wanted the *avío* and its crew sent to the capital. He planned to travel in two coaches and one wagon. He would require seven servants, but only three teams of mules, because he already had fifteen mules in Mexico City (Harris 1964, 45).

At Patos, headquarters of the latifundio, preparations were hastily made. The mules received an extra measure of corn daily to be fit for the long journey, and the coach was inspected by the hacienda black-smith. Meanwhile, Jacobo wrote Arizpe again, telling him that he would be accompanied by his mother and his brother's family, and asking for twenty-nine additional mules. By April 13 the preparations were com-pleted. A permit for the servants to carry arms was secured and on April 20 the *avío*, eight servants, and thirty mules left the hacienda for the capital, which they reached on May 6. Two mules died on the way, and the "remainder arrived quite thin" (Harris 1964, 45–46). The Sánchez Navarro family set forth on May 12 and was to arrive in Saltillo on June 1, but by the time they reached San Luis Potosí, several mules were in such bad condition that Jacobo had to write home for two more teams to meet him on the road. The remainder of the trip was uneventful.

The Gordoas had a somewhat similar organization when traveling. Mine foreman Domingo Martínez, writing from Catorce, mentioned in a letter dated February 19, 1844, a possible trip to Mexico City to meet with his employer, Luis Gordoa, indicating that he intended to take two servants and six horses or mules for the journey (Gordoa Family Pa-pers). Travelers seldom rode alone. Wealthy Mexicans, as well as illus-trious personages such as the Calderón de la Barcas, were always accom-panied by a long retinue, and sometimes by a military escort; and foreign visitors usually joined forces before setting off on a journey across Mexico.

ROBBERS . . .

Bands of highwaymen infested the roads. Robbers were the main topic in the conversation of travelers, and robber stories occupy a prominent place in their journals and diaries. Wherever they journeyed, travelers were reminded of their presence. "At every place we stopped," wrote Albert M. Gilliam, "accounts of murders and robberies are detailed" (Gilliam 1847, 208). William Parish Robertson, an English gentleman who visited Mexico in 1851, agreed that the "universal theme of conversation between Vera Cruz and the city of Mexico is that of 'The robbers' " (Robertson 1853, 1:301). And American trader Josiah Gregg said that when he rode with his wagons on the *camino real* from Chihuahua to Zacatecas all the frightful stories he had heard about robbers began to flash upon his memory (Gregg [1844] 1926, 258).

Many crosses marked the burial places of victims of highwaymen. Occasionally one saw a bandit hanging from a tree or a home-made gallows by the road. They were left rotting—or drying—as a warning. On the road to Guadalajara, Bayard Taylor passed a spot where eleven traders and soldiers had been killed by highwaymen eighteen months before. Black crosses were planted by the roadside, and directly above stood a rough gallows, on which three of the robbers, eventually caught, swung in chains. "Their long hair hung over their faces, their clothes were dropping in tatters, and their skeleton-bones protruded through the dry and shrunken flesh." On a board above the swinging bodies was written, "Thus the law punishes the robber and the assassin" (Taylor [1850] 1949, 278).

Most robbers were products of the civil war, in which many had taken an active part as insurgents for the independence of Mexico. These armed bands eventually robbed all whom they met, although they were not bloodthirsty either. They killed more out of necessity than cruelty, were gallant with the ladies, and, said Frances Calderón, could be "easily moved to compassion" (Calderón de la Barca [1843] 1931, 343).

It is true that Bayard Taylor had the misfortune of being robbed on the Guadalajara road; however, his assailant, "a ferocious looking native," gave him a dozen tortillas before abandoning him, tied to his horse. "Perhaps you may get hungry before the night," he said (Taylor [1850] 1949, 275–77). B. M. Norman, while exploring around Tampico with a party of Indians, was suddenly surrounded by a band of "gentlemanly looking" highwaymen. They seized Norman's party, searched them carefully, then "drew forth from their bags . . . an ample store of substantial food, and invited us to partake of their supper" (Norman 1845, 125–26).

Nineteenth-century observers also stressed the highwaymen's sense of honor. When offered a pardon on the condition that they give the names of their accomplices, they usually preferred death (Thompson 1846,

Stagecoach attacked by bandits. Engraving by M. Serroma and Casimiro Castro in J. Decaen, ed., *México y sus alrededores; colección de monumentos, trajes y paisajes* (1864).

21). Nor were they devoid of sardonic humor: Blanchard reports that the great Spanish tenor Manuel del Pópolo Vicente García was robbed of "all his savings" by a band of highwaymen who, moreover, "forced him to sing one of his favorite tunes" (Blanchard and Dauzats 1839, 129).

Yet highwaymen were not left to rule the road unchallenged. The *Diario Oficial* in 1856 announced that a special armed escort of fifty mounted guards led by army officers was to accompany all stagecoaches on the Mexico City–Veracruz route, for as long as necessary. The management felt confident that their passengers would not object to increased fares in the interest of safety.

INDIANS

In northern Mexico the roads were rendered still more perilous by the constant hostility of Apache and Comanche Indians who raided Mexican caravans of traders and parties of travelers. As the years passed, they became more and more bold, and although much of their activity was confined to border states, large bands plunged down into Mexico as far south as Zacatecas and San Luis Potosí.

According to Joel Poinsett, the government of Mexico saw no difference between robbers and Indians. In a confidential letter addressed to U.S. Secretary of State Henry Clay on April 13, 1827, about claims of two American citizens who had been robbed by Comanches, Poinsett writes that Indian tribes living within the borders of Mexico were not considered as "independent people in any respect whatsoever but as a component part of the populations. . . . The Comanche Indians therefore, can be regarded only in the light of a lawless banditti that attack indiscriminately the inhabitants of this country and foreigners who come within the reach of their incursions" (United States Legation in Mexico Papers). However, it seemed to Poinsett that the Indians were more disposed to plunder Mexicans than Americans.

As the Comanches were about ten times more numerous than the Apaches and were among the best horsemen in the world, and as they possessed a great number of firearms and went about in large bands, they were far more dreaded. They would attack daringly and impetuously, unlike the Apaches, whose tactics were those of surprise and ambush. They advanced in a column and, when near their objective, split into two groups, charging simultaneously from opposite directions. Keeping their horses in constant motion, they threw themselves over the side, leaving only a small portion of the body exposed, and in this position discharged their guns or shot their arrows. Even for a sharpshooter, it was very difficult to hit a Comanche brave. When Albert M. Gilliam left Durango for the Pacific coast, he was told that Indians were committing depredations in all directions. But he was persuaded that, "if there was any correctness in the Indian intelligence, my traveling was rendered the more safe, for the dreaded Indians would only drive home the ladrones, and my chances would be lessened for a rencounter, in having none but the Camanches for my enemies, and I looked upon them as the lesser evil of the two" (Gilliam 1847, 224). Between Santa Catarina and the Boca, he met "six mules, each loaded with the melancholy freight of a dead man. . . . They had come to their end mostly by Indian arrows." The over-confident Gilliam then wisely decided to wait a few days in the Boca before proceeding to the coast, in order to recruit a large company, "which was accomplished by the arrival of some more travellers" (Gilliam 1847, 227).

The Apaches also were dangerous. We are told by John R. Bartlett that, although escorted by Mexican soldiers, he had to sustain a full-scale attack from Lipan Apaches as he was slowly riding over the broad and boundless plain south of El Paso, with his train of wagons. They were suddenly startled by "the most terrific yells and shouting," and to their horror saw a band of Indians coming from the arroyo they had just passed. They numbered about thirty or forty and were armed with bows and lances. As they passed, they discharged their arrows at the teamsters. The firing was general, wrote Bartlett, "but the constant motion of the enemy enabled them to escape. . . . The spare animals were all stampeded and lost," and one Mexican was killed (Bartlett [1854] 1965, 2:412–14).

More trouble lay ahead. While Bartlett was in Chihuahua a band of Comanches made a daring raid against a large train of wagons with 140 mules. No sooner had they camped for the night than the Comanches suddenly "stampeded the whole caballada, and succeeded in driving every animal off" (Bartlett [1854] 1965, 2:448). The most dangerous part of the route was between Cuencamé and Parras, for the great pass there leading to the Bolsón of Mapimí was the winter stronghold of the Comanches, and "the little heaps of stones surmounted by crosses, where murders have been committed by Indians, are met with at every mile" (Bartlett [1854] 1965, 2:475).

No, indeed, it was not like traveling in England.

CHAPTER FOUR

SEAPORTS, CITIES, AND TOWNS

The Spaniard, then, was by tradition a town dweller. . . . His town, or at most his province, was his patria chica, which he loved (and loves) with an astonishing strength.—Lesley Byrd Simpson

To the Spaniard the organization of society into urban communities was the established and accepted way of life, predating even Roman rule. The Spanish village, or *comunidad*, provided both defense and an adequate food supply. The citizens, or *vecinos*, lived in a designated area, farmed their outlying land, and shared the work of harvesting and threshing. Public granaries served all. Common woods and common pastures were shared by all. The village was governed by a town council, the *cabildo*, and a mayor or mayors, the *alcaldes*. The *cabildo* was composed principally of elders, the *regidores*, and it also served as the court of justice (Simpson [1941] 1966, 92–93). Such was the basic municipal unit that quite naturally was introduced into New Spain, as well as into all Spanish America. An important modification was a quarter, or *barrio*, for Indians who provided domestic service and who were under the jurisdiction of their own *cabildos*.

While some Indian towns became Spanish towns, as in the case of Tenochtitlán, more often the Spaniards founded towns in new locations, with fertile land and sufficient water, places not already chosen by Indians, who preferred sites they could defend. A municipality might be established to secure land gained in subduing the Indians, as was San Cristóbal de las Casas in Chiapas; or as a defense of trade routes, as was Querétaro; or to exploit silver mines, as was Zacatecas.

Once the site was selected, the new town was marked out as close to a set pattern as the topography permitted, with a central plaza, a church and a town hall facing the plaza, and streets at right angles forming squares 600 feet to a side, called *manzanas* (Sartorius [1858] 1961, 115). Residential lots and agricultural lands would be assigned, and the existence of the new town confirmed, by the Audiencia in Mexico City. The size of the governing *cabildo* varied according to the importance of the town. Mexico City, for example, had twelve *regidores* and two *alcaldes*. A *regidor* originally was elected, but later the office came to be sold and could be resold or inherited. *Regidores* in turn chose *alcaldes* for one-year terms. The responsibility of the *cabildo* was to regulate the markets, arrange food and meat supplies, supervise artisans' guild activities, and provide police protection. The jurisdiction of a municipality extended far beyond the limits of the urban settlement (MacLachlan and Rodríguez O. 1980, 108).

Towns might pass through various legal classifications as development progressed. Thus Querétaro, within six years of its founding in 1531, was called *pueblo de indios*, or Indian village; then by 1655 it had attained recognition as a Spanish *villa*, or town; and the following year was designated a *ciudad*, or city (Altman and Lockhart 1976, 232).

To say that all Mexican towns and cities shared a common cultural heritage, and more specifically a common architectural heritage, would be to state the obvious. To be sure, the same elements were immediately apparent in them all—the flat roofs, the balconies, and the multitudinous church spires from whose belfries the ever-tolling bells called the faithful to masses, vespers, and prayer. Yet the communities were by no means identical. Each urban area developed in its own peculiar way, according to circumstances of geography and history. Each had by the early nineteenth century its own personality, and no two looked alike: no two churches boasted the same architectural details; no two promenades were shaded by the same trees or ornamented with the same shrubs; no two fountains duplicated each other; and many houses presented a fanciful display of frescoes on their walls that enlivened their otherwise dull and prisonlike appearance.

FROM VERACRUZ TO TAMPICO

Most foreigners were first introduced to Mexico through the seaports: Acapulco, San Blas, and Mazatlán on the Pacific coast and Campeche, Tampico, and Veracruz on the Gulf. All of these cities shared certain characteristics. They were unhealthy, and except for Acapulco, they were poorly endowed with the natural features that make convenient and safe harbors. And without exception, they were all hotbeds of smuggling and bribery.

Veracruz was the oldest, the most notorious, the most enviable of all the seaports. There a corner of Spain had thrived while the fate of Mexico still hung in an uncertain balance. During most of the colonial period Veracruz had enjoyed the exclusive right to foreign commerce on the Atlantic coast. It was the funnel through which passed three-fourths of all the silver bound for Spain, as well as items of trade from the Orient that had arrived in Acapulco and had been shipped across the country. From the other direction, it was the heralded gateway into New Spain for people and products coming from the home country.

Hernán Cortés would surely have been surprised to find the city he had named Villa Rica de Vera Cruz back in its original location across from the island Ulúa after he had moved it to the mouth of the Río Antigua, and to see the early wooden buildings, which had burned down several times, rebuilt with coral scraped up from the harbor. Confined within a wall, the city assumed a crescent shape on the sandy shore (Pasquel 1969, 72).

Despite its fame, the harbor of Veracruz offered only unreliable, insecure anchorages to shipping, exposed as it was to the violent winds called *nortes*. Not infrequently, hapless vessels were driven ashore and the breakwater where cargo was discharged was damaged. And the formidable old fortress of San Juan de Ulúa, built of coral on a sandbank a half mile off shore from Veracruz, did not always play the role in defending the city for which it had been designed. The Spaniards, who occupied the island until 1825, had bombarded the city from San Juan de Ulúa, and the French in 1838 blew up the fortress. Veracruz in the nineteenth century retained little of the glories of its past.

The finest view of the city was from the harbor, as Judge Wilson asserted, "and the best time to look upon it is when a bright sun, just risen above a watery horizon, is reflected back from the antiquated domes and houses, which are visible above the old massive city wall" (Wilson 1855, 15).

On reaching land and getting a closer look, the visitor was likely to apply adjectives such as "forbidding" or "disagreeable." The ravages of war were readily apparent in Veracruz. Ward remarked upon the melancholy appearance of the town in 1827; recalling that it had been under siege from the fort, he noted that the houses were riddled with shot and the churches in ruins (Ward 1828, 2:173–74). The population had declined from a peak of 19,000 in 1804 to a mere 6,500 in 1842 (Boyer 1973, 48).

When she first viewed the city, Frances Calderón could not imagine anything more forlorn. "On one side, the fort, with its black and red walls," she said, "on the other, the miserable, black-looking city, with hordes of large black birds, called *sopilotes*, hovering over some dead carcass . . . not a tree, or a shrub, or flower, or bird, except the horrid black *sopilote*" (Calderón de la Barca [1843] 1931, 24–25, 29). Vultures by the hundreds perched on the roofs of churches, where they passed the night. Protected by law, they, along with city prisoners, were responsible for keeping the streets clean. To quote Brantz Mayer: "The galley slaves and the zopilotes constitute a large part of the most useful population of Veracruz, the former being the city authorities' laborers, the latter the city authorities' scavengers" (Mayer 1844, 3–4).

In most ways Veracruz was little distinguished in style from other Mexican cities. The central plaza was flanked by a large cathedral, an impressive *palacio municipal*, and *portales*. After morning mass the plaza would fill with ladies wearing mantillas of shining black satin, with women of lower rank wrapped in rebosos, and with black-gowned priests. Men appeared in immense yellowish hats, shirts of cotton, and trousers of linen, all appropriate for the climate.

The houses—some were palaces three stories high—had the usual flat roofs, courtyards, and balconies, and also, as particularly noted by Orbigny, windows with panes of glass (Orbigny 1836, 408). The coral building material of which the whole town was constructed, including roofs and "foot pavement," was so hard that in places it became polished like marble (Bullock 1824, 21). Walkways frequently were sheltered under piazzas that provided protection from the sun and rain. Water for drinking, a precious commodity, was preserved in tanks or cisterns, though the poor often had to resort to ditch water.

Although there were numerous churches, monasteries, and convents, only six remained in use in 1824. At the side of one deserted church was a battered stone image that day after day suffered new deterioration—by young girls of marriageable age. A stone thrown by a "fair hand" that hit the image in the face would assure a husband, or so they believed (Wilson 1855, 17–18).

The market presented a spectacle of diverse people and costumes. For example, a dark-skinned African might add a dash of color to the usual crowd of Mexicans. Although the market provided a somewhat inferior assortment of fruits and vegetables, fish were in abundance—"hundreds of various species glowing in all colours of the prism," said W. Bullock of the London Museum (Bullock 1824, 19). And Orbigny declared that the markets of Veracruz had a "better aspect than its promenades" (Orbigny 1836, 407).

Small wonder! The paseo of Veracruz, a paved walk outside the city gates designed for promenading on foot, on horseback, or in a carriage, had lost all of its trees under the bombs of the various assailants (Koppe [1835] 1955, 60). Many nearby houses also were lying in ruin because of war. But war was not the only cause of desolation in Veracruz. The *vómito prieto* was a more deadly menace.

Yellow fever took that name from one of its symptoms—the black vomit. During the months of heat and rain, from the end of April to the beginning of October or later, anyone not native-born to the *tierra caliente* was in grave danger of being stricken by the fever, with death likely by the third day. B. M. Norman reported that 2,000 died of the black vomit in 1842—most of them Indians rounded up to be soldiers (Norman 1845, 94). Travelers took careful note of the season in planning their itineraries. Some sought to avoid the danger by proceeding immediately to Jalapa after reaching the beach, only to die on the road. In Tampico, where it had little effect before 1821, the disease was as prevalent as in Veracruz by the end of the decade.

Tampico suffered yet another difficulty as a seaport: contrary winds and an ominous bar at the mouth of the Pánuco River often prevented ships from docking safely upriver for as much as three days (Barinetti 1841, 2). The port had the advantage, however, of being the closest point on the coast to the mining districts inland, and from it quantities of specie were exported, as well as dyewoods and hides.

Tampico was located about three leagues, upstream, at a point on the river where the water was sufficiently deep for anchoring close to shore. This location was preferred by business interests to the original site downstream (Norman 1845, 99). And so by the 1840s there was a bustling town of some 6,000 persons where only a few Indian huts had stood in the 1820s, and the old Spanish seaport was but a ghost town. There were in effect two Tampicos with at least three names: Pueblo Viejo was the old original town, and Santa Anna de Tamaulipas was the new one, which also was called Pueblo Nuevo or Pueblo Nuevo de Tampico. The new seaport was more or less a bachelors' city: because of the unhealthy climate, few women came with their husbands.

Although laid out in regular squares, Tampico claimed no uniformity of architecture or "pretensions to beauty" (Norman 1845, 102). As

the commerce of the town was chiefly in the hands of foreigners—
Americans, English, and Spanish—various styles of buildings sprang
up. Some houses were built with pitched roofs, shingles, and even
weatherboarding (Gilliam 1847, 267).

Frances Calderón, who journeyed to Tampico on her way to Havana
after her husband's tour of duty, was quite charmed with what she saw
and considered it a "slandered place." She liked the houses, which from
a distance appeared like "coloured bandboxes, some blue, some white,
which a party of tired milliners have laid down amongst the rushes."
Walking through the town, she could have fancied herself "in a New
England village." She afterwards heard that these houses "were actually
made in the United States and sent out here" (Calderón de la Barca
[1843] 1931, 534).

True to Spanish tradition, however, there were as many as four plazas,
of which the principal one was on the river fronting the customhouse.
In the mid-1840s plans were under way for the erection of an expensive
monument in honor of Santa Anna and his victory over the Spanish
forces in 1829. It awaited only the marble column to be sent from New
York (Norman 1845, 105).

The marketplace was on a bluff overlooking the Pánuco. From the
spot one could discern at some distance downstream, amid lagoons and
woodlands, the remnants of Pueblo Viejo.

To that abandoned place went numerous travelers in search of the
tranquility that pervaded the forsaken streets and byways, in contrast to
the relative activity of its neighbor. B. M. Norman, echoing nearly ver-
batim earlier words of Charles Latrobe, gave a nostalgic description of
the old town: "The houses are low-built, with flat roofs. The facades of
some of them show, in the faded gaiety, and dubious taste of their col-
oring, what they were in the palmy days of Pueblo Viejo's early glory.
Many of them had *court-yards* and *porticos*. One group of old buildings . . . shows many marks of its ancient grandeur, even in its present
state of desolation and decay" (Norman 1845, 108).

Both Norman and Latrobe sought out one idyllic spot at the edge of
town—a half-hidden spring called La Fuente, tucked away under the
protective reaches of a hill. The place was covered with vines, and there
luxuriated birds, butterflies, and alas, ticks! Water filled a large stone
reservoir that served the women of the area as a picturesque place for
washing clothes. It was also "the lounge and trysting place of the town,
and many a youthful dark-eyed gallant might be seen at times lolling
upon the stone wall which hemmed in the reservoir" (Latrobe 1836, 35).

But if humble Pueblo Viejo bespoke romance and nostalgia, how much more so did Acapulco, on the Pacific coast. There one might dream of the bygone days of the Manila galleon.

ACAPULCO AND THE PACIFIC PORTS

Beginning early in the colonial period, Acapulco was for a brief time each year the most important seaport of New Spain. Its population mushroomed from about 4,000 to 9,000 people. The annual galleon from the Philippines arrived about Christmas day, bringing the cloves, cinnamon, and nutmeg, the silks, cottons, velvets, satins, damasks, and taffetas, the porcelain, the gold and silver work, the fine jewelry, ivory, furniture, and pearls that Spanish buyers had purchased at the trade fair of Parián, near Manila. A similar fair of international renown was set up in Acapulco from January 10 until February 25. Church bells in Mexico City heralded the ship's arrival, and merchants from all corners of Mexico hastened to attend. Caravans of mules then transported the Spanish portion of the cargo to Veracruz. In return, Spanish wine, Saltillo wool, Oaxaca cochineal, and cocoa from Tabasco and Chiapas were sent to the Orient (Varona 1956, 27). In 1820, however, the days of glory ended abruptly when the Manila galleon made its last voyage and Acapulco was left to doze in the sun, forgotten in its tropical splendor.

Unlike Veracruz, its rival of old, Acapulco had a very safe harbor. It appeared to Judge Wilson in the 1840s "like a nest scooped out of the mountains, into and out of which the tide ebbs and flows through a double channel riven by an earthquake in the solid rock" (Wilson 1855, 135). The panorama of this land-locked harbor, protected from the open water by small islands, backed by granite mountains and rugged cliffs, and watched over by the fortress of San Diego on a high promontory, was so grand that it scarcely fit within the scope of one's vision.

The little town itself, periodically destroyed by earthquakes, lay at the western edge of the bay between hills and the harbor. Although it was credited with having "only one good house" ([Forbes] 1851, 223), that of the American consul, the town must have made a charming picture. Row upon row of houses, forming horseshoe-shaped rings, climbed the sides of the mountains of La Quebrada and El Vigía. Their red-tiled roofs were accented by palm trees in the irregular terrain, as steep, narrow lanes twisted into intricate, labyrinthine curves (Varona 1956, 37–38). Acapulco was not at all a well-planned city. And, said Wilson, it was one of the hottest and most disease-ridden places on the continent (Wilson 1855, 136). The California gold rush brought a brief revival of activity because Acapulco was a regular port of call for Panamanian and Nicaraguan steamers going north, and passengers flocked ashore to stock up on food and provisions (Lewis 1949, 228).

Mazatlán on the north, as well as San Blas, was also affected by the mad surge of gold seekers. Because of the closeness of Mazatlán to California, houses were going up in all parts of town in 1850, and so did prices. Bayard Taylor found them truly outrageous and refused to buy.

The young American journalist did leave a vivid account of the little port as it was at mid-century. Built at the base of a hill on the neck of a stony volcanic promontory, Mazatlán faced the sea on two sides. Part of the town looked toward the California Gulf, and the other part looked south toward San Blas. Most houses were of stone, one story high, painted white, pink, or cream. Arched entrances and courtyards from which the feathery tops of palms could be discerned produced an Oriental effect. On the "clean and cheerful" main streets stood some magnificent taller buildings with "massive cornices and large balconied windows," and the "principal shops" were as "tastefully arranged" as any in Paris or New York (Taylor [1850] 1949, 246).

By night the shops were brightly lighted, with doors and windows open and shawls and serapes displayed within. The whole population, which numbered some 5,000 souls (Mason 1852, 2:41), seemed to be out to enjoy the air. With a band playing in the distance and the gleam of the paper lanterns of fruit vendors at every corner, women in *rebosos* and men in white shirts milled about while aristocratic señoritas smoked their cigars on the balconies above (Taylor [1850] 1949, 247). The scene could not have presented a gayer aspect.

The Mazatlán market was held in a small plaza on the side of a steep hill. It was filled with square, umbrellalike canopies of palm leaves, under which were spread all varieties of native produce. Particularly desirable were the oysters and shellfish, roasted or pickled (Mason 1852, 2:41). At night the market was lighted with torches of a resinous wood.

Concerning the merits of the harbor itself, there were few comments, but during the first half of the nineteenth century Mazatlán became the seaport of most importance on the Pacific, an honor previously held by San Blas, which had been opened for trade in 1812.

The town of San Blas was perched on the top of a rock 150 feet high. Sheer cliffs dropped away on three sides, and the fourth was very steep. A low, swampy plain at the base of the rock was completely submerged in water during the rainy season (Hall 1824, 2:183–84). San Blas was the final stage of a long and arduous journey for the numerous would-be prospectors who traveled the route across Mexico to reach California, as well as a stopping place for the steamers and sailing ships going up and down the coast. Nearly every week some vessel would sail from San Blas to San Francisco with provisions and passengers. Fruits and vegetables were the chief exports. Onions were in great demand—eaten like apples by the Yankees up north ([Forbes] 1851, 208), it was thought.

The town of San Blas had a cosmopolitan tone, but many foreign merchants had their place of residence in nearby, inland Tepic, which was considered more healthful. Some even lived as far away as the provincial capital of Guadalajara.

GUADALAJARA AND PUEBLA

Guadalajara was believed by some to be the second-largest city in Mexico. Others thought the honor belonged to Puebla. Census figures were highly inaccurate, but by the 1850s the scales tilted toward Puebla at 71,000, compared to 63,000 for Guadalajara (Boyer 1973, 37,47). Both cities easily surpassed Mexico City in the cleanliness of their streets, and rivaled it in the beauty of their architecture, while they shared many similarities with each other.

Both had occupied positions of significance in the colonial system. Guadalajara, founded in 1530 or 1531, lies at the western edge of the central plateau, surrounded by arid plains. At an altitude of 5,100 feet, it has a mild and dry climate. As capital of the Audiencia of Nueva Galicia, it governed an area that extended into the present-day southwestern United States. Puebla also was founded in the early 1530s, and although it was south of Guadalajara, its higher altitude of 7,000 feet resulted in a moderate climate. Its principal importance lay in its strategic position on the route between Mexico City and Veracruz, which caused it to become a military post. Both Guadalajara and Puebla were divided by streams flowing through their midst.

Bayard Taylor referred to Guadalajara as "the most beautiful city in Mexico" (Taylor [1850] 1949, 282). Its streets were laid out in the typical squares, and though rather narrow, they were all paved (Carpenter 1851, 210). Convicts were kept at work sweeping the streets all day long. It is not surprising that they were "a model of cleanliness and order" (Taylor [1850] 1949, 282).

Puebla too was praised as a city that would be considered exceedingly beautiful in any part of the world (Koppe [1835] 1955, 119). Not only were the streets broad and straight, crossing at right angles and edged with sidewalks of porphyry (Tayloe 1959, 40), they were paved in a "peculiar and highly ornamental manner." Large, thin stones were placed edgewise in beds of sand and arranged with other square stones to form diamond-shaped patterns (Bullock 1824, 83–84).

Most observers noted the magnificent houses of Puebla They were spacious and elegantly constructed, with the usual flat roofs, iron balconies, barred windows, courtyards, and great wooden doors. Many were decorated with mosaics of glazed tiles in different colors and designs, usually of biblical subjects. The overhangs of roofs also were lined with tile (Bullock 1824, 84). Other houses were painted with various motifs of flowers and columns, while a few tastefully mixed "frescos and azulejos [glazed tiles]" (Blanchard and Dauzats 1839, 135). Water was conveyed to residences in earthen pipes, which supplied many fine fountains.

In Guadalajara the houses were "two and three stories high, well finished, and beautifully painted," according to William Carpenter (Carpenter 1851, 210), a soldier of the American army stranded in Mexico. Unfortunately, the whitewash would wash off toward the end of the rainy season, detracting considerably from the general appearance.

The central plazas of both cities were much admired and followed plans similar to that of the capital: the cathedral and government buildings occupied two sides of the square, while buildings with *portales* bordered the other two. The plaza of Guadalajara was well cared for, with trees planted in the center ([Forbes] 1851, 113). Of the busy and pleasant scene presented each day under the protection of the plaza's *portales*, Bayard Taylor wrote: "The intervals between the pillars, next the street, are filled with cases of toys, pictures, gilt images of saints, or gaudy slippers, sarapes, and rebozas. Here the rancheros may be seen in abundance, buying ornaments for the next festivals. Venders of fruit sit at the corners, their mats filled with fragrant and gleaming pyramids" (Taylor [1850] 1949, 282).

The cathedral of Guadalajara was of majestic proportions. It exhibited various architectural styles, with twin spires relieving a rather severe facade. During Taylor's visit in 1850 it was constantly filled with worshippers. Remembering the epidemic of cholera that devastated the city in the 1830s, the faithful sought deliverance in "solemn religious festivals" and sent up rockets "to propitiate the Virgin" (Taylor [1850] 1949, 282). Many other churches with beautiful works of art affirmed the faith of the people. It was here, in the archdiocese of Guadalajara, that a member of the Gordoa family, José Miguel Gordoa y Barrios, was bishop in 1831 and 1832.

But if mere numbers of churches and the richness of their endowment are indications of religious dedication, then surely Puebla deserved to be known as the most pious of Mexican cities. Here the compulsion in the colonial period to build sacred edifices had run wild, producing sixty churches, nine monasteries, and thirteen nunneries. In consequence, Puebla was a city of priests, monks, and nuns, whose influence may have produced the somber and taciturn people noted by one traveler (Koppe [1835] 1955, 122). Frances Calderón suggested that taking the veil was as common among the young ladies of Puebla as getting married (Calderón de la Barca [1943] 1931, 333). The magnificence of these buildings is certain. The cathedral rivaled and perhaps surpassed in elegance that of Mexico City. It was elevated on a stone platform where its authority could be felt below. Its towers soared two hundred feet heavenward, and its interior was rich in ornamentation beyond description.

Puebla in the 1840s was still developing a paseo for a public promenade, which Fanny thought one day would be pretty, when the young trees grew (Calderón de la Barca [1843] 1931, 334). It was nonetheless a place for relaxation at the end of the day or on Sundays and holidays for people of every station, from the *china poblana* in her dress of bright colors to the lady of society, whether on foot or in a fine carriage.

Guadalajara by contrast boasted a "beautiful square" at the edge of the city, "shaded with fine trees, and traversed by pleasant walks, radiating from fountains in the center," with "a hedge of roses, which bloom throughout the whole year." The drive around the alameda attracted some "handsome turn-outs," according to Taylor. Even more fascinating was the scene at night when the paseo moved to the plaza and fashionable folk appeared on foot—a custom unique to this city. As he recalled:

> We sat down on one of the benches, so near the throng of promenaders . . . that their dresses brushed our feet. The ladies were in full dress, with their heads uncovered. . . . The faint clear olive of their complexion . . . the deep, dark, languishing eye . . . the ripe voluptuous lip—the dark hair whose silky waves would have touched the ground . . . and the pliant grace and fullness of the form, formed together a type of beauty which a little queenly ambition would have moulded into a living Cleopatra. (Taylor [1850] 1949, 285–86).

After independence Guadalajara and Puebla both struggled for economic recovery and development. Both had a measure of success in the textile industry, and Guadalajara undertook the manufacture of carriages, while Puebla produced glass, bricks, and soap in quantity.

MINING CENTERS

Communities of quite a different type were the mining centers of Zacatecas, Guanajuato, and Catorce, which were shaped by the mountains that gave them birth.

Like many a mining town, Zacatecas just happened. A mining camp materialized where the first discoveries were made in 1546, and by 1585 it had received the official title of city. Blessed with a healthful climate at an altitude of 8,000 feet amid barren mountains, the town thrived and became one of the major silver-producing areas of New Spain, as well as an important outpost of the Franciscan order for the Christianization of the northern regions. In the 1840s Zacatecas had a reported population of some 25,000 people (Lyon 1828, 1:265).

The city, when viewed from a distance, had "a most beautiful and imposing appearance" as it lay at the foot of an "abrupt and picturesque porphyritic mountain" (Lyon 1828, 1:265). The mountain, called La Bufa, was neatly crowned with a little church dedicated to the patron saint of Zacatecas, Nuestra Señora del Patrocinio. Because of the uneven terrain, streets were short and crooked, but they were all well paved and clean. An aqueduct was stretched across the city of flat-topped houses, but even so, to obtain a supply of good water was a serious problem for Zacatecans. A stone fountain in the center of the main plaza, which bore the inscription "Upon thee I shower abundance," had, in fact, long been without water when it was noticed by Lieutenant Hardy in 1827 (Hardy 1829, 492).

The city extended over and around and through the mines. The wealth extracted provided for the construction of large and imposing public buildings that attracted the eyes of travelers: the remodeled Mint of Zacatecas; the Ayuntamiento, which was in a handsome private dwelling on the *plaza mayor*; the substantial post office; and the customhouse. Another elegant building on the plaza was the town house of the Gordoas. It was rumored that some houses were actually situated over mines that the owners worked at night, quite illegally, stealthily throwing the refuse into the street (Hardy 1829, 492).

The only trees that the citizens had planted in this desolate locale, according to Lyon, were along the narrow alameda on the outskirts of

Plaza Mayor of Zacatecas. Engraving by Carl Nebel, *Voyage pittoresque et archéologique dans la partie la plus intéressante du Mexique* (1836).

town (Lyon 1828, 1:265). However, the place popular as a promenade was the Portal de Rosales, across from the *plaza mayor*. This portal was dedicated in 1827 to the Zacatecan hero of the war of independence, Víctor Rosales, in what has been called "one of the many examples of a cult for honoring defeats which is so linked to the Mexican character" (Hoyo 1960, 138).

The jewel of Zacatecas was the parish church on the main plaza. Although the rich miners spared no expense, it was not to become a cathedral until 1862; nor would the second of its two towers be completed until 1904. The main facade, in glorious baroque, resembled an immense shield with three horizontal divisions, each with Solomonic columns that enclosed niches for small statues.

The city supported many other churches and convents, including the extensive Franciscan convent at the nearby village of Guadalupe. Was it the influence of the many priests or the isolation of the region that caused some Zacatecans to look with suspicion and overt hostility on all strangers? Lyon was pelted with stones. He noted in his journal that the

English and all foreigners were believed to be Jews and as such were supposed to have tails (Lyon 1828, 1:267).

No less important in the mid-1800s was the mining city of Guanajuato, founded in 1545 northwest of Mexico City. The mountains there seemed to afford an inexhaustable source of wealth, and even the poorer classes appeared better dressed and in better circumstances than in other places, because of the quantity of money in circulation (Carpenter 1851, 141).

This town was, in the words of Bayard, "of all places in Mexico . . . the most picturesque and remarkable. It lies like an enchanted city, buried in the heart of the mountains" (Taylor [1850] 1949, 290). The entrance was through a narrow pass that ultimately ended in a cul-de-sac, so that the only exit was by the same route. Beyond the city gates, which were closed at night, one passed high adobe walls, above which rose tier upon tier of windowless, sunbaked houses. The roofs of these houses were planted with grass, so that anyone looking down from above was astonished to see little but a field of green, interspersed with painted spires and domes (Carpenter 1851, 140–41). The road wound past the substantial stone facilities of the mining companies and the many imposing public buildings. Streets ran up and down the mountains in all directions, narrow and crooked, leaving no room for proper plazas or alamedas. A small triangular area in front of the cathedral made a pretense of being the *plaza mayor*. At night it was lit up by the smoky torches of the corner fruit stands. Water was brought to town on burros and sold for six cents a load (Poinsett 1824, 161).

The setting of the younger town of Real de Catorce, which lay in the bleak mountains of the Sierra Madre Oriental, was no less spectacular, and even more inaccessible. *Real* in the name of a town indicated that it was a mining center; *catorce* perhaps refers to fourteen bandits, or possibly fourteen Spanish soldiers, slain by Indians.

The town was a veritable eagle's nest (Cabrera Ipiña [1970] 1975, 34), which took shape on the lofty shoulder of an isolated mountain, Barriga de Plata, or "Silver Belly." At 9,000 feet it was the highest town in all of Mexico. The first great discoveries of silver and gold had been made in the 1770s, and at the beginning of the nineteenth century Catorce was third in the country in the production of silver. Antonio María Gordoa made his fortune there with the development of the mines La Luz and Refugio, which continued to produce even during the hard times of the 1830s and 1840s, when a mine employee lamented to Luis

Approach to Guanajuato. Engraving by Carl Nebel, *Voyage pittoresque et archéologique dans la partie la plus intéressante du Mexique* (1836).

Gonzaga Gordoa that "Catorce was becoming sadder every day" (Juan Mata to L. G. Gordoa, 28 April 1844, Gordoa Family Papers).

The Real had attracted the attention of Humboldt in 1803, and later that of the English minister Ward, who ascended the precipitous trail to the summit of Barriga de Plata and spent five days there in 1827. His wife sketched the road to this out-of-the-way little city, which at the time numbered some 8,000 inhabitants. Catorce, as the Wards saw it, was built layer upon layer up the side of the mountain from the ravines that intersected the plain below. Houses and public buildings were of stone with stone carvings. Many were two stories high with wrought-iron balconies and entrances at different levels. Because of the severity of the cold, the Wards were glad to be lodged in a house with a fireplace, something of a rarity in Mexico. Despite its remoteness and the difficulty of the approach, Catorce was amply supplied with provisions—meat, fowl, fruit, and grain—from the tableland and the *tierra caliente*. Even luxery items, such as French wine and Virginia tobacco, found their way into Catorce homes through a complex system in which silver was exchanged for contraband. Many homes were, in effect, storehouses for illegal goods (Ward 1828, 2:486, 510–11).

The principal plaza was built on a not-quite-perpendicular slope, with the Palacio Municipal looking down from the top and the parish church looking across from the side. Streets were narrow and steep, so steep in fact that some seemed to climb directly up the mountainside, and many were paved in interesting cobblestone patterns. There was the evidence of diggings everywhere around. In Santa Anna's time the few remaining trees were falling under the woodman's ax, leaving the mountains completely bare (Díaz-Berrio Fernández 1976, 10).

NORTHERN CITIES

Of the four major cities on the north, Durango, Chihuahua, Saltillo, and Monterrey, all but Durango were mining centers, and by the end of the century it too would be. Yet the mountains did not completely surround them or limit the opportunities for other enterprises. They were all agricultural centers as well.

Durango was "one of the handsomest cities in the north" (Gregg [1844] 1926, 254). Located nearly 200 miles northwest of Zacatecas on a level plain at 6,200 feet, and surrounded on all sides by low mountains, it appeared to Albert Gilliam to occupy as much space as the City of Mexico and to have buildings just as large if not as high. His figure of 30,000 for the population in those days (Gilliam 1847, 210) was probably, however, much inflated. As a bishopric, Durango had a fine cathedral and other splendid churches, as well as one of the nine government mints.

The alameda was "as lovely and delightful a retreat as I had ever in my life enjoyed," Gilliam commented. On the outskirts of town, it commanded a picturesque view of the city, the plain, and the mountains around. A grove of trees shaded the clean walks and benches, while a fountain of water refreshed the air (Gilliam 1847, 209). Water for the fountain was supplied by open aqueducts leading through the streets from a large spring a mile or so away. Gardens could be irrigated, but since much pollution found its way into the canals, drinking water was purchased from *aguadores*, who packed it in on asses (Gregg [1844] 1926, 254).

Tropical fruits appeared at the market in great abundance and were sold on the street by vendors. Their cries mingled with those of the

Urban marketplace. Engraving by Casimiro Castro and J. Campillo in J. Decaen, ed., *México y sus alrededores; colección de monumentos, trajes y paisajes* (1864).

pulque sellers. Pulque, made from the maguey plant, was cultivated in fields and also grew wild. It was sold everywhere in jugs and goblets when it was in season (Gregg [1844] 1926, 255).

The population of Durango, as well as that of Chihuahua and Sonora, Ward tells us, was predominately white, unmixed with the blood of the Indians (Ward 1828, 2:556–57). He praised the manners and character of these Mexicans, which he said contrasted favorably with the prejudices against foreigners held by some of their countrymen. Gilliam also commended the people of Durango, who seemed to him to be of a "better order" than the citizens of other places. He credited this to the influence of the very pious and beloved bishop of Durango, a man faithful to his vows, who had never allowed a woman to enter his house and retained only men as servants. The bishop's father confessor accompanied him always, and three times daily he made his confession (Gilliam 1847, 215–16).

A word now about the scorpion, the *alacrán*, inasmuch as Durango was the unofficial capital of the scorpion nation. The sting of this venomous creature was reputed to be more poisonous in Durango than anywhere else, and some families at that time made their living there by catching scorpions and collecting the bounty offered by the government (Gilliam 1847, 215).

Farther north, on a high tableland surrounded by low, detached mountains, lay Chihuahua, a town of perhaps 10,000. When compared to Spain's northernmost outpost, Santa Fe, Chihuahua was grand. It sank in significance when compared to the cities of the south (Gregg [1844] 1926, 281), and yet was not without its merit. The streets were laid out with the proper regularity, and by 1850 some of them were paved and had paved sidewalks. Many houses were quite handsome. Most were built of stone or adobe around courtyards, and though they had but one story, the ceilings were so high, the walls so thick, and the windows so few that, with their brick floors, they were perfectly adapted to the hot climate (Bartlett 1854, 2:433). Chihauhua's cathedral was said to be "second to the great cathedral of Mexico" (Bartlett 1854, 2:433) or "to equal in architectural grandeur anything of the sort in the Republic" (Gregg [1844] 1926, 282). Its towering steeples and intricately carved columns gave evidence of the million pesos collected in levies against the mines of Santa Eulalia a century before to build it (Gregg [1844] 1926, 282).

In a land where water was often dearer than silver, no city was better supplied than Chihuahua. An aqueduct of many arches stretched for three and a half miles across rough terrain to bring its treasure within easy access. And there was also a stream running along the northern edge of town. Both sources of water provided irrigation for fine gardens of fruit and vegetables—apples, pears, peaches, figs, melons, and grapes, and beans, peas, maize, red peppers, tomatoes, onions, lentils, beets, and cabbages in abundance (Bartlett 1854, 2:433, 437).

Another highly regarded product of the area was the Chihuahua dog, a sagacious little animal of three or four pounds. In Chihuahua in the 1850s the dogs cost between five and sixteen pesos, but in the capital they would bring as much as fifty (Bartlett 1854, 2:440).

Also bordering the desolate Indian country on the north were the rival towns of Saltillo and Monterrey. Both had about 15,000 inhabitants at mid-century; both had been founded in the late sixteenth century as outposts to pacify the Chichimecas. Soon after the founding of Saltillo, friendly Tlaxcalan Indians were settled in the adjacent village of San Esteban, and of the two settlements, surprisingly, the Indian town prospered more, as we shall later see in chapter 8.

Saltillo, set in a broad valley amid the Sierra Madre Oriental, was a well-built, mile-high city with an ideal climate. Its streets, though somewhat crooked and not very wide, were paved with stone, and many houses were of two stories and painted in warm colors. Large trees filled the alameda, and its walks were lined with agaves and roses (Bartlett 1854, 2:498). The cathedral compared well with that of Chihuahua, although the exterior was incomplete; the tower would not be finished until 1897. Older than the cathedral was the adjoining chapel of the Cristo Crucificado with a churrigueresque facade and a delicate spire. It had been built with gifts of the miners of La Iguana, who donated the silver they extracted on Saturdays (Alessio Robles 1934, 121).

About 3,500 feet lower was the town of Monterrey, situated on a plain at the edge of the last link of the mountain chain. Monterrey was one of the very few places visited by travelers at that time that seemed to be thriving. Improvements were being made; fine houses were under construction; the streets were paved and clean. In fact, declared John Russell Bartlett, who traveled in this area in the 1840s, Monterrey was an example for the street inspectors of New York City (Bartlett 1854, 2:504).

QUERÉTARO AND OAXACA

The role that Indians played in the history and development of Saltillo was unusual in the northern states, but Indians were an integral part of society in many towns farther south. One of the founders of Querétaro in 1531 was an Otomí Indian, and a large, diverse Indian population lived there throughout the colonial period, contributing to the growing manufacturing enterprises of the city. By 1810, of the 50,000 inhabitants of Querétaro, possibly one-third were Indian (Altman and Lockhart 1976, 231–32). The population declined after independence, but in 1824 it was no less than 30,000, of whom 11,000 were Indian (Poinsett 1824, 139).

Querétaro was beautifully situated on the gentle slope of a hill in the fertile country known as the Bajío. An extensive aqueduct of more than sixty arches brought water into the town, where the streets were narrow and irregular but well paved, (Tayloe 1959, 141) and sidewalks were laid with slabs of porphyry (Poinsett 1824, 141). The town was, in all, well built. The handsome public edifices created a general impression of an industrial town. Half of the houses, which were usually of one story, had shops opening onto the streets, and a large proportion of the people worked in textile mills (Orbigny 1836, 433–34).

Querétaro was famous for its numerous religious buildings. In fact, some observers judged the number of churches and convents to be excessive and even unnecessary, and Lieutenant Robert Hardy wrote that "Querétaro and La Puebla de los Angeles are said to be the most fanatical towns in the republic of Mexico" (Hardy 1829, 503). Worthy of note were the church and convent of Santa Clara. This very large complex was similar to a small town, with streets and squares laid out in straight lines. Contained within its confines were no less than 250 smaller churches (Orbigny 1836, 433).

The influence of the church and the superstition in which the clergy held their flock show in some of the carefully preserved letters that young Mariana Gordoa received in Mexico City from her sisters in Querétaro. In a letter written June 28, 1842, Dolores Rubio tells her sister that "the Virgin del Pueblito is here and they are having a novena for rain. In these days it has rained a lot." But another sister, Carmen, who often expressed very independent ideas, had remarked on May 22, 1841, that despite her petitions to the saints her sister had not recovered her health, and that now more than ever she had doubts about the saints' ability to work miracles. On the following June 19, 1841, Carmen confided to Mariana, "You say that it is a miracle that I confessed. I tell you that I am tired of being bad, and I'm going to be good" (Gordoa Family Papers).

Even more Indian in character was the very old town of Oaxaca, set in a green semitropical valley in the foothills of the Sierra Madre del Sur. Cortés had arrived in the Valley of Oaxaca in 1526 at the invitation of the Zapotec ruler, who offered submission in exchange for protection against the Mixtecs. The settlement, with buildings erected over an ancient *templo mayor*, was first called Segura de la Frontera. Then it assumed the name Antequera, and as such was granted the title "Most Noble City" by Carlos V. Only later did it take the name Oaxaca. Benito Juárez, the Zapotec Indian who was to become president of the republic of Mexico in 1861, gave the somewhat forgotten town its moments of glamour and celebrity.

This southern city of 18,000 or 20,000 souls was not on the itinerary of most nineteenth-century travelers, but the Frenchman Mathieu de Fossey ventured there in the 1830s. He noted its location between two rivers and the streets that stretched to the four cardinal points. Along the more important of these streets ran fast little streams, supplied with water from the aqueduct of San Felipe. Houses were of but one story because of the frequent and intense earth tremors. Most, Fossey said, were white both inside and outside, and to remedy the almost unbearable reflections of the sun, unbleached cloth was placed at the windows instead of panes (Fossey 1857, 349–50).

Fossey gave scant importance to the architecture, little noting the characteristics that distinguish it as "Oaxaca Baroque": the use of beautiful green stone on important buildings, the charm of details, the decorations based on plant themes (Varona 1957, 15–16). In fact, some of the colonial houses of greenish hue, with wrought-iron railings and lavishly ornamented entrances, were unique in Mexico (Varona 1957, 31). Fossey remarked that the Convent of Santo Domingo, while remaining a convent, was also a citadel where troops and important residents took refuge in time of danger (Fossey 1857, 352). He might well have added a few words about the gigantic tree in high relief with branches that extended in all directions over the arch of the vault supporting the choir, and the images of important historical figures—Saint Peter, Ferdinand and Isabella, Joan of Arc, the Cid, Cortés, and Charlemagne—which appeared among the leaves (Varona 1957, 21).

Some of the inhabitants of Oaxaca were rich Indians "who spent considerable sums of money for keeping up their houses." Fossey had dinner with several of these and wrote: "I often saw silver dishes there and other precious objects. They also had good wines of Bordeaux, Malaga, and Xeres, that they generally served to their guests; their tables were covered with the best viands cooked in the Mexican fashion, while they ate a frugal meal, and drank water seated on a matting in the kitchen, surrounded by their families" (Fossey 1857, 353).

In general, Fossey found the people of Oaxaca "amiable" and "kind to strangers." The women he called "genteel" and of "a good natural disposition." On his first visit he did not think that their manners and language compared with those of Mexico City, but on his return in 1849 he said "they seemed to me as advanced as the ladies of the capital" (Fossey 1857, 354).

MÉRIDA

With gusto, John L. Stephens described the distinctive attractions of Mérida, the capital of Yucatán, which he called "a little nook almost unknown to the rest of the world" (Stephens [1843] 1963, 1:19). It was, in truth, very far removed from the greater part of Mexico. The population in that year of 1842 numbered some 23,000, most of them

Mayan Indians. Mérida had been founded exactly 300 years before on the site of an ancient Mayan city located on a massive plain of limestone.

Mérida was laid out with perfect Spanish regularity, and the general appearance of the town was Moorish. The principal plaza was bounded on the east by a fortresslike cathedral, on the west and north by offices of government, and on the south by a large stone house, the Casa Montejo, built by the son of conquistador Francisco de Montejo. Its richly ornamented facade displayed two knights in armor standing on the shoulders of defeated naked figures. Most houses were of stone and of only one story, but they had balconies at the windows and large courtyards. Eight streets extended from the plaza, two from each corner. A few blocks beyond, on every street, were gates, dismantled by 1842, and beyond those were the Indian barrios (Stephens [1843] 1963, 1:48).

Street names were indicated in a curious way typical of Yucatán. High at the angle of the corner house was placed a painted wooden image of an animal, bird, or some recognizable object. One street with the image of a bespectacled old woman was the Street of the Old Woman; another with a flamingo was Flamingo Street. This system of course benefited the masses of 'inhabitants, universally the Indians,'' who could not read (Stephens [1843] 1963, 1:48).

The alameda of Mérida was a wide, paved avenue with stone seats on either side, and on each side of it were carriage roads shaded by trees. Adding a picturesque quality to the scene were the ruins of a fortress, the Castillo, from which rose the spires of an old Franciscan church. Every Sunday a promenade such as the one that attracted Stephens took place around the castle and along the alameda. Most striking, he said, were the *calesas*, the special little carriages painted red with gaily colored curtains for protection against the sun. Each was drawn by a horse with a boy astride. Two, sometimes three, ladies rode in the *calesas*, their hair beautifully arranged without hat or veil, in perfect contentment. Mestizas and Indian women, in costumes of white with red borders at the neck and on the skirt, were part of the quiet but unforgettable picture (Stephens [1843] 1963, 1:19).

The ladies of Mérida in the evening paseo held great charm for Stephens. He wrote that they had such an "air of modesty and simplicity" that their very gentleness was a protection and shield from insult, and that mestizas and Indians also had "the same mild and gentle expression" (Stephens [1843] 1963, 1:19).

TEPIC AND JALAPA

Innumerable smaller towns dotted the huge territory of Mexico. Tepic, on the Pacific coast, and Jalapa, near the Gulf of Mexico, seem to have been favorites of both Mexicans and foreigners.

Tepic was set on a plain amid moist meadowland and small streams, at an altitude of 3,000 feet, a short trip inland from the port of San Blas. The extinct volcano Sángangüey loomed in the background. Pleasant gardens surrounded the town, obscuring everything from the view of a visitor just arriving except the towers and dome of the cathedral (Taylor [1850] 1949, 265). The population at mid-century was perhaps 8,000, mostly mestizo, with the blood of the Indian dominating ([Forbes] 1851, 127, 136). The population increased each May when San Blas, because of rains, excessive heat, and the threat of sickness, became uninhabitable. Then, en masse, the population "took the high road to Tepic" (Hall 1824, 2:278–79) and rich and poor, on horses or on foot, trekked across the plains to summer homes.

Most houses in Tepic were of one story, massive, and well built. As many had adjoining stables and corrals, the town spread out over much land ([Forbes] 1851, 128). Streets ran at right angles and were kept at least tolerably clean. The plaza at the end of one of these streets was judged by Bayard Taylor "the most beautiful in Mexico." An old stone fountain was in the center, and giant trees grew around all four sides, giving shade to the arched *portales* where vendors displayed their wares. "All the gaiety of the city seems to concentrate in the plaza," added Taylor (Taylor [1850] 1949, 265). For the English traveler Basil Hall in the early 1820s, "the gay world of Tepic" (Hall 1824, 2:191) was seen in the evening exodus of the women of the town, who took the broad public walk leading out to the little church of Santa Cruz, chatting merrily on their way to services.

Tepic was well provided with delicious drinking water, not from the aqueduct but by carriers who brought in a constant supply from several nearby wells ([Forbes] 1851, 138–39).

Jalapa was the eastern counterpart of Tepic, matching it in the quality and abundance of its water, in its lush garden setting, and in the refuge it provided for coastal residents every summer. Just as the people of San Blas fled to Tepic, those of Veracruz made the seventy-mile journey inland to Jalapa, with the added incentive of escape from sieges and bombardments. Those temporary residents regularly expanded the number of Jalapa's usual population, which was variously recorded at 13,000 to 20,000 (Bullock 1824, 48; Taylor [1850] 1949, 324).

The location of the town at 4,700 feet on a slope halfway between the sea and the high tableland, under the majestic shadows of the mountains Orizaba and Cofre de Perote, gave Jalapa the "extreme softness of its climate" (Ward 1828, 2:193). Here was a spot of rare fertility and luxuriant vegetation, "a piece of heaven let down to earth," said an old Spanish author (quoted in Wilson 1855, 57).

The city indeed presented a charming picture—"no filthy alleys, no squalid poverty," wrote Wilson (Wilson 1855, 57). The steep streets were laid out with no regard for chessboard regularity, but were "as clean as a Dutch cottage" (Taylor [1850] 1949, 324). Houses of one or two stories, buried in gardens, were built of stone and were neatly whitewashed and trimmed in pink, red, blue, yellow, or green. They enclosed courtyards of trees and flowers and, unlike the flat roofs of Veracruz, had curious slanting roofs of red tile (Bullock 1824, 48).

Along the banks of a little stream at the foot of town was the alameda, a broad, paved parkway lined with stone benches and stone urns. Strollers in the evening could cross over a bridge and take one of a dozen footpaths that branched off among the shaded glens and orange orchards (Taylor [1850] 1949, 325). No wonder that travelers who stopped over in Jalapa en route to the higher elevations of Mexico or the low lands of Veracruz left this enchanted spot with regret. And as for the Indians who lived there, they had a saying, "Jalapa is Paradise" (quoted in Wilson 1855, 57).

CHAPTER FIVE

MEXICANS AT EASE

For those who would understand Mexico in one quick glance, there was no scene comparable to the Festival of the Holy Spirit at the celebrations of San Agustín de las Cuevas.—Guillermo Prieto

The diversions in the daily lives of Mexicans were remarkably the same in large towns and small, from one side of the country to the other. Most places of any size at all had their theater, their bullring, their cockpits, and as we have seen, their alameda or paseo. Socializing at balls or dances, *tertulias,* and weddings was engaged in, to some degree, by all levels of society everywhere, while a variety of extravaganzas attracted crowds in towns and cities. Patriotic celebrations were decreed for all. Everyone had the same church calendar which provided a never-ending cycle of holidays, while each town had its particular patron saint to honor. In view of this grand array of celebrations, one foreign critic was led to complain that "the *fiestas* and half *fiestas* are of such frequent recurrence, that at least two working days out of six are lost to labour" (Beaufoy 1828, 142). And, it must be added, at every celebration and nearly every social gathering an integral part of the entertainment was gambling, the universal passion of the people.

SAN AGUSTÍN DE LAS CUEVAS

It is safe to say that no other church celebration so excited and captivated the hearts of Mexicans as did the feast of the Holy Spirit, or Pentecost, as it was observed in San Agustín de las Cuevas, or Tlalpan, a village just south of Mexico City. There for three days in May or June, seven weeks after Easter, were concentrated all the joys of cockfighting, dancing, dining, fashionable dress, and most of all, gambling, which was the great attraction of the occasion. Church bells pealed, church doors opened, and masses were sung, but it was the prospect of sudden riches at the *monte* tables that brought the people streaming out from the capital. They came, the mighty and the humble, by carriage, cart, or hackney coach, on horseback, muleback, or foot, descending upon the normally quiet community, which overnight became "the gambling emporium" of the country (Calderón de la Barca [1843] 1931, 146). Dolores Rubio in Querétaro recalled with nostalgia in her letter to Mariana Gordoa of October 2, 1841, the happy times that they had enjoyed together in San Agustín de las Cuevas (Gordoa Family Papers). For the ladies of society the fete offered the opportunity to display their elegant gowns—first at the ten o'clock mass, a second time in the Plaza de Gallos, a third time at the alfresco ball at the Calvario, and a fourth time at the evening ball. Of course the dresses had to be different on each successive day (Mayer 1844, 78).

The center of festivities in the plaza of San Agustín could scarcely have been more animated. Banners were strung from rooftop to rooftop, flags flew, music and rockets filled the air, booths were set up to serve ices and drinks, and people in bright colors were constantly arriving and milling about, bent on pleasure. Everywhere, under makeshift awnings, were tables for the games of chance: *monte*, simple dice games, roulette, and a bingolike game called *lotería* or *rifa de cartones*, in which numbers had names. In the latter, the number twenty-two was "the little doves," seventy-seven was "the spikes," and eight "the spectacles of Pilate." *Carcamán*, played with special dice, attracted players as much for the risqué verses chanted by the *carcamanero* as for the game itself. The game of the "three little cards," which relied on sleight of hand, soon separated the credulous from his coppers (García Cubas 1904, 350–52).

Street games were patronized mostly by the tattered *lepero* and the blanketed Indian, playing small sums. The piles of money on the tables— copper *tlacos* or the lowest silver coin, the *medio*—did not exceed a total of more than twenty or twenty-five pesos. For people of less modest means other opportunities beckoned.

Around the plaza were the great houses opened for the festival by private bankers. These were supplied with as many as thirty thousand doubloons—a doubloon equaled sixteen pesos. In the most exclusive houses only gold was accepted, while in the lesser ones both gold and silver, or silver alone, were played. The accommodations were lavish, with sumptuous dinners and refreshments. Liquors, chocolates, coffees, and sweets were always at hand.

Meanwhile, on green-covered tables, there was the game of *monte*. The name referred to the pile of money or the stack of cards, and the fascination lay in risking large sums for the chance of matching cards with those already drawn from the stack. Fortunes were made or lost at the flip of a wrist, but it was nearly impossible to guess by the expression on the faces of the players whether they were winning or losing. It was said that a certain Matías Royuela placed a 20,000 peso bet on a particular card, and, when his loss was announced, he did not interrupt for one moment the interesting story he was telling his friends (Prieto 1906, 2:152).

And who were the players? Just about everyone. The politician, the businessman, the soldier, the *hacendado*, the priest, and even at times the fine lady. They all participated in this most respectable of vices, deporting themselves with perfect decorum and honor.

Gambling of another sort flourished in the afternoon at the cockfights in the Plaza de Gallos, where the money was on the birds. This primitive sport, which was sanctioned by tradition and accepted by the gentle sex, was a popular part of daily life in every corner of the republic. Yet even then it was condemned as repugnant by some thoughtful Mexicans (García Cubas 1904, 356). As for Santa Anna, who was often observed at the cockfights of San Agustín, he was in his glory, placing bets on his fowls, overseeing the action, and mingling with the throng (Prieto 1906, 2:153). Brokers of the unwashed variety circulated in the arena accepting bets from one and all and seemed never to make an error or to be guilty of the slightest dishonesty. Seven sets of cocks, armed with deadly knives strapped to their legs, faced each other every day. Tail feathers were pulled to infuriate them, water was poured on their heads to refresh them, and then the hapless creatures were released to fly to the attack. After two or three brief rounds one or the other cock would be pronounced dead, bets would be paid off, and the next pair brought forth (García Cubas 1904, 356).

After the last cock had met his fate, some of the crowd would join the gamblers at the *monte* tables, while others repaired to the ball at the hill of the Calvario just west of the village. There in the open air, surrounded by all the natural beauty of a garden of Eden, they danced to the sounds of sprightly martial music, or simply sat and watched. Children on the

Cockfight. Engraving by Claudio Linati, *Costumes civils, militaires el réligieux du Mexique; dessinés d'apres nature* (c. 1829)

green meadow played the innocent games of childhood and lovers exchanged glances, while others entertained themselves with picnics of tamales in the woods (García Cubas 1904, 357).

The crowning event of each day was a gala ball held in the evening at the Plaza de Gallos. It was a ball for all people, where the tailors, the hatters, the shop boys, and the carpenters danced on an equal footing with the elite, and the white-gloved hand of the gracious señora was not withdrawn from the dirty brown palm of the stableboy. And yet the ultrafashionable people of *mucho tono* preferred to take box seats and amuse themselves from the sidelines without even bothering to dress for the occasion (Calderón de la Barca [1843] 1931, 378).

Meanwhile, in the plaza, by the light of dripping oil lamps and greasy tallow candles, the rage for gambling continued. As copper coins exchanged hands and pulque flowed freely, the soothing strains of the guitar created an agreeable feeling. All was peaceful and harmonious, without fighting or harsh words (Calderón de la Barca [1843] 1937, 379–80).

When the three-day gambling spree at San Agustín ended each year, most folks returned home with empty pockets. Yet the gambling on this characteristic national feast day was just a fraction of the gambling that took place daily in gaming houses in Mexico City and towns everywhere, most often among those who could least afford to lose what little they had.

For festivals of a more truly religious nature we must look elsewhere. And yet, though the church calendar was replete with holy days the year round, some of which were of a very solemn nature, almost all of them had their frivolous and secular aspects as well.

THE DAYS OF CARNIVAL AND LENT

Unleashed gaiety and high spirits prevailed in the capital on the three days preceding Ash Wednesday, which marked the beginning of Lent. On those days the streets were thronged in the afternoon with people going to the Paseo de Bucareli, where elaborate carriages paraded along with quite ordinary ones. Groups of masquerading gentlemen, called *comparsas,* rode about in open *calesas,* lavishing flowers and candy on the ladies in carriages. Or dressed in grotesque costumes, they brought laughter to the crowds as they sallied forth in carts or on burros.

At night more masqueraders of all kinds and colors appeared. Moors and Christians, and some in domino cloaks of black taffeta, filled the *portales* and pressed on to Vergara Street, where the Teatro Nacional was aglow with hundreds of little lights that outlined the doors and windows and encircled the columns. A great lantern illuminating allegorical paintings hung from the second floor. Those with invitations entered to attend the carnival ball (García Cubas 1904, 308–10).

Before eleven the boxes would be full of spectators and the salon crowded with maskers, while the orchestra struck up a light-hearted tune. The ball managers, in long, black capes and red sashes, would signal each new dance with a thump of their canes. A diverse crowd it was: men dressed as women, women as men, with a sprinkling of knights in armour and *china poblanas.* Among the women the most popular disguises were the dominoes, for they provided the most concealment; it was not, after all, according to Fanny Calderón, "very creditable to be there" (Calderón de la Barca [1843] 1931, 115). Insults directed by anonymous maskers toward attending dignitaries, or anyone at all, were the rule and were expected, yet at times they were quite offensive, revealing a lack of education on the part of the perpetrator. And many a practical joke or case of mistaken identity was played out among lovers at the carnival balls.

If we accept the recollections of Antonio García Cubas as he wrote of the Mexico of his youth, we will admit that neither the dawn of Ash Wednesday nor the ensuing forty days of Lent summoned forth the universal spirit of fasting and self-denial that the church decreed. Not at all: the mass for the faithful on Wednesday morning was accompanied by the shouts of street vendors hawking their special fish for the day, their special flour for sweets, their vegetables and their spices, while the merry custom of cracking eggshells filled with bits of colored paper on the heads of friends was enjoyed everywhere.

Fasting during Lent had once been austere, but in the nineteenth century the days of *vigilia* seemed meant more for recreation than for penitence, and the abstinence from eating meat had its compensations. From the richest table to the poorest, the assortment of dishes for Lent was astonishing: fish, salmon, oysters, and lobster in succulent soups, ravioli stuffed with spinach and sardines, pastries, liquors and wines, fruits and sweets. If the consumption of salty fish and seafood produced an unbearable thirst, refreshing drinks of lemon and pineapple were prepared at home, ice creams were sold from the vendors on the street, and delicious sherbets were served at the crowded Gran Sociedad and El Bazar (García Cubas 1904, 312–14).

The doors of the theaters were closed during Lent to performances of music and drama. But the theatrical companies used this time to prepare new repertories, and the theaters remained open on Sundays for such carnival-like entertainments as piñatas, and bullfights continued as usual in the great arenas.

CORPUS CHRISTI

The procession of the Holy Eucharist on the day of Corpus Christi, celebrated in the late spring on the Thursday following Trinity Sunday, was one of great pomp and solemnity. Many more people observed the procession than were a part of it, and it became an occasion for high fashion among the wealthy, who watched from their balconies, and for holiday dress among the general throng of spectators below. Schoolboys rejoiced in a one-day vacation from books. The streets of Mexico City were covered over with awnings where the procession was to pass, as were streets throughout the country. Lengths of white linen edged in red extended across the streets from above one second-story level to the other, allowing spectators on the balconies a clear view of activities below (Sartorius [1858] 1961, 160).

A twenty-one-gun salute marked each of the nine phases of the ceremony. The first was at the break of dawn, the second at the beginning of mass, the third at the elevation of the Eucharist, the fourth at the end of mass, and the fifth as the Eucharist was escorted by the archbishop out of the cathedral in a grand procession composed of all the dignitaries of the church, the religious communities, the employees and administrators of the civil government with their alternates, the rectors of the schools, the seminarians and students, and the rank and file of the military. A sixth salvo was fired as the procession passed through Vergara Street in front of the Teatro Nacional, a seventh when the procession reentered the cathedral just as the last of the officials were leaving, the eighth at twelve noon, and the ninth and final salute at sundown (García Cubas 1904, 359).

Never was the pageantry more magnificent, nor the dress code for city officials and the military more flamboyant, than when it was decreed by Santa Anna in 1854. Public employees appeared in blue dress coats embroidered in gold, white trousers with stripes of gold, and gold-decorated vests set off by ornaments appropriate to the individual's rank, plus plumed hats and rapiers. What a bonanza it was for the tailors of the city! They received monthly payments deducted from the salaries of employees for the required uniforms, which, depending on the wearer's rank, cost from 250 to 1,000 pesos. Of course, the military were just as colorful in green frock coats with yellow piping, deep blue trousers with sky-blue piping, and caps with green pompons. Even their horses had to be of a minimum required height (García Cubas 1904, 365–68).

THE DAY OF SAN JUAN

In contrast, the day of San Juan on June 24, in honor of John the Baptist, was a private affair and was celebrated in two curious ways: many people attended public baths, and young boys dressed up as soldiers to take part in mock battles. The two customs seem to have had nothing to do with one another.

Daybreak and the sound of church bells brought a jolly crowd out to the streets singing the endless verses of the *mañanitas* on their way to the baths:

> Now the little birdies sing.
> Now hidden is the moon.
> Open, my love, your dear, sweet eyes.
> Look, it is morning now.[1]

To be sure, the baths themselves were of various sorts. Some provided the luxury of private cubicles with steamy hot water brought in by carriers. Others were supplied with cold water only. Women and children seem usually to have shared one dimly lighted room which lacked not only cleanliness but privacy too.

However, on the day of San Juan all baths were scrubbed clean; patios, doors, and windows were adorned with willows, and flowers and festive banners were displayed everywhere. The holiday mood of the bathers was matched by the exuberant music of stringed instruments. It was the custom on this holiday to reward all bathers with little gifts of fruit, soap, and esparto-grass scrubbers, which might be presented in clay baskets or simply added to the water that filled the baths. Celebrations thus continued, but in a less-animated way, until the day of San Pedro on June 29 (García Cubas 1904, 374).

The upper class, like the rest of the population, enjoyed bathing that day. Letters from the sisters of Mariana Gordoa, written from Querétaro on May 12 and 22, 1841, recall a time when they bathed with Mariana in Tacubaya on the day of San Juan (Gordoa Family Papers).

Meanwhile, young boys in the capital dressed up as soldiers on the day of San Juan. The Portal de Mercaderes in the Plaza Mayor was full of tables and stands where vendors sold military paraphernalia of every sort, from plumed hats to wooden swords and false beards. In the afternoon youngsters from all sections of Mexico City assembled in their assorted uniforms and marched to the plazas, where they practiced maneuvers and battles. These at times degenerated into real fights. Sometimes groups organized themselves in accordance with actual political parties so that federalists confronted centralists and liberals faced con-

---

[1] Ya cantan los pajaritos
Ya la luna se metió,
Abre mi alma tus hojitos
Mira que ya amaneció (García Cubas 1904, 374).

servatives. The custom dated far back to the early days of New Spain when *encomenderos* were obliged to defend their own property and periodically to present military reviews (García Cubas 1904, 375–76).

CHRISTMAS POSADAS

Another very typically Mexican celebration was the series of *posadas* on the nine nights preceding Christmas, representing the wanderings of Mary and Joseph in search of shelter after their arrival in Bethlehem. The *posadas*, or inns, offered refuge for the birth of the Christ Child. No other celebration more charmingly combined the human with the divine, or as it was commonly expressed "the opera with the sermon" (García Cubas 1904, 294). Fanny Calderón thought the *posadas* "extremely pretty" (Calderón de la Barca [1843] 1931, 293), and although she considered them an amusement for children, they seemed to appeal to the young of all ages.

A different family took reponsibility for each night of the *posadas*, a custom that naturally led to competition for the best in decorations and the finest in entertainment. For families who aspired to a higher social level, the acceptance of one of the *posadas* could mean financial hardship or even a trip to the national pawnshop, the Monte de Piedad. The wealthy, of course, prepared with ease festivities for fifty or sixty guests, including prominent people such as the Calderóns. The more truly representative *posadas*, however, were those of the middle class, according to Antonio García Cubas, who described in full the progression of an evening's activities (García Cubas 1904, 296–98).

Guests entered a house filled with the fragrance of pine branches and lighted with the brilliance of a multitude of paper lanterns, candelabra, and chandeliers. Each arrival knelt and crossed himself, and the litany of the Virgin was intoned as the group assembled into a procession. At the front went the children, holding little tallow candles that dripped on the carpets and corridors. Then came the young people, followed by the adults, everyone with a candle; and following them were the children who had been chosen to carry a board on which rested the Holy Pilgrims, an angel, and the indispensable mule, all on a silver base under silver arches representing the winter season. Behind them walked the musicians—the guitarist, the mandolin players, the flutists—and last of all the servants. As they marched about the house, their singing was accented with the deafening sound of rockets.

When the litany was concluded, the singers divided into two groups,

the smaller of which withdrew into a room, leaving the larger group
outside with the Holy Pilgrims to seek shelter, or *pedir la Posada*. Those
outside would sing:

> From our long journey
> Exhausted we arrive.
> We implore you for shelter
> In order to rest.

And the answer would come from within:

> Who comes to our door
> To annoy us
> So imprudently
> On such a stormy night?

The verses continued back and forth until at last those inside relented
and opened the door with an exultant:

> Open the doors
> Throw off the veils
> For the King of Heaven
> Has come here to rest![2]

At that point total pandemonium would break out. But still the holy
board had to be placed on a table, knees had to bend in prayer, and
seven Ave Marías had to be sung. At long last a piñata could be broken,
toys and refreshments could be distributed, and dancing could begin.

Posadas in the tenements were much the same, but ended far earlier
because of the workday in the morning.

On the last night, which was Christmas Eve, or Noche Buena, the
posada was generally held at the home of the head of the family. It

---

[2] De larga jornada
Rendidos llegamos
Y así lo imploramos
Para descansar.

Quién á nuestras puertas
En noche inclemente
Se acerca imprudente
Para molestar?

Abranse las puertas
Rómpanse lo velos
Que viene a posar
El Rey de los cielos (García Cubas 1904, 296–97).

differed in two ways from the preceding nights. First, a nativity scene was prepared for the eyes of the weary travelers to behold when the door was opened. It held the figures of Mary and Joseph kneeling at the manger bed of the Baby Jesus, while shepherds, angels, and the Wise Men stood guard amid animals from all countries and plants from every clime and season. These *nacimientos* were often considered family treasures and proudly displayed all year long (Campos 1928, 105). Second, instead of presents this night, a midnight feast was served. Or the family might attend midnight mass—the *misa del gallo*—after which joy at the birth of the Savior would burst forth in the unrestrained tooting of water whistles and the sounding of noisemakers by the children, and the playing of popular Mexican tunes by the organist. Unfortunately, this aspect of the Christmas celebration would fade away toward the end of the nineteenth century (Campos 1928, 105).

PATRIOTIC CELEBRATIONS

A similar feeling of unbridled spirit and fervor found an outlet in patriotic celebrations. And at the height of Santa Anna's rule there was an abundance of patriotic occasions. Mexico City seemed to revel in a constant fiesta of parades, artillery salvos, drums and bugles, fireworks, and high masses. The dictator's birthday and saint's day were obvious times for rejoicing. Even Dolores Rubio, in a letter of June 21, 1842, to Mariana Gordoa in the capital (Gordoa Family Papers), mentions how happy she is that Mariana had such a good time at Santa Anna's recent saint's day, on June 13, though she does not happen to mention just how they celebrated.

Various other civic holidays of a somewhat transient nature were observed under the Santa Anna regime. On September 11 the victory over the Spanish under General Isidro Barradas in the battle of Tampico was remembered. September 27 was not only the anniversary of Iturbide's triumphal entry into Mexico at the head of the Army of the Three Guarantees, the Trigarante, but also the date chosen in 1842 for a most singular celebration, the funeral for Santa Anna's leg.

The drama of this unique historical event did not fail to impress Brantz Mayer, who wrote that he had arrived early at the city gates just as the "cannons were firing in honor of the day which is to be celebrated by the '*entombment of the remains of Santa Anna's leg that was shot off at the battle of Vera Cruz in 1838!*'" (Mayer 1844, 207). The grisly appendage, which for four years lay buried at Manga de Clavo, had been dug up, placed in a crystal vase, and carried in a full military dress parade to the cemetery of Santa Paula. There it was laid to rest in a monument built for the purpose. Santa Anna acknowledged the speeches, poems, and salvos in his honor wearing a new cork leg (Simpson [1941] 1966, 248–49), doubtless oblivious of the caustic epigraph that Brantz Mayer claims appeared soon afterward on a nearby tomb: "*Protest of the dead bodies of the cemetery against the reception of the limb among them*" (Mayer 1844, 207).

The one regular civic holiday during the early days of the republic was Independence Day on September 16, a day instituted by decree in 1822. It probably evoked more genuine patriotic feeling than any other, as it marked the anniversary of Father Miguel Hidalgo's historic Grito de Dolores in 1810 and the beginning of the struggle for freedom.

In those days the celebration in the capital, as Antonio García Cubas recalled it, began with a solemn mass in the cathedral attended by the president, his ministers, and various high functionaries. It continued with a so-called *paseo cívico,* or civil promenade, which originated at the Palacio Nacional and made its way around the Plaza Mayor and down Plateros and San Francisco streets to the Alameda, where a small, templelike structure was improvised. There the president and his retinue would hear the oration of the day. It was such a somber procession, with nearly all participants dressed in black and marching slowly, that if it had not been for the joyful pealing of bells, the music, and the happy crowds, one would have thought it a funeral. The oration itself was usually of interminable length and full of diatribes against Spain with allusions to "the chains of oppression" and "the dark Inquisition." At night there were more speeches in ceremonies at the National Theater, attended by the first families. And not only speeches, but poetical recitations and musical performances as well. Indeed it was at the Teatro Nacional on September 16, 1854, that the national hymn of Mexico was sung for the first time (García Cubas 1904, 378–79).

Patriotic anniversaries often provided the excuse, if one were needed, to stage elaborate balls. As we have mentioned, September 27 was Iturbide's birthday, as well as the date of the funeral for Santa Anna's leg. The residents of Chihuahua in the 1830s, willing to forgive their fallen hero, enjoyed an annual ball given there by the governor and other high officials for Mexicans only. No Americans were invited, complained Josiah Gregg, the visiting businessman from the north, except for a rare Mexicanized American or two, whose invitations clearly stated that the price of admission was twenty-five dollars (Gregg [1844] 1926, 286–87).

SOCIAL PLEASURES

People of the upper classes often felt disposed to hold balls for any number of reasons, and they often staged gala events similar to those of San Agustín de las Cuevas or carnival. Charity was often stated as the purpose. Such was the dance mentioned by María Francisca Rubio in a letter of October 2, 1839, to Mariana Gordoa. It was held in the plaza of San Luis Potosí for the benefit of *léperos* (Gordoa Family Papers). Charity also occasioned the great costume ball that Frances Calderón attended on January 8, 1840. Unfortunately, the expenses of this gala event were so great that little or nothing was left for the poor (Calderón de la Barca [1843] 1931, 66 and 80).

Much more frequent than balls were *tertulias*, the purely social gatherings of friends in the evening. Captain Basil Hall of the Royal Navy, among other early travelers to Mexico, described one such *tertulia* he attended on an April night in 1824. The room was dimly lighted by a tallow candle, behind which, in a glass case, was displayed an image of the Virgin of Guadalupe. In one corner rested a guitar, and there was always someone ready to play a popular tune or accompany the ladies in song. Our English visitor noticed that music never interrupted the conversation, but instead acted as a stimulus. In another corner was a card table where men played *monte*. The center of the room was left as a playground for the children. Nurses and old servants walked in and out at will, which prompted Captain Hall to remark that "a degree of familiarity is allowed between the servants and their superiors, of which in England there is no example in any rank of life" (Hall 1824, 2:196–98).

This mingling of the classes was noted by Fanny at the hacienda of her rich friends the Adalids. While the Señora de Adalid played the piano one evening, a whole party of servants and masters gathered to perform the dances of the country—*jarabes, palomas,* and *zapateados.* They maintained always, however, the proper respect between the ranks (Calderón de la Barca, [1843] 1931, 156).

For the people of a lower social level, these popular dances provided easy and spontaneous entertainment. No dance was mentioned more frequently by travelers than the *fandango*, an ancient dance of Spanish origin. The name of the dance was taken by William Carpenter to apply as well to the fiesta. He explained that, once the *fandango* was decided upon and musicians engaged, the firing of a few rockets would be invitation enough for one and all to flock to the selected location (Carpenter

Fandango. Engraving by Casimiro Castro and J. Campillo in J. Decaen, ed., *México y sus alrededores; colección de monumentos, trajes y paisajes* (1864).

1851, 267). The dancing could take place inside or out and was performed with the couple facing each other, hands elevated, tripping lightly a few steps forward, then a few backwards, and round and round (Mason 1852, 1:163). Music, dancing, and drinking could continue thus until dawn, with always a chance that aroused jealousies might lead to violence.

Of the same family of dances were the equally popular *jarabes*, one of which, the *jarabe tapatío*, would later be recognized as the national dance of Mexico. The *jarabe* and the *fandango* were typically danced by the *china* and her counterpart the *charro*; their traditional dress would by the end of the century become the national costume.

It was this dress of the *china poblana* that Fanny Calderón, thinking to honor Mexico, chose as her costume for the charity ball early in 1840. But persuasive critics dissuaded her from her plan with the admonition that such apparel was not appropriate for the wife of the Spanish minister, inasmuch as it was the dress of a woman "of no character" (Calderón de la Barca [1843] 1931, 76–77). Could such criticism have been inspired merely by envy of the frankly attractive and sensuous *chinas*?

Less complicated surely were the lives of ordinary citizens, and less pretentious their pleasures. Few pastimes were more pleasurable and healthful too than that of bathing, indulged in by all people wherever there was a sufficient supply of water. Gilliam was prompted to remark that "the Mexicans are as fond of bathing in water as are the Spanish poodles" (Gilliam 1847, 142–43). And Josiah Gregg, in recording his visit to the famous warm springs of Aguascalientes, lamented: "The water was precisely of that agreeable temperature to afford the luxury of a good bath . . . but every few paces I found men, women, and children submerged in the *acequia* . . . it was so choked up with girls and full-grown women, who were paddling about with all the nonchalance of a gang of ducks, that I was forced to relinquish my long-promised treat" (Gregg [1844] 1926, 260).

It has been noted that the Rubio sisters went bathing on the day of San Juan. Their letters of May 12 and 22, 1841, also tell of a festive outing at the baths of La Cañada, perhaps a natural spring or pool. Carmen mentions her pleasure in finding that she could still swim. Both men and women bathed two times and were also entertained with music for dancing.

Those activities of bathing, dancing, and socializing, to which may be added picnics, country outings, weddings, and dinners, were the day-to-day private pleasures of Mexicans at ease. Other more stimulating entertainments beckoned as well.

PUBLIC SPECTACULARS

Sundays and holidays were occasions for bullfights in city, village, and hacienda. Nothing else in the New World could quite compare with this legacy of popular entertainment from Spain. While basically the same as in Spain, bullfights in Mexico exhibited their own peculiar characteristics. Indeed, a certain Mr. Forbes, writing at mid-century, insisted that the "Mexican bull fight is very different from the Spanish, less cruel, but at the same time [it] does not produce the same feeling of excitement in the spectator" ([Forbes] 1851, 162). He explained that Mexican bulls were small and young, compared to the Spanish, and had the tips of their horns sawed off, thus inflicting less damage on the horses, which were wretched animals in either country. But he noted, as did other observers, that in Mexico fireworks were a particular torment: the banderilleros affixed them, along with paper flags and streamers, to the necks of the beasts ([Forbes] 1851, 164–65).

While Forbes asserted that at the bullfight "all ranks are on an equality" ([Forbes] 1851, 164), quite the opposite must really have been the case, as bullrings accommodated two types of spectators: those who could afford comfortable seats in the shade and those who could not and sat instead in the sun. Nevertheless, all levels of society were addicted to the sport.

Antonio García Cubas provides first-hand recollections of the principal bullrings in Mexico City at mid-century. The most ancient was that of San Pablo near the church of the same name in the southeastern part of the city. Built at the end of the eighteenth century with two tiers of shaded balconies, this spacious structure was renovated after independence. Young Antonio's first sight of the life-and-death encounter was in the Plaza de Toros de San Pablo, where seventeen horses and one picador lay stretched out dead in the sand. The sight left an indelible impression (García Cubas 1904, 269–73).

Somewhat more agreeable were Garcia Cubas's memories of another bullring, called the Plaza del Paseo, erected in 1851 near the equestrian statue of Carlos IV. This beautiful, grand plaza was as full of the social elite, in their 272 boxes and shaded seats, as of commoners in the sun. It was demolished during his lifetime, but in October, 1853, García Cubas witnessed a very festive event there in honor of Santa Anna himself, who attended with his wife, Doña Dolores Tosta. García Cubas recalled the opening maneuvers in the plaza by a colorful corps of grenadiers, the dazzling appearance of the famous *torero* Barnardo Gaviño with his *cuadrilla* of brilliantly dressed *picadores* and *banderilleros*, the salute to the authorities and the crowds, and the first charge against the bull by two mounted picadors. And he noted the part played by the comics dressed as clowns, who entertained between fights, dancing, cavorting, and juggling in a role later to be eliminated from the proceedings. Sartorius described a similar amusing performance by clowns and *léperos* who teased the bulls, tried to sit at prepared tables to eat all sorts of tasty dishes in the face of the galloping bulls, or attempted to climb a greased pole to seize a prize while the bull descended upon them (Sartorius [1858] 1961, 152–53).

García Cubas, who in truth found the spectacle of the bullfight horrifying, was nevertheless fascinated by its splendor. He concluded his remarks about the bullfight in honor of Santa Anna by describing the elegant carriage that entered after Gaviño had dispatched the final bull. It circled the arena, stopped, and two girls alighted and offered the *torero* a crown encrusted with gold coins, all amid music and deafening applause. Gaviño then joined the girls in the carriage and made a triumphal turn around the plaza. At the conclusion of the function Santa Anna and his entourage in another magnificent carriage, accompanied by mounted grenadiers fore and aft and mounted aides on both sides, departed at a gallop for the palace (García Cubas 1904, 273).

The Mexican populace was not content to be entertained solely with the thrill of the bullfights. Other exhibitions, such as races of men against animals, fights between bulls and tigers, and wrestling matches also were arranged to please them (Salvat Editores de México, S.A. 1974, 7:196).

For many, entertainment meant blood, as we can see in the following account of a troup of French gymnasts performing in the Teatro Nacional in 1848. To accommodate the crowds, the show was moved to the bullring, where it was announced that strongman Turin would do the impossible: with his arm in a vertical position he would stop a horse at a full gallop. And this he did, to loud applause. But then the audience cried out that the horse was weak and he should repeat the feat with a strong one. Turin agreed. He wrapped a cord around his arm and ordered the horse released. Turin was about to subdue it too when his arm doubled, the cord snapped loose, burning and tearing off the skin, and he fell in a faint. The shouting crowd demanded that he finish the program, which had called for him to fight a Mexican who had challenged him. A clamor arose. Turin, once he had regained his senses, walked out into the arena with his arm bandaged and took on the challenger, whom he defeated without effort. Did this placate the mob? Not at all. It only infuriated them to see their compatriot lose to a foreigner, and they would have lynched him on the spot if the guards had not restored order (Reyes de la Maza 1972, 37–38).

Not all diversions were of such a violent nature, of course. Very popular on Sunday afternoons, in Mexico City and elsewhere, were the circus and acrobatic acts called *maromas* performed in outdoor areas. Families gathered to watch the skills of tightrope walkers and the antics of clowns. Amidst the ear-splitting strains of a brass band, these jovial fellows with pointed hats, floured faces, and long, curled hair mimicked the other performers and directed satirical verses to the audience (García Cubas 1904, 254–57.

A number of firsts in entertainment took place in the early years of the century. In 1832 an enterprising showman arrived in Veracruz with the first elephant to set foot in Mexico. The poor beast was exhibited in all villages from the coast to the capital, but because of old age and the climate, he soon expired. Undaunted, his owner had him mounted and continued to display him for two reales (Salvat Editores de México, S.A. 1976, 7:196). Just one real was the price to pay in 1843 to see Mexico's first trained chimpanzee play the violin and sweep and brush the clothes of his master (Reyes de la Maza 1972, 28).

The same year, 1843, marked the beginning of an astonishing fore-runner of the cinema. Crowds at number four in the Portal de Merca-deres in Mexico City were amused with a diorama of pictures illu-minated from within with gradations of light that produced optical illusions. The viewer faced a picture not unlike a modern film screen and the light, broken down into a thousand tones, created scenes such as the interior of the convent of Monserrat in Spain lighted by the sun. Slowly, evening approached, and with darkness the moon and stars ap-peared, while lamps of the convent came on. Nine different pictures were presented in this way (Reyes de la Maza 1972, 27–28).

Surely the most extraordinary spectacles of the time were the balloon ascensions of the Frenchman Eugène Robertson. In February, 1835, to the amazement of a full house in the Plaza de Toros de San Pablo, Rob-ertson in a wicker gondola ordered the lines loosed, and up he floated, slowly at first, then faster. In less than ten minutes he was out of sight. Fear gripped the spectators and the whole city, until it was learned the next day that he had landed safely in a tree in Chalma, having traveled some sixty miles in two hours. A hero's welcome awaited him in the capital, where he was received by Interim President Miguel Barragán, since Santa Anna was absent at Manga de Clavo.

A repeat performance in a larger balloon was made on September 13 to commemorate the 1829 defeat of General Barradas by Santa Anna, who was on hand for this occasion, watching from his place of honor. First an enormous portrait of the dictator was sent aloft in a smaller balloon. Then the intrepid Robertson boarded his gondola and, as he majestically rose heavenward, he waved a Mexican flag and threw out printed poems lauding the victor of Tampico. After a leisurely cruise over the city, the balloonist landed smoothly at Potrero de Balbuena to the cheers of thousands—a hero again. "It was the greatest spectacle produced by science in the century," proclaimed the newspaper La Lima de Vulcano on September 19 (Reyes de la Maza 1969, 358).

But his most glorious exploit was yet to come. On October 11, Robertson was aloft again, in a balloon bedecked with the flags of Mexico and France. And he was not alone. A lovely young Mexican señorita was at his side, smiling and casting down flowers and verses, hiding well whatever terror she may have felt. A gasp escaped the crowd as Robertson narrowly maneuvered past a church tower. Then the duo sailed on to a safe landing in a nearby pasture. After all, he had promised the girl's mother that it would be a short ride. So enthusiastic was the throng that they all but tore the balloon apart, while Robertson and his lady fair mounted horses to return in triumph to the city. Thus it was that the honor of being the first Mexican ever to make a trip by air was won by a woman (Reyes de la Maza 1972, 19–23).

THEATER

Most women were satisfied to be entertained by less exhilerating means. Universal in its appeal throughout the country, in cities and rural areas alike, was theater of all varieties—comedy, tragedy, opera, farce, and religious representations. Travelers recorded in generally approving terms the theatrical events they witnessed in small towns and haciendas, which often were performed by itinerant troups.

Basil Hall described one such play, presented on a balmy Sunday evening in Tepic early in the century. The audience sat on benches in the open air; the stage was made of planks with walls of cane and plaster, and the scenes consisted of pieces of cloth pinned together. There was no lighting other than the moon. The play itself, a comedy by Calderón, "caused great mirth" (Hall 1824, 2:195–96). The playwright probably was the Spanish dramatist Pedro Calderón de la Barca rather than the Mexican Fernando Calderón.

Later in the century, Bayard Taylor was traveling in the same vicinity and came upon a reenactment of the Christmas story staged by the villagers of San Lionel. The procession of characters included two harlequin figures who amused the onlookers with their antics. Ingeniously, a cord had been stretched from a platform at one end of the plaza to a hole in the front of the church. On it was suspended a tinsel star that could be moved along by means of a string. It preceded the three kings, leading them to King Herod, the Virgin in the manger, and then away. Afterwards there was a *fandango* with bonfires and rockets, the ringing of bells, "and high mass in the church, with the accompaniment of two guitars" (Taylor [1850] 1949, 266–68).

The theater was without question even more a part of the daily lives of city dwellers, especially in the capital. While the wealthy often rented

Paris fashions in Mexico. From *El Liceo Mexicano* (1844).

boxes for an entire year whether they attended or not, the less affluent
were willing to stand through entire performances, crowded together at
the back of the theater.

To attend the theater after the promenade was not merely an occasional diversion but an accepted routine for many. Waddy Thompson
recalled how he once asked a very accomplished and elegant lady, the
mother of eight or ten children, with an extended family of as many

more: "'Do you go, Madam, to the theater every night?' 'Oh yes, Sir,' she answered, 'How else could I possibly get through the evenings?'" (Thompson 1846, 127). It is not surprising that the Gordoa letters frequently mention the theater, in general if not specific terms: Mariana had gone to the opera, or Mariana did not enjoy the latest comedy—her sisters in Querétaro were always interested in such news.

A succession of theaters in Mexico City rose and declined in popularity as the century progressed. At the time of independence there was only one, the Coliseo Nuevo, also called the Principal. It was followed by the Teatro de Gallos, or Provisional, the Teatro de Nuevo México, and others. In 1844 the enormous and sumptuous Gran Teatro de Santa Anna appeared—a theater with glittering chandeliers and five tiers of boxes, "one of the finest theatres in the world," in the opinion of Bayard Taylor (Taylor [1850] 1949, 300). As historical circumstances dictated, the Santa Anna became in turn the Gran Teatro Nacional, the Santa Anna again, the Teatro Imperial, and in 1901 at the time of its demolition, simply the Nacional.

The opulence of the Santa Anna in its prime contrasted sharply with the conditions that the audiences had been likely to find in earlier theaters. Speaking of the Teatro Principal as it was in 1825, Luis Reyes de la Maza painted this vivid picture in his book on Mexican theater: "Because of the indolence of the managers, it had been neglected for many years and the porters were reluctant even to sweep. From the restrooms emanated such foul odors that the spectators in their boxes and seats were constantly obliged to hold perfumed handkerchieves to their noses; but in contrast, there existed a tiny chapel at the entrance which was always very clean" (Reyes de la Maza 1972, 11–12).

Reyes de la Maza recorded that theatergoers were not as a rule very well mannered. Indeed, sometimes discussions carried on in a box reached such a pitch that the voices of the actors could not be heard and the audience forgot about them and listened instead to the conversation in the box. Stage settings were frayed and costumes for a Greek tragedy were the same as those for a Spanish comedy. Add to those annoyances the unpleasant smell of the oil lamps that lighted the hall and the fact that "those suspended over the spectators constantly dripped their viscous liquid, which spotted the dresses of the señoras (Reyes de la Maza 1972, 11–12). Indeed, the theatergoer had to be a hardy soul.

Little had improved by the time Frances Calderón first went to the theater. She complained about the darkness, the bad odors, the dirtiness, and even more about the smoking: "The whole pit smoked, the galleries smoked, the boxes smoked, the prompter smoked" (Calderón de la Barca [1843] 1931, 67–68). And Bayard Taylor, who felt the performance he saw at the Santa Anna could have withstood even Paris critics, noted that between acts "the gentlemen lit their *puros*, the ladies produced their delicate boxes of cigaritos. . . . By the time the curtain was ready to rise, the air was sensibly obscured, and the chandeliers glimmered through a blue haze" (Taylor [1850] 1949, 301).

The theater was above all a diversion, a distraction, a place to go and be seen, something for Mexicans at ease to do. Without a doubt for some it was the source of genuine cultural enrichment, and perhaps a few took seriously the words written in large letters on the curtain of the Teatro de Nuevo México:

The theater is no vain pastime.
It is a school of virtue and useful example.[3]

[3] "No es el teatro un vano pasatiempo / Escuela es de virtud y útil ejemplo" (García Cubas 1904, 259).

CHAPTER SIX

MEXICANS AT WORK

*The four elements of antiquity, fire, air, earth and
water, conspired against the miner: fire threatened
in explosions; air thinned or mixed with harmful
gases; the earth caved in and water flooded.*
                                    —Octavio Cabrera Ipiña

In the years immediately after the conquest the labor
supply available to the Spaniards seemed inexhaustible. The Indians
numbered in the millions, and their labor constituted wealth under the
encomienda system: Spanish conquistadors were granted the goods and
services of large numbers of Indians, though not the land itself. The
system made possible the first steps in the development of the colonial
economy (Brading 1971, 2).

Indians tilled the soil and worked the mines. They were so grievously
mistreated that the crown saw fit, in the New Laws of 1542, officially to
terminate the *encomienda*. But in effect, the practice lingered on into the
eighteenth century, and by the mid-1500s the native population had
taken a demographic nose dive, caused principally by the diseases imported from Europe. The survivors, now drastically reduced in numbers, were often resettled into small villages, while the Spaniards, always
the city dwellers, founded towns, to which Indians, mestizos, and blacks
also gravitated. Thus much land formerly occupied by Indians was left
vacant and the Spaniards, through grants, purchases, or appropriation,
legal or otherwise, quickly filled the void. The way was open for the
cultivation of wheat and maize and for the raising of livestock on a
grand scale. But always the labor of the Indians, no matter how deci-
mated, was essential.

A draft of labor, called the *repartimiento*, was implemented to supply
laborers for work that was considered necessary for the commonwealth

(Simpson [1941] 1966, 115). Native villages, especially those in the central valleys, were forced to furnish annually a quota of workers for an established number of days. They labored on haciendas, in textile mills and silver mines, in building churches and roads, or digging drainage ditches—most kinds of work seem to have been necessary for the commonwealth—and they were paid small wages in return. Many Indians chose to escape the forced labor and became free servants or artisans in town, independent workers in the northern mines, or resident peons on haciendas, where they were welcome.

The backbone of the economy of New Spain was the export of silver. Silver provided the means to import the fine textiles demanded by the Spaniards, the wine, the paper, and the weapons. Productive mining commenced in the 1550s in Zacatecas, Real del Monte, Guanajuato, Pachuca, and elsewhere, and profoundly affected the local economies. Mines had to be provided with quantities of horses, mules, leather, lumber, charcoal, and food, and nearby haciendas supplied those needs. Mineowners often used their wealth to buy their own haciendas. Thus the mines depended on the haciendas for their necessities, and the haciendas used the mines as the principal consumers of their products. Haciendas also provided the wool for the textile mills that in turn produced the coarse cloth worn by nearly all workers. Thus the different segments of the economy were mutually dependent.

After Mexico achieved independence in 1821, as in the years before, the masses of laborers included agricultural workers, miners, artisans, and textile workers. The agricultural workers were by far the most numerous. Statistics indicate, for example, that in Zacatecas in 1829 the number of agricultural workers exceeded 45,000, or 78 percent of the work force, while the miners and the artisans each numbered approximately 6,000, or only 10 percent each (Cross 1980, 260). But of all the workers, the miners were the elite. They considered themselves something of a class apart and looked in contempt on all other occupations (Sartorius [1858] 1961, 197).

THE MAGNETISM OF MINING

It is true that at one time slaves and the Indians drafted into service provided much of the labor needed in the mines, especially in those close to Mexico City. Subhuman conditions were commonplace, but most miners were free men—Indians, mulattoes, and mestizos—whose skills were in demand and who were actively sought by mineowners (MacLachlan and Rodríguez O. 1980, 174).

Even under the best of circumstances, the miners' lot was not an easy one. Those who labored in the bowels of the earth spent sunless days in immediate danger. Yet, if we are to believe the English authority H. G. Ward, mining exerted a magnetic attraction on many among the laboring classes. "A mine in Bonanza, in whatever part of the country . . . ," he asserted, "is sure of a sufficient supply of workmen, because the system of payment by Partido, (a share in the ore raised) . . . is always preferred to regular wages" (Ward 1828, 2:145). According to Ward, certain groups of Indians regularly traveled from mine to mine seeking out the more productive ones because the work for shares was so profitable (Ward 1828, 2:145).

A gambling spirit most certainly prevailed among the miners. With luck, the poorest muleteer might parlay a modest investment in a mine into a kingly fortune, as indeed happened to a certain man named Zúñiga in the Real de Catorce (Ward 1828, 2:508–9) and to countless other uneducated fortune hunters. Likewise, someone such as our Licenciado Antonio María Gordoa could invest capital that he already possessed in the precarious business of claiming and developing a mine, as he did in Catorce. He struck a bonanza and accumulated wealth enough for generations to come. He might as easily have lost it all.

Gordoa took advantage of the Mexican law of the time to denounce the mine of El Refugio. In doing this, he laid claim to an unworked mine, as anyone was priviliged to do; he registered his claim and, within the time prescribed by law, actively undertook mining operations.

Gordoa's willingness to risk it all did not continue with him into old age. Instead he reached a point where he would spend nothing unless the mine could pay for it (Ward 1828, 2:500). This was not typical: with most miners it was easy come, easy go. Common miners were known to lose 2,000 or 3,000 pesos in a single cockfight (Ward 1828, 2:509).

For the ordinary miner, however, the lure was not so much the prospect of owning a mine as it was of earning more than the average worker did elsewhere. Mineowners had to spend more for labor than for any other single expense, including the indispensable mercury used in the refining process (Cross [1976] 1980, 258). According to one report, when the mines of Catorce were at their peak, many of the miners earned as much as $1,000 a week, but that, of course, was unusual (Sartorius [1858] 1961, 200).

Wages varied, and even the method of payment varied from time to time and from mine to mine. Topside workers and most underground refinery workers were paid straight daily wages that ranged from four to ten reales. A peon might earn four reales, while a *cajonero* who operated a hoist might receive ten reales (Cross [1976] 1980, 264). Compare those wages with the 1½ to two reales paid daily to hacienda peons (Brading 1971, 147).

Sometimes work was done by contract, or a certain price was paid for a certain amount of work. In this way a group of *barreteros*, the pickmen with skills in blasting, could agree to excavate ore by the weight or by the yard at a prearranged price. The hardness of the rock would then determine the actual amount earned; wages could vary 100 percent from one week to the next (Cross 1980, 262).

But the greatest inducement in mining, as indicated by Ward, was the *partido* system whereby the *barreteros* received not only their fixed wages but also a portion of the ore. This could be between one-eighth and one-third of the cut, depending on its grade (Cross 1980, 263). Not surprisingly, the *partido* was avoided if possible by mineowners, who paid dearly if a rich strike was made. It was militantly and successfully defended by the miners.

The administrator of the Gordoa mine El Refugio, Fermín Mata, submitted weekly *memorias,* or reports, in 1835, listing the types and names of the approximately 100 workers employed at that time. They were paid on a very uneven scale. Some were on fixed salaries: the carpenter Ximénes always received his six pesos a week, while the *barreteros* Echevarría, Yañes, Valdés, and Frutos received a peso for each day worked, or five pesos for five days. The night shift earned no more than the day shift. The administrator and perhaps a few other top employees received a percentage of the production as well as a salary of thirty pesos weekly. Meanwhile, interestingly enough, two and sometimes three miners earned much more because they were paid by the yard, according to the amount that they excavated: fifty-six pesos each one week, seventy pesos another week, forty-six another week (Gordoa Family Papers, mining reports, 1835). All possible formulas were used for payments to mine workers.

Mining also presented the irresistible temptation to smuggle pieces of ore, or even pure silver, out of the mine under the noses of the authorities. Sartorius claimed that in many places the miners were required to work naked so that nothing could be concealed, oftentimes to no avail (Sartorius [1858] 1961, 196). The tricks and ruses were infinite. Ore could be crushed into powder, mixed with tallow, and rubbed into the hair, or inserted in hollow handles of tools; or bits could be hidden in body orifices. In one case which Sartorius recounts as true, a dog got into a mine. The foreman objected and the dog's owner, to avoid trouble, killed the animal with his hammer and threw the body aside. Later when the stench became unbearable, the foreman demanded that the man remove the carcass. With apparent reluctance he complied and flung the body onto a refuse heap. Only then was it discovered that it was filled with ore and that the whole incident had been planned (Sartorius [1858] 1961, 196).

And what of the mines themselves, those great caverns in which so many chose to work entombed for so much of their lives?

EL REFUGIO

The Socabón y Mina de Nuestra Señora del Refugio near Catorce well represents the approximately 3,000 mines that existed in the new republic. It was not a major mine such as the famous Valenciana in Guanajuato or the renowned mines of the Real del Monte near Pachuco, but it was no shoestring operation either. Producing silver enough to make its owner, Licenciado Gordoa, "notoriously rich" (Dahlgren 1887, between 102 and 103), it was admired by H. G. Ward during his 1827 visit.

Like most of the mines, El Refugio had perpendicular shafts cut down from the surface to the vein. Although the mine had experienced a bonanza beginning in 1806, the main shaft had reached such a depth by 1815 that it was difficult to extract the ore. Doubtless, it had filled with water as did so many of the mines. But measurements were made, remedies were undertaken, and by 1822, five years after the work had begun, an immense and awesome tunnel, called a *socabón,* had been cut 715 *varas*[1] to the main vein from below (Ward 1828, 2:499). The water easily drained off, and another shaft was sunk, which was 150 *varas* deep when Ward saw it. He explained that "the ore is raised by a malacate (hoist), erected in a large excavation made for the purpose in the side of the socabon" (Ward 1828, 2:499). This *socabón* was so wide and so high—seven *varas* by six *varas* high—that wagons could go in and out with ease (Cabrera Ipiña 1975, 62). The ore was brought out to a receiving room in carts, and a canal ran along one side to carry away the water from the shaft. "The ventilation is excellent," said Ward, "and we were much struck with the order and regularity apparent in every

[1]A *vara* is a unit of length varying from about thirty-two to forty-three inches, or approximately one yard.

part of the establishment, in which from four to six hundred men are employed daily" (Ward 1828, 2:500).

At that particular time the mine was not producing very high-grade ore; in fact, it was operating at a deficit of 3,000 to 4,000 pesos a year. The history of El Refugio alternated between bonanzas and near busts, but it was still in business as late as 1980.

The 1835 inventory of El Refugio reads like a description of a small community, complete with a chapel and houses.[2] The first item mentioned is an image of the patron saint of the mine, Nuestra Señora del Refugio, with curtains—value 35 pesos. One can assume that the saint was placed above the mine entrance or just inside, as small altars were present in all mines. Further down the list were 80,000 pounds of tallow made up into candles, valued at 320 pesos; powder, 174 pesos; and the 366 steps down into the mine, 732 pesos. Listed next were the carpenter shop with all the equipment, then the blacksmith's shop, followed by the granaries and other storerooms.

The chapel was "*bien construida*," with a wooden roof, a fine tower, a main altar, a choir, and the chaplain's room. It was valued at 15,000 pesos. The long lists of furnishings included another image of Nuestra Señora del Refugio, worth 100 pesos. The stable housed twenty-eight horses and five mules—worth another 324 pesos. The final major entry was the administrator's house of six rooms and a patio—valued at 1,600 pesos. The mine equipment and buildings were valued at 24,974 pesos, no insignificant sum.

One wonders how the conditions in this indestructible old mine affected the lives of those who worked in or near it. No one thought to write on the subject, but the correspondence and reports of the administrators yield many clues. Once their fortunes were secure, the mineowners, from Licendiado Gordoa through later generations, chose not to live in the inhospitable climate of Catorce. Bleak and barren and unbearably cold in winter, the mountains seemed determined to break the health of all who dared to stay. The several administrators who assumed responsibility for the mine's operations in the 1830s and 1840s succumbed one by one to ill-defined maladies. Administrator Fermín Mata complained of a "horrible attack" and pain in his heart in 1843 and was dead in 1844. His successor, Ygueravide, had difficulty with

---

[2] The information on the El Refugio inventory and the correspondence and reports of the administrators of the mine are in the Gordoa Family Papers, Latin American Library, Tulane University, New Orleans, Louisiana.

his lungs and, despite time spent away to affect a cure, soon followed Mata. Of those left in charge, head miner Domingo Martínez carried on resolutely and went to the mine daily despite complications resulting from an unspecified accident, while Juan Mata, Fermín's nephew, suffered debilitating rheumatism that prevented him from riding a horse.

Through all the letters that reached Luis Gonzaga Gordoa in Mexico City runs a thread of accusations and recriminations, jealousies, and fears. Left to his own devices for years to run the mine as he pleased, the supposedly loyal Fermín Mata, once he was dead, was found to have misappropriated large sums. His chief accuser was Juan Mata, who in turn was called a gossip. Domingo Martínez, ever complaining, was convinced that all were against him and "for what did he serve anyway?"

However, all of the men wrote with great optimism about the mine's prospects, whether the weekly receipts indicated profits or deficits. Very little was mentioned concerning the ordinary workmen, who at this time, a decade after Ward's visit, were much reduced in number. We can assume that there was no general dissatisfaction, only hints of unrest. Martínez admitted that two miners, one a veteran of eight to ten years of night work and the other of thirty years of day work, protested his proposed change of routine. At one point another miner wrote to Martínez on a fine grade of blue paper calling him a demagogue and accusing him of "killing his sheep," but with what effect we do not know. Miners regularly worked a twelve-hour day, six days a week, with Sundays and certain holy days off. A special celebration in honor of Nuestra Señora de la Ascención was planned in nearby Cedral in August, 1844, with fifteen *corridas* of bulls. Such holiday breaks may have helped reduce tensions and frustrations among workers at all levels.

OF OTHER MINES AND DAILY DRUDGERY

Of the many who followed after Alexander von Humboldt in the early years of the nineteenth century and studied the mines of Mexico, Henry George Ward was doubtless the most notable. But every bit as knowledgeable, if not as popular, was the United State minister Joel Poinsett. He visited one of the greatest and deepest of mines, the Valenciana, and later recorded:

> We were conducted to the first flight of steps; and preceded by four men carrying torches, we descended to the first parallel, and stopped where four galleries branch off.
>
> Our torch bearers were sent off to the extremity of these galleries, that we might form some idea of their extent in a straight line. They are both

extensive and solid; the vaults are of porphyry, and the bottom of gray
slate. . . . These galleries have been blasted out, and must have cost great
labour, for the whole mountain is of porphyry to a great depth. . . .

On our return, we plodded painfully up these stairs, which the *carga-
dores* (porters) ascend with ease, with a load of ten or fifteen arrobas on
their shoulders. They are paid according to the quantity they bring up; and
some of these men will ascend . . . from the perpendicular depth of five
hundred yards, carrying the enormous weight of twenty-four arrobas (six
hundred pounds). (Poinsett 1824, 158–59)

The trip made by Judge Wilson down into another mine was by way
of ladders that extended from floor to floor in half the shaft. The shaft
was divided by a partition that reached from the top to the bottom of
the mine. Through one side all the materials needed were let down and
ore was drawn up in large sacks, each made from the skin of an ox.

Wilson wrote that, when his party had reached the limit of its descent
and they had turned aside into a gallery, they made their way "among
gangs of workmen, silently pursuing their daily labor in galleries and
chambers reeking with moisture, while the water trickles down on every
side on its way to the common receptacle at the bottom" (Wilson 1855,
358–59).

Indeed, water was a constant enemy in most mines. Huge sums were
spent on shafts through which water could be hauled up in leather bags
by a windlass powered by horses or mules; or as we have seen in the
Gordoa mine, in the excavation of long adits, or *socabones*. Even so, at
times miners were obliged to work in cold, numbing water up to their
knees, which was likely to induce rheumatism (Cabrera Ipiña 1975, 44).

Another nineteenth-century visitor, William Parish Robertson, declined to join the miners in their descent "by a difficult spiral stair," but
he remarked that during their entire twelve-hour shift they ate no food
(Robertson 1853, 2:175–76). This seems unlikely. There are other reports of miners drinking water distilled from the rocks and eating
their cold *gordas* (Cabrera Ipiña 1975, 42), which probably were filled
tortillas.

Fanny Calderón, not surprisingly, was eager to investigate the Real
del Monte mine, but was not allowed to do so. Instead she watched the
"men go down with conical caps on their heads, in which is stuck a
lighted tallow candle." And she admired "all the great works which English energy has established here: the various steam engines, the buildings for the separation and washing of the ore" (Calderón de la Barca
[1843] 1931, 172–73). To be sure, the English had invested heavily in

Mexican mines after independence and had introduced many modern techniques and machinery, only to lose it all eventually.

Carl Sartorius witnessed a change of shift at daybreak. When the night workers emerged and handed their tools over to the smiths, the ore was brought up and the paymaster registered the work done. Then the day workers paired off, received their tools, candles, and powder, and the "procession" started. Everyone crossed himself before the patron saint at the entrance and echoed the overseer in singing an Ave María. Sartorius added that there was a landing place in every mine where the workers had built a stone altar which was decorated each morning with fresh flowers and lighted candles (Sartorius [1858] 1961, 197).

Small wonder that miners became hardened and ill-tempered. They spent their lives laboring in the semidarkness where one slip of the foot could send them plummeting into an abyss, or an explosion could fill the air with flying rocks. After a day's work most miners wished for nothing more than home and a hot meal and bed, though on Sundays they were ready for drinks and an exchange of stories at the local bar (Cabrera Ipiña 1975, 45). Small wonder that they were a superstitious lot, fearful of evil spirits who they believed dwelled in the far recesses of the mines, but equally devoted to their patron saints. They were a special breed.

TOPSIDE WORKERS

The mine workers above ground did not share the characteristics of those below. Theirs was the wearisome task of processing the ore that the miners had excavated. Refining took place in *haciendas de beneficio* that might or might not be a part of the mines. Of the two possible methods of refining, smelting was faster but required more elaborate equipment. It was used for high-grade ore. Although it was slower, the patio process of amalgamation was more efficient, and by the turn of the nineteenth century it had predominated in refining all grades of ore (Brading 1971, 140).

While visiting the Valenciana mine, Poinsett described the amalgamation process, for which thirty-five mills were grinding ore at the time. Mules were used to turn grindstones that revolved in circles eleven feet in diameter. Women were employed to separate the ore from the refuse. Working with dispatch, they discarded worthless stones and chipped off small pieces of ore (Poinsett 1824, 164). Forbes also observed how men, women, and children were all engaged in the sorting and breaking of ore ([Forbes] 1851, 98), but it should be mentioned that children never

Refining ore in the hacienda of Salgado. Engraving by Mrs. H. G. Ward in H. G. Ward, *Mexico in 1827* (1828).

worked inside the mines, and rare was the instance of a woman who did so. Indeed, it was considered bad luck if a women so much as entered a mine (Cross 1980, 279–80).

The ore was put into a mill, ground to a powder, perhaps mixed with a little mercury, then taken to an open, paved courtyard. There mercury was added in proportion to the supposed yield of silver, plus murate of soda and iron and copper sulphates, to form an amalgam, which Poinsett noted was "trodden by mules, which are driven round for hours together; or by men, who tread the mass with naked feet" (Poinsett 1824, 165). The amalgam was examined from time to time, and a little of this or that was added every other day or so until the process was judged complete. The resulting mixture was then washed—the refinery had to be located on a river—and the remaining amalgam burned to separate the silver from the mercury (Brading 1971, 138).

Lyon mentioned that old women, called *apuranderas,* would carry off the refuse and wash it again, and they were paid one real the ounce or two dollars a pound for the amalgam they could retrieve (Lyon 1828,

2:286). This whole washing operation was strictly monitored, and workers leaving were carefully examined to make sure none of the precious substance was being spirited away.

A refining mill could be a major enterprise requiring the investment of thousands of pesos and employing hundreds of people, or it could be limited to a very simple operation. Refiners bought at auction the ore from the mines that had no facilities of their own. Such auctions were held on a weekly or semiweekly basis and, according to Forbes, were conducted in a "curious manner," with bidders "going up and each whispering to the auctioneer what he will give for such a heap, and the latter merely calling out the name of the highest bidder and the price" ([Forbes] 1851, 98).

The mountainous terrain and the lack of water at Catorce precluded the establishment of refineries at the mines. Instead, they were set up at lower elevations at Matehuala and Cedral. The Gordoas consequently were obliged to sell at weekly auction the ore extracted from El Refugio. Or at least their employees did so: by the 1830s the Gordoa family had long since left the mining community to become absentee landlords of both their haciendas and their mines.

THE MEXICAN HACIENDA

The Gordoa haciendas of Malpaso and Maguey, near Zacatecas, were *haciendas de ganado* dedicated principally to the raising of livestock. The stock were sheep, as was typical of haciendas in the north, where the land was too poor and too vast for extensive cultivation. In the fertile valley of Mexico, at Puebla, Atlixco, Tlaxcala, and Oaxaca, *haciendas de labor*, or farming estates, produced wheat and maize on a large scale, as well as beans, chilis, and maguey; and at the lower altitudes, at Cuernavaca or Cuautla, haciendas grew sugarcane, rice, cotton, and tobacco.

In general, the size of the hacienda, which could range from a minimum of 2,000 acres to as many as 500,000 (Brading 1978, 21), distinguished it from the small *rancho*. Haciendas were often subdivided into smaller units for administration, or combined with other haciendas to form huge, all-encompassing latifundios. However, the identifying characteristic of the hacienda was its organization. The *hacendado*, or owner, more often than not lived elsewhere—in a nearby town, Mexico City, or even abroad—and left the operation of the hacienda in the hands of the administrator. Under his direction was an administrative staff responsible for different functions, and below them, on the bottom level, was a large assorted company of peons. This sizeable congregation of people lived together in the central *casco,* or compound, of the hacienda, which constituted a small town.

Scholars have long accepted without question the existence in nineteenth-century Mexico of what is known as debt peonage, a system by which peons were bound to the hacienda by continual advances on their wages for food, clothing, or obligations, which they could never pay off. These advances were made primarily through the hacienda store, the *tienda de raya.* Supposedly this system assured a constant supply of cheap labor because workers were not free to move away.

Sartorius gives us a contemporary analysis of the system when he observes that, "should they [the workers] be hindered from working by sickness, or if the master makes special advances for weddings, christenings or burials, they are forced to incur debt, and are naturally obliged to work it off" (Sartorius [1858] 1961, 173). And Charles Harris, writing of conditions at the Sánchez Navarro latifundio in Coahuila in the 1840s, states that "everything the peones received, even down to the meat from an occasional steer slaughtered for them, was entered on their accounts, and it was almost impossible for the peones ever to become free from debt" (Harris 1964, 39). He later describes the severe treatment meted out to one particular shepherd who had fled the hacienda. Not only was he "soundly beaten," but the cost of hiring a guard to bring him back was added to his account (Harris 1964, 42–43). Recent investigations by recognized authorities, however, strongly suggest that debt peonage may not have played such a universally pernicious role in prerevolutionary Mexico as is generally believed. For example, historian Harry Cross, who studied records and accounts of the hacienda of Maguey, is convinced that it did not (Cross 1980, 313). At least, not at Maguey.

HACIENDA DEL SEÑOR SAN JOSÉ DEL MAGUEY

The Gordoa Hacienda del Maguey was typical of many of the Mexican haciendas, much as their mine El Refugio represented other mines. Located approximately fifteen miles west and north of Zacatecas, it covered about 416 square miles of flat valley land. This would seem today to be an enormous estate, but it ranked only seventh or eighth in a state whose largest hacienda extended over 3,000 square miles (Cross 1980, 299). In its inventory for 1835 the total Maguey assets are listed at $411,924.40. That figure included 89,000 sheep, 4,000 horses and mules, 12,000 goats, and 100 cattle (Gordoa Family Papers). The human population at Maguey during the century fluctuated between 500 and 900 people (Cross 1980, 301, 295). The *iguala,* the negotiable levy paid annually to the state, was set at 300 pesos in the 1840s. Compared to other estates, these figures represent the average and are indicative of a full-fledged working hacienda.

To understand the everyday lives of the workers on Maguey, it would be ideal to gather details from a journal or diary written at the time, but no such document has been found. We must glean what we can from extant business correspondence and inventories of Maguey, and from personal inspection. We can also consult the findings of Harry Cross, who had extensive records at his disposal (Cross 1980). Those resources, plus observations of other haciendas left by travelers, will enable us to reconstruct a picture of hacienda daily life.

The *casco* was the center of all activity, a cluster of stone buildings, large and small, pressed together for comfort and protection in defiance of the isolation and danger outside its confines. Unlike its neighbor the hacienda Malpaso, Maguey had no surrounding outer walls. At the first streaks of dawn in the sky the great bell in the chapel at the corner of the plaza would begin to toll, and workers would prepare for the new day. They streamed across the broad, dusty plaza, numbering 200, 300, 400, or more, from their humble dwellings on the outskirts. These so-called *acomodados* lived permanently rent-free on the hacienda. Their day might seem long—from six until six, when the bell sounded again—but with breaks for eating and a siesta, the number of working hours totalled only eight or nine.

Their tasks as gatekeeper, groom, coachman, house servant, or cook would take them at one time or another past the domed chapel with its high bell tower. It was the most imposing building on the hacienda. Perhaps they would stop to chat with the resident priest, or they might enter to pray before the statue of the patron saint, Señor San José, or one of the many other saints who adorned the chapel. When the bell for mass rang out, worshippers would overflow the chapel, but at other times they merely came and went.

The main house, or *casa principal*, faced the plaza adjacent to the chapel. With stone walls two stories high, it had the solid appearance of a fortress, and indeed it may have served as such, since a permanent detachment of guards was employed to protect the hacienda from marauders. Although this was the house where Luis Gonzaga Gordoa and other family members stayed while visiting Maguey, it was never their permanent home. Probably that was just as well. Although it was ample in size, its furnishings were Spartan: two large, old wooden chairs, a table, and a wardrobe were among the few items listed on the 1835 inventory. But one imagines the lively bustle whenever the master was to arrive: the fresh-slaughtered kid roasting on the grill, the bread baking in the oven, and the slap, slap of the tortillas being prepared in the partially covered, arched courtyard at the rear of the house. Activity extended from the near side of the courtyard, where two doors led to convenient inside privies, to the far side where a handsome wrought-iron gate opened to a garden and a well. The house was always scrubbed and spotless in readiness for visitors, but most hacienda hands were ordinarily kept busy elsewhere.

Diagonally across the plaza from the *casa principal* were the ample houses of the administrator and the priest, and along the sides were the lesser houses of the clerk, the *mayordomo*, and the guard. Those dwellings, with the coach house, the stable, the storerooms, and the granaries, completely surrounded the plaza, although an inn was nestled somewhere among the other buildings. The inventory mentions a bed frame and well-worn mattresses and bedclothes. Apparently, accommodations there were no better than those encountered by Captain Lyon at Malpaso when he "procured a room in its very miserable meson" (Lyon 1828, 2:244). Inns brought in a few pesos monthly and provided at least basic shelter to the traveler.

There was also a school at Maguey. Not every hacienda could say as much. In fact, a schoolmaster was a regular member of the Maguey hacienda staff and was well paid at seven to twelve pesos a month. It is likely that, besides teaching the children of the administration, he held general classes for laborers' children as well (Cross 1980, 354–55).

The principal business of the hacienda was the shearing of sheep for wool, the slaughter of sheep and goats for tallow, and the making of soap. Doubtless, those labors were directed from the central plaza. We are informed by Sartorius that the flesh of the slaughtered animals was "stewed down" in a building set apart (Sartorius [1858] 1961, 190) and the tallow was wrapped in sheepskins for sale in packages weighing 220 pounds. The mines of Zacatecas were a ready market for the tallow of Maguey.

Here too in the plaza the peons came each week to receive their wages, which for the least-skilled amounted to four pesos a month. Farther up the scale, a foreman or a mason could expect to earn as much as ten pesos. Wages were paid out in cash and in credit at the *tienda de raya*, which was actually a convenience, as there was no other store in the area. For each worker or staff member there was also a weekly allowance of eighteen liters or more of maize, depending on their rank. The *hacendado* was obliged to provide this regardless of the market price.

Harry Cross has determined that the maize ration supplied 75 percent of the basic energy requirements of an average family at Maguey (Cross 1980, 340). With the purchase of beans and mutton, which were well within the means of the lowliest worker, a minimum diet was complete, although additional food was at hand. Small plots were available to grow more maize, beans, or squash, or to raise pigs or chickens (Cross 1980, 344). And sugar, chilis, cheese, and even chocolate and tobacco, could be obtained at the *tienda de raya*. Prices in the *tienda* of Maguey at no point exceeded those charged in Zacatecas; in fact, they were usually lower. For example, rice, which cost twelve reales at Maguey, cost sixteen in Zacatecas (Cross 1980, 305).

At some distance from the *casco* were two orchards, the Huerta de Picón and the Cieneguilla, which produced pears, apples, quinces, blackberries, peaches, figs, walnuts, cherries, grapes, and plums. As these fruits were not listed in sales, they must have been consumed on the hacienda. And what of the maguey, the namesake of the hacienda? Without a doubt, there was a good supply of pulque made from the fermented juice of this ubiquitous plant. In all it seems that the workers had access to a diet sufficient for their daily needs. Cross asserts that the level of activity on a sheep hacienda was not very vigorous. In fact, except for shearing in March and August and small-scale slaughtering weekly, most of the work consisted of sitting, standing, and even sleeping (Cross 1980, 336).

Not everyone lived in the *casco*. There were numerous houses built on the outer reaches of the hacienda. There were seven for the cowboys and their foreman at the Estancia de Organos, where horses and mules were raised, and several more near the Río Frío and the Peralito, which had been dammed to create reservoirs. *Vaqueros* such as those at Maguey were "the boldest horsemen in existence," declared Sartorius. "They lead a poor life . . . they live in wretched huts, their feet bare. . . . Still they would not change with any other mode of life. Half their time is passed in the saddle, and their delight is to race with the other herdsmen, to cast the lasso, and to mount the untamed horses and mules" (Sartorius [1858] 1961, 187–88).

It is easy to picture the cowboys of Maguey engaged in the rough-and-tumble sport of *colear* the bulls, which Frances Calderón declared the whole republic adored. She explained that "he who is most skillful catches the bull by the tail, passes it under his own right leg, turns it round the high pummel of his saddle, and wheeling his horse round at right angles by a sudden movement, the bull falls on his face." A dangerous pastime! Many accidents occurred, but it was not considered bloody or cruel, and even boys of ten took part (Calderón de la Barca [1843] 1931, 476–77).

Solitary was the life of the shepherd, spent under the sun and the stars and exposed to the dangers of robbers and marauding Indians. A mat and a blanket might be his only shelter, his dogs his only companions. As extra compensation at the time of slaughter, the shepherds in some places were given the heads and intestines for food and gut strings (Sartorius [1858] 1961, 190).

Records show that some of the more enterprising workers at Maguey went into business for themselves, although it was on a small scale to be sure. Taking advantage of short-term loans provided by the hacienda, some families bought quantities of cloth or wool to make into clothes or blankets to sell. More common was the purchase of goats or pigs or extra maize for feeding animals or for planting. Although temporarily in debt, they thus acquired assets over and above their regular wages.

There is no evidence that the credit induced debt peonage, nor any indication that those who lived and worked at Maguey could not have left if they had wished. In fact, some did. But most must have been content with the security of the simple rural life where rent was free, wages assured, and maize provided. The debts incurred were most often those imposed by the church, not the hacienda. Mandatory fees for baptism, burial, and marriage were "especially severe at Maguey" (Cross 1980, 321). It cost the income of five months to marry.

Not everyone who worked at Maguey was a permanent resident. As much as a third of the labor force at any one time worked only periodically. Some were employed as day laborers with pay a bit higher than the *acomodados,* but with no extra benefits. Others were hired from among the approximately 100 renters of Maguey land, who increased their income by working for the hacienda when they were needed (Cross 1980, 351–52). Their position as tenants was not very different from that of the *rancheros* who owned and cultivated the small *ranchos* scattered over the territory of Mexico.

THE RANCHO

The Mexicans who dedicated themselves to agriculture received high praise from Carl Sartorius, who called them the "flower of the Mexican

Rancheros in their finest. Engraving by Carl Nebel, *Voyage pittoresque et archéologique dans la partie la plus intéressante du Mexique* (1836).

population" and their occupation the "noblest" (Sartorius [1858] 1961, 166). *Rancheros* for the most part were part of the broad class of mestizos, who were highly regarded by foreign observers for their independence and their industry. They, not the *hacendados* or the peons, were the true agriculturalists, "the typical Mexicans of the rural districts" (McBride 1923, 84). They might be the owners of quite prosperous irrigated farmlands, or even large stock ranges in the northern states, or just two or three acres on which they eked out a living. They and their families lived on their own land. The title might be obscure, but they planted their own crops and depended on their own efforts to survive.

The origin of many *ranchos* could be traced to land grants made during the early colonial period, and though many holdings had been swallowed up by haciendas, others remained intact or were subdivided. Throughout the nineteenth century the number of *ranchos* steadily increased from less than 7,000 in 1810 (McBride 1923, 89) to 15,000 in 1854 (Brading 1978, 149). A group of *ranchos*, even though somewhat dispersed, formed a *ranchería*.

Perhaps Sartorius would have refused to use the word "industrious" to describe the *rancheros* of the tropical regions, where help from nature seemed to take most of the back-breaking work out of farming. Besides planting his field of maize and his plots of beans, peppers, and tomatoes, the ranchero could raise yams weighing fifty to eighty pounds, sweet potatoes, and manioc with very "little trouble." In fact, said Sartorius, "if he cultivates half an acre of them, [he] thinks he has done much" (Sartorius [1858] 1961, 179). Bananas yielded year-round fruit with a minimum of effort and were a favorite food, raw or cooked, dried, roasted, baked, ripe or green. Even the fibers were useful as fabric, and the leaves for shade.

Sartorius's description of a *rancho* in the tropics tells the daily life of the *ranchero* and his family (Sartorius [1858] 1961, 179). A simple bamboo hut with a roof of palm leaves was set on a low hill somewhat removed from the fields below. Nothing was allowed to grow within twelve feet of the dwelling, as a protection against fire. Chickens roosting on a ladder against a tree and a sow suckling her litter nearby gave evidence of two mainstays of the family diet. Inside the hut the light filtering through the windowless walls revealed a few essential implements grouped around the central fire: the ever-present *metate* for the women's work grinding maize, some earthen pots, cups, plates, and gourds, a few knives, a water jug. On the wall hung a flintlock gun with a jaguar-skin shooting pouch. Dried meat on a rope extended across the room above a basket of fruit and vegetables and a supply of firewood.

The *ranchos* of the central plateau or the highlands were likely to include a more substantial dwelling of stone or adobe, but everywhere the methods of cultivation were most primitive. Plows were homemade, with or without iron parts, and the usual draft animals were oxen, as indeed they were even on the haciendas (McBride 1923, 85). Waddy Thompson wrote: "The plough in universal use is that used two thousand years ago—neither more or less than a wooden wedge, without a particle of iron attached to it. The hoe is a wooden staff, with an iron spike in the end. What is more remarkable, the only animal used in ploughing is the ox; a planter with twenty thousand horses . . . will use his oxen in the plough" (Thompson 1846, 18).

Another common denominator between the hacienda and the *rancho*, and among all *ranchos*, was the presence and use of the wonder plant *Agave americana*, the maguey or century plant. Maguey was cultivated as a domestic plant most extensively on haciendas on the central plateau, but it thrived in poor soil as well as fertile, springing up wild as a weed, and was also grown in little patches (Wilson 1855, 82). The poorest Indian or *ranchero* could benefit from its multiple uses. Planted in a row as a fence, it marked off a man's property. Beaten into a pulp, the thick, oversized leaf became a form of cloth or paper. The fiber of the leaf could be used as thread; woven into cloth, sacking, or rope; or cut as straw for brooms and brushes. Even sandals and hair combs could be made from maguey, and the points of the leaves served as nails or needles (Wilson 1855, 82).

Beyond those attributes, maguey was the source of the intoxicating pulque, which Fanny Calderón called "the most wholesome drink in the world" (Calderón de la Barca [1843] 1931, 94). To make pulque required vigilance on the part of the worker, for at the moment the maguey was about to flower, he or she had to cut out the heart and cover the center with the side leaves. The juice that would have nourished the flower then flowed into the empty basin and could be collected three times daily for several months. This honey water, sweet and scentless, was siphoned off through a long gourd into a bag made from the skin of a hog, which when full, was shaped like the animal. A little old pulque would be added, and within twenty-four hours it would be fermented and ready to drink.

OF *OBRAJES* AND MORE

We have seen the extent to which the Gordoa family interested itself in the business of haciendas and mines. It is entirely possible, although difficult to prove, that the family also had a connection with the textile enterprises that were the most important industry in Mexico aside from mining. We know that quantities of Maguey wool were shipped to Aguascalientes and Querétaro for the manufacture of cloth (Cross 1980, 291–93). We know too that Dolores Rubio, the sister of Mariana Gordoa, lived in Querétaro, where her husband was in charge of a factory or mill. Querétaro and centers such as Puebla and Mexico City had textile mills employing thousands—in fact, as many as 30,000, according to Mason (Mason 1852, 2:215)—and reputedly the largest mill in Mexico was that of a Don Cayetano Rubio in Querétaro (Taylor [1850] 1949, 295). What conditions were like in the Rubio mill or mills we have no way of telling, except to mention that Poinsett in 1824 held the opinion that many of the Indians in the textile factories of Querétaro were still kept in a brutal state of bondage by the manufacturers (Poinsett 1824, 139).

It is not surprising that the textile industry enjoyed the same unsavory reputation regarding labor as did the mines and the haciendas. Indeed, conditions perhaps were worse in the mills. Throughout the colonial period Indians had continued to practice their preconquest skills in weaving, first in cotton and then in wool. The colonists soon entered the textile business too. With only a loom or two they could operate a *trapiche* employing a few workers, or they could expand to a full-scale *obraje* requiring many. The enterprise could contain all the operations required for manufacturing cloth—the carding of wool, the dying, and the weaving—under one roof. *Obrajes* turned out the coarse, common fabrics that were made up into the *mantas* and *rebosos* worn by the great masses of the poor. Humboldt had particularly harsh words for such an operation. He wrote that the traveler was unpleasantly struck by "the unhealthiness of the place and the bad treatment the workers received there. Free men, Indians and people of color, are mingled with convicts who are dispatched to the mills to work every day. All of them are half naked, covered with rags, emaciated and ashen" (Humboldt 1822, 4:10).

Nothing seems to have changed by the time of independence, when the British traveler W. Bullock described the industry in terms similar to those of Poinsett: "The wretched system in which public manufactories are conducted is of itself sufficient to disgust even the most degraded and lowest of human species" (Bullock 1824, 223). He likened the factories to prisons, and indeed some workers were confined there because of crimes, and others because of debts they had pledged to pay off in labor. Such debts seldom were liquidated, because the proprietors would supply the workers with alcohol and tobacco, thus increasing the original debt.

Bullock expected reforms in the future. He said that "this state of things cannot long remain: a liberal Government like the present will surely devise a remedy for so great an evil" (Bullock 1824, 225). And perhaps his optimism was warranted.

Forbes, writing at mid-century, described a cotton factory at Tepic which had been in operation for ten years and which he considered "admirably managed" ([Forbes] 1851, 143). It was an English factory run by Americans with American machinery, and it employed about 200 Mexicans, who worked in two gangs day and night. The whitewashed brick building was situated along a river, which presumably was used for power. The rooms were large, well ventilated, and lighted at night with coconut-oil lamps. Workers were paid every Saturday night, and other aspects of the operation were conducted as regularly as in

England or the United States ([Forbes] 1851, 145). It seems that there was no forced labor here, but we must keep in mind that working conditions in England and the United States in the nineteenth century would be far from acceptable by our standards today.

Nonetheless, a sense of enterprise and modernity was beginning to flourish among Mexicans too. Determined to promote public industry and open a new cotton mill, Don Esteban Antuñano bought the old mill of Santo Domingo in Puebla and set about rebuilding it, making use of a loan from the Banco de Avío, a government assistance bank. He ordered 3,840 spindles from the United States for the sum of $178,000 and subsequently was forced to live most frugally with his "numerous family" (Calderón de la Barca [1843] 1931, 335) while he awaited the machinery, which arrived in August, 1833. Although "ignorant foreign workmen" declared the machinery bad and the cotton worse, production began in 1835 at the mill, which was rechristened Constancia Mexicana (the Mexican Constancy). When more machinery was required, a machinist was sent to New York to obtain it. He embarked on the return trip in February, 1837, but was shipwrecked off Key West. Saving what he could of the machines, he sailed north in the *Argos* only to be shipwrecked again, this time losing all the machinery. New machines had to be made in Philadelphia, and in August he headed south once more in the *Delaware*. Unbelievable as it seems, this ship too was shipwrecked, off Key Alcatraces, and the hapless machinist was lucky to escape with his life. Still the undefeated Antuñano persevered. New machinery was again ordered, and at last, despite even further difficulties, was finally installed.

When Fanny Calderón toured the factory in 1841, she declared it "beautifully situated," with "more the air of a summer palace than of a cotton factory." She applauded its "order" and "airiness" and the "large fountain of the purest water" in the courtyard (Calderón de la Barca [1843] 1931, 336).

Fanny said not a word about the workers or the working conditions at the Constancia Mexicana, but her description conveys so little of the prisonlike atmosphere mentioned by Humboldt that it is evident that times were changing. In truth, Esteban Antuñano was enlightened as well as persistent. He established schools for the workers' children in his factory—he was not the only factory owner to do so—and he, along with the workers, contributed to a medical fund to provide a doctor and an apothecary (Potash 1983, 160). He believed, contrary to existing prejudice, that women could work alongside men in factories. Only 10 percent of the employees in the Constancia, however, were women, whereas in other factories the women outnumbered the men.

In general, the life of the factory worker was easing considerably over what it had been in the oppressive colonial *obrajes*. Yet the twelve-hour shift was typical, and strict discipline was enforced. Conversation and smoking were forbidden. Workers were free, however, after hours and could enjoy the many religious holidays. And if orphans sometimes were apprentices in textile factories, that at least meant that they were exempt from military service (Potash 1983, 160).

The growing number of textile mills seems to have caused the number of artisans in other fields to increase as well. The statistics for Orizaba, where the large factory Cocolapam was built, support that contention. Skilled workers, masons, and carpenters were required during the construction, and when the mill reached full production in 1841, 1,200 workers were employed, each of whom received five pesos a week. The workers on this $6,000 payroll all needed goods and services. Where in 1831 there were only 90 shoemakers, there were 192 in 1839. The number of painters increased from 16 to 18. Bakers increased from 48 to 55, and tailors from 75 to 111. In 1831 there were no soapmakers at all, and no millers, no gunsmiths, no silversmiths, no watchmakers, no singers, and no fireworks makers; but in 1839 millers numbered 15, gunsmiths 6, silversmiths 16, watchmakers 3, singers 6, and fireworks makers 15 (Potash 1983, 155–57). It is obvious that, as soon as they were able, the Mexicans were willing to pay for entertainment and comfort.

Our nineteenth-century observers could not help noticing the labor of some of the less-numerous types of workers and commenting accordingly. We hear of the "much-prized" candies of Puebla and Guadalajara, a specialty of the nuns ([Forbes] 1851, 57); and of the popular soap made in a "thousand fantastic forms"—like fish, birds, beasts, and fruits—that was sent all about the country (Bullock 1824, 108). We learn from the French traveler Orbigny that tailors' workshops were few and that men operated the fashion workshops. Men sewed muslin gowns "nearly in the middle of the street," making ruffles, flowers, bonnets, and linens, while poor young girls on their knees were busy at the long, hard task of grinding chocolate (Orbigny 1836, 428)

Santa Anna himself gave great impetus to the painting business when a decree of his government required that houses in Mexico City be painted or whitewashed every twelve months. Gilliam watched as Mexico City took on a "cheerful" and "gay appearance," and remarked, "I was often astonished at the feats of ability and strength, as also of daring, which the Mexicans had in ascending and descending the high walls of their buildings by the aid of a *petre*, a rope made of the maguey plant" (Gilliam 1847, 91). He looked on as a man painting the walls of a convent ascended a rope hand over hand for fifty feet. When he reached the cornice, a co-worker awaiting him reached down with one hand and, grasping him under the arms, lifted him with ease to the top. Such a feat drew cheers from the onlookers. Sometimes a painter could be seen suspended at the end of a rope in a special basket, lowered over the top of a wall. Gilliam also noted the fatal fall of one unfortunate painter near his lodgings. This was a hazardous occupation (Gilliam 1847, 91).

THE *FERIAS*

No discussion of Mexicans at work would be complete without mention of the annual trade fairs attended by multitudes, such as the famous fair at Jalapa or the one held in Saltillo every September and October. By far the most important was the *feria* of San Juan de los Lagos in the state of Jalisco.

The Mexican writer Manuel Payno, in his novel *Los bandidos de Río Frío,* described perfectly the ambience of the fair at San Juan de los Lagos. For eleven months of the year San Juan was nothing but a sad and dusty provincial town. But come December, its inhabitants would put forth new paint and make repairs, and the community would expand suddenly into the surrounding hills with all kinds of hastily assembled structures. These would include a cockpit, a theater, a stage for puppets, cafés, and inns where none existed before, including the flimsiest and most comical hotels. The latter consisted of long, covered galleries that were divided into rooms by curtains of such loose weave as to make peepholes unnecessary. The wind and rain played havoc with the dividers, but fortunately the lighting was very dim. If they required privacy, the occupants had to hang up their own ponchos. For four pesos a night, or three if renting for the season, the guest had a small wooden bed, two chairs, a candle holder, and a chamber pot (Payno [1889–91] 1964, 561–62). Thus these temporary hotel keepers did a good business. Their accommodations were for those not rich enough to stay in a regular building or lucky enough to have arrived with their own facilities, as many did in the caravans of wagons from Chihuahua or Texas.

However obscure the origins of the fair in San Juan, its fame had spread throughout the republic and to Europe as well. Merchants sailed from France with fine silks and jewelry, and from England and Germany with crystal and china. Of course, Mexican goods, such as clay dolls from Colima and crockery from Guadalajara, were also for sale. Wagons, carts, horses, and mules from all parts of Mexico converged on San Juan with their loads of fabrics, leather, hardware, precious metals, and everything else imaginable. Animals brought along for sale—and there were many—were placed in special corrals.

The action would begin about eight in the morning. Travelers who had arrived dusty and dirty put on their finest outfits and began to circulate along the improvised streets and plazas. Vendors of all sorts of breads, biscuits, and hot drinks provided breakfast. In their shops, merchants displayed little flags telling their names, the articles for sale, and appropriate slogans, such as "very cheap" ([Forbes] 1851, 110). Muleteers who had deposited their cargo looked around for other goods to haul back.

At this fair, which was above all an occasion for business, quantities of merchandise exchanged hands to be distributed around the country. Forbes reported that as much as $300,000 worth had been sent to San Juan by a single merchant ([Forbes] 1851, 110). The San Juan fair was also a great socializing event. People from as far away as Oaxaca became acquainted with residents of New Mexico or Veracruz. They found plenty to entertain them, including the inevitable *monte* tables. The fair also became one long religious celebration, since December included the special days of Guadalupe, Noche Buena, Christmas, and New Year's Eve. The priest "blessed the thousands of people who gathered in San Juan at that time of year" (Payno [1889–91] 1964, 563).

CHAPTER SEVEN

MEXICANS AT WAR

Peace! Peace, Eternal peace among Mexicans! War, war, eternal war against Texans and the barbarous Comanches!—Mariano Arista, General en Jefe del Cuerpo del Ejército del Norte, January 3, 1841, to the inhabitants of the departments of Tamaulipas, Coahuila, and Nuevo León.

On reading such a proclamation, one might think that the Mexicans in general, and General Arista in particular, were excitable, hotheaded, and sanguinary. Excitable and hotheaded they may have been, but sanguinary they were not. Their belligerence sprang from their weakness. A feeling of insecurity led Mexicans to declare war against an enemy even when they did not have sufficient strength to resist an attack. As they were neither well disciplined nor well organized, the results were in most cases disastrous. Bravery made up for their anarchic inclinations, because generally they fought with gallantry, but their military science would have horrified Karl von Clausewitz, the Prussian military philosopher.

American minister Waddy Thompson looked upon the Mexican army with a critical eye. According to him, Mexican troops never attempted a tactical evolution in the face of an enemy, satisfying themselves with "mere melées" that they terminated with a charge of the cavalry—"which is, therefore, the favorite corps with all Mexican officers." Because of the small size of the Mexican horses and the "equally diminutive stature and feebleness of their riders," Thompson regarded the cavalry corps as "utterly inefficient against any common infantry" (Thompson 1846, 170).

The American expressed that opinion one day in a conversation with a reputable Mexican colonel. To his amusement, the colonel replied that there were no impregnable squares of infantry for the Mexican cavalry because of the lasso—"the cavalry *armed* with lassos rode up and threw them over the men forming the squares, and pulled them out, and thus made the breach." Waddy Thompson was not convinced: "The Mexican army, and more particularly their cavalry, may do very well to fight each other, but in any conflict with our own or European troops, it would not be a battle but a massacre" (Thompson 1846, 170–71).

The lasso perhaps was used more effectively to "recruit" soldiers. Impressment of soldiers and seamen was not unusual in the nineteenth century, but in Mexico the recruiting detachments were not satisfied with the criminals collected in jails or the drunkards rounded up in the streets; they also went into the mountains to hunt Indians in their fields and villages, and they did not hesitate to use lassos to catch the fleeing peasants and force them to "volunteer" in the Mexican army. Indians, in fact, formed the bulk of the Mexican army, and there was scarcely a day, noted Waddy Thompson, that droves of the poor wretches, chained together, were not seen marching through city streets to the barracks (Thompson 1846, 172–73).

In 1853, Santa Anna issued a law on conscription that substituted a system of drawing lots for the cruel practice of impressment. But on the first day of drawing lots for service in Guanajuato, Mathieu de Fossey witnessed a compulsory levy in the nearby village of Mellado in which "a score of miners were thus dragged from their families in defiance to all humanitarian law" (Fossey 1857, 495, n. 19). And Ernest Vigneaux, a French adventurer in the Raousset-Boulbon filibustering expedition in Sonora in 1854, noted that in spite of a law that exempted from military service Indians who paid a poll tax, all the soldiers he met were Indians (Vigneaux 1863, 353).

Once rounded up in barracks, recruits were dressed in a uniform made of "linen cloth or of serge" and were "occasionally drilled—which drilling consists mainly in teaching them to march in column through the streets" (Thompson 1846, 173). The military bands, according to Thompson, were good, but the soldiers never managed to march "with that jaunty, erect and graceful air which is so beautiful in well-drilled troops." Only one soldier out of ten had ever seen a gun, and probably only one out of a hundred had ever fired one before being dragged to the barracks. Their arms were "generally worthless English muskets" that had been thrown aside, "purchased for almost nothing," and sold to the Mexican government (Thompson 1846, 173). The powder was just as bad. During the Pastry War, the powder used by the gunners of the fortress of San Juan de Ulúa was of such poor quality that the biggest cannonballs scarcely reached the French ships; they usually fell halfway to their targets.

Seaward defences were utterly inadequate. At the time of the 1835–36 Texas war, José Valadés wrote: "[The] harbors, with the exception of Veracruz, were without artillery. Although Tampico had various cannons, they were useless for lack of ammunition; only San Blas and Acapulco retained something of their colonial past as fortified ports. Mazatlán was defended by two antiquated cannons. . . . Veracruz itself, with San Juan de Ulúa, looked indeed like a fortress, but could hardly resist an assault, as some of its cannons were useless" (Valadés 1979, [1936] 148).

Soldiers were not regularly issued rations; they were paid every day and were their own commissaries. But lack of money was chronic in the Mexican army: "they are well satisfied," said Waddy Thompson, "if they receive enough of their pay to procure their scanty rations, which was very rarely the case" (Thompson 1846, 169). Men often fought on empty stomachs.

Ernest Vigneaux, captured soon after he set foot in Mexico, left very interesting comments on the Mexican army. At Guaymas, for example, the soldiers, "all Indians," were scantily dressed in white cotton coats and trousers, and wore sandals. Vigneaux was surprised to discover that there was no furniture of any kind in the barracks—no beds, no cots, no tables; a big nail in the wall was used to hang the pouch. The soldiers slept on the floor, "wrapped in their *fresadas* [blankets]" (Vigneaux 1863, 156–57). Vigneaux pitied the poor recruits. Soldiers, he wrote, continually received rebukes and blows, while scanty food and forced marches wore them out, and many died along the road (Vigneaux, 1863, 353).

Discipline was poor; desertion, commonplace. A report from Matamoros dated January 2, 1837, said that the soldiers there, not having been paid for two months, were "stating they would not march for Texas until their arrears were paid up, and measures taken to have a regular commissariat behind the army, after having marched" (quoted in Nance 1963, 32). In a letter of December 12, 1836, from San Luis Potosí, Francisco Ignacio Gordoa had made some telling statements: "Bravo passed through here as general in chief of a new army against the Texans, much better than the one Santa Anna had, that is, more men, better equipped and provisioned, with a convoy of the best artillery. If this expedition fails as the last did, we can forget about Texas, not for lack of justice, but of strength, as it won't be possible at least for some years to raise another army its equal" (Gordoa Family Papers).

How right he was.

ON THE WAR PATH

The misery of the Indians increased in time of war because their men were used as cannon fodder. The plight of the foot soldiers did not trouble the officers. They rode ahead mounted on beautiful horses, dressed in gaudy uniforms, while the troops walked behind, sometimes half naked and half starved, followed by their women. Nothing matched the ordeal of the long treks northward, whether to crush the Texas rebellion in 1836 or to meet the invading forces of General Zachary Taylor in 1847. On both occasions Santa Anna set forth in the dead of winter.

Without money or provisions, and with only meager armaments, Santa Anna left Mexico City with 3,000 men in September, 1846. By the beginning of October he had reached San Luis Potosí, where he immediately set about creating an army. The 4,000 survivors of General Pedro de Ampudias's Army of the North, who had capitulated at Monterrey, were ordered to join him. This was an absurd move, since they arrived totally exhausted. Vito Alessio Robles wrote: "Thus was created an army of 7000 men. . . . Ammunition was lacking; arms were badly maintained; pieces of artillery dismantled, and there were no funds or credit to pay for the rations of the troops. In the midst of a thousand hardships and difficulties, and with incredible speed, Santa Anna increased his strength to twenty thousand men. All the recruits were superficially drilled in San Luis Potosí, but had no target practice because of the lack of ammunition" (Alessio Robles 1934, 209).

General José Vicente Miñón, with a vanguard, started from San Luis Potosí on January 27, 1847, and on February 2, Santa Anna followed with the bulk of the army: "Twelve thousand infantrymen, four thousand dragoons and sixteen pieces of artillery were to cover the 450 kilometers of desolate and inclement steppeland that stretches between San Luis Potosí and Saltillo" (Alessio Robles 1934, 210).

A detachment of American prisoners, who had been captured near La Encarnación, met Santa Anna's army on the road. Their attention was attracted by the *generalísimo*, "seated in a chariot of war drawn by eight mules and surrounded by his staff elegantly and gorgeously equipped." He was followed by a number of women and a train of pack mules, among which five were said to be carrying his fighting cocks (Rives 1913, 2:339).

Soldier in dress uniform. Engraving by Claudio Linati, *Costumes civils, militaires el réligieux du Mexique; dessinés d'apres nature* (c. 1829)

The Mexican army suffered from the unusually harsh weather. They had to endure in turn torrential rains and heavy snow, entirely without shelter, since no tents were provided. Food was scarce and water bad. Many died on the road from cold; and hunger, exhaustion, and disease also took their toll. Others deserted. The last stage of the long trek was through an uninhabited and waterless region, and the army marched well into the night.

Santa Anna expected to find the American troops at the hacienda of Aguanueva, south of Saltillo, but General Taylor had retreated a few miles north to La Angostura, near the hacienda of Buena Vista, which was in a narrow pass through a range of mountains between the valley of Saltillo and that of La Encantada. Without even giving his troops time to get a drink of water, Santa Anna ordered them to continue their advance on the double.

On February 22 the well-fed and rested American troops moved into position. Santa Anna had sent Taylor a note, telling him to surrender because he was surrounded by a force of 20,000 men. Taylor declined, and the battle began. The Mexicans outnumbered the Americans, but the Americans had better guns. Cannonades did little damage to either party. When night came, the combat ceased and both armies bivouacked in their respective positions without fires, although a fierce, cold wind blew all night. Reinforcements were sent to the Mexicans, and at dawn on the following morning the battle resumed.

At a distance, the Mexican troops presented a brilliant appearance with the glitter of arms and the flutter of pennants as the cavalry came into view. When the American artillery opened fire, the Mexicans wavered but did not break ranks. Combat was fierce, casualties were heavy on both sides, and the North Americans were unable to check the Mexican cavalry. In the afternoon the American artillery concentrated their fire on the soldiers marching down the plateau, throwing the ranks into disorder. At three o'clock, Santa Anna ordered forward his reserves.

In the steppeland, General Julián Juvera drew his troops into battle array. They formed a long line of 3,000 prancing horses and impetuous dragoons. The spectacle was impressive. The erect shafts of the lances stood out against the sky, banners floated in the wind, and the steel of armor and saber glittered in the sun (Alessio Robles 1934, 221). They galloped to the hacienda of Buena Vista. With their trumpets sounding, the cavalry charged, and the notes rang through the invaders' position like a knell.

Men and beasts fell, but the proud Mexican cavalry moved on. They fought savagely with sabers and lances. Under the ardor of the assault the North American infantry and artillery reeled back behind the walls of the hacienda of Buena Vista. And from that good defensive position they battered the Mexicans. Juvera was compelled to retreat, but the Indian recruits at La Angostura bravely attacked the American lines. The infantry regiments of Illinois and Kentucky were destroyed immediately, and American cannons were silenced by the thrusts of bayonets. The air rang with cries of joy, while in the pass of La Angostura military bands jubilantly announced the Mexican victory.

But, though the American forces had suffered heavy losses, a Mexican victory it was not. Supported by the regiments of Mississippi and Indiana, the North American artillery pounded the Mexicans, who fell back from the position that they had so painfully won. In the failing light and the darkness, the Americans launched attack after attack on the Mexican forces, who held their ground. From the fiery Creole officers down to the poor Indian recruits, they fought magnificently. Santa Anna constantly exposed himself to danger, mounting a new horse when one was killed beneath him. The Mexicans fought to the limit of their strength; they fought until they dropped from hunger and thirst and fatigue. Then, during the night, Santa Anna gathered his army and retired to the hacienda of Aguanueva. The Americans did not follow. Taylor, whose troops were exhausted, waited for a new attack on the morning of February 24. It never came.

The knell had tolled for many. Dead upon the battlefield lay 591 Mexicans; 1,048 were wounded, and 1,894 were missing (Alessio Robles 1934, 225–26). Santa Anna departed in his carriage, proclaiming victory, and leaving his army shuffling along the road to San Luis Potosí. Cold, hunger, dysentery, and desertion played havoc with the soldiers: 3,000 died or disappeared on the way back to the Potosina capital.

During the battles for Mexico City, Mexican troops again fought like devils, and "for the first time," said Henry Bamford Parkes, "the Mexican army consisted no longer of Indian conscripts but of creole and mestizo volunteers who were prepared to die in defence of their capital city." As for Santa Anna, he recklessly exposed himself in the forefront of every battle (Parkes [1938] 1950, 219).

Santa Anna would surely have agreed with that assessment. He described the action after the defeat of General Gabriel Valencia by Winfield Scott as follows: "My seasoned troops moved quickly to check with heroic efforts Scott's triumphal march to the capital. Fighting still while in retreat, I arrived at heavily fortified Churubusco, where I confronted Scott's troops. The firing continued from nine in the morning until five in the afternoon. Leaving the strength of the enemy somewhat reduced, I fell back to the plaza for the night. The battle of Churubusco was a glorious one for the Mexicans" (Crawford 1967, 100).

However, writer Guillermo Prieto, who took part in the battles for

Mexico City, had faint praise for either Valencia or Santa Anna. He retained horribly painful memories of their rage and envy and personal passions and the ruin that they caused (Prieto 1906, 2:222). Later he went on to say that Santa Anna "wasted his efforts, he fearlessly defied danger, and though one could not call him a traitor he could not without injustice be considered a good general, or Statesman, or a person equal to the situation" (Prieto 1906, 2:237).

Indeed, mistakes and jealousies, plus the lack of discipline and of tactical sense, caused the Mexicans to lose control of the action. The gallant boys from the Military College at Chapultepec, the "Niños Héroes," fought to the death but did not save the day.

Summing up the results of the campaign in the Valley of Mexico, General Scott declared that his force had beaten

> the whole Mexican army of (at the beginning) thirty-odd thousand men—posted, always, in chosen positions, behind entrenchments, or more formidable defences of nature and art; killed or wounded, of that number, more than 7,000 officers and men; taken 3,730 prisoners, one-seventh officers, including 13 generals, of whom 3 had been presidents of this republic; captured more than 20 colors and standards, 75 pieces of ordnance, besides 57 wall-pieces, 20,000 small arms, and immense quantity of shots, shells, powder, etc. (General Scott's report quoted in Rives 1913, 2:564–65)

Whenever a Mexican region or town was threatened by invaders, inhabitants voluntarily joined the army or formed a batallion to harass the enemy. Thus the guerrilla force was formed by citizens of Saltillo and its vicinity in 1846 (Alessio Robles 1934, 207). Yet one is surprised by the general apathy of the Mexican population when battles were fought far from their homes. National sentiment was by no means widespread. Mexicans seldom felt concerned about the woes of their country unless their own state was faced with a war or blockade.

A most curious incident occurred during the long conflict between Mexico and Texas when on October 23, 1840, the inhabitants of Saltillo were invited to attend a battle that was to be fought on the Mesa del Ojo de Agua, between Landín and Buena Vista. It was not to be a mock battle, but a true military engagement that men, women, and children could attend without danger. Groups of officials indicated seats for the guests on the site of the battle, booths were set up, and vendors plied their trade in fruit and refreshments (Alessio Robles 1934, 231–32).

In the conflict over Texas many citizens made voluntary monetary contributions. For example, the *Diario Oficial* of Mexico City on September 3, 1836, printed long lists of those who gave amounts from one to fifty pesos. Often, however, the only contributions of the more affluent were forced loans. On the hacienda of Malpaso, near Zacatecas, the Gordoa family paid a substantial forced loan of 1,500 pesos in 1833, and another of 250 pesos in 1835 (Gordoa Family Papers, Records for 1833 and 1835). The *Diario Oficial* on July 21, 1836, printed long lists of such loans, in four categories ranging from 100 to 1,000 pesos.

Some even managed to profit by war. The Sánchez Navarros speculated in beans, and negotiated to supply the Mexican army with flour and horses. Then, when the invaders occupied the state, the *hacendados* assumed a neutral attitude. Practical considerations so outweighed patriotism that they procured supplies for the American forces. "Largely as a result of this *rapprochement*," said Charles H. Harris, "the Sánchez Navarros' property suffered comparatively little damage." It was, nevertheless, on one of the haciendas of their latifundio that the battle of Buena Vista was fought, and the buildings were seriously damaged (Harris 1964, 12–15).

GAMES OF CHESS

Contrary to the rule elsewhere, Mexican revolutions were seldom sanguinary. Contemporary observers even had the feeling that Mexicans fired upon each other from safe distances in order to avoid casualties.

When the Americans entered Mexico City, snipers fired on the victorious troops. General William Worth said that it was no time for "halfway-measures," and the Americans retaliated with heavy battering guns, "together with musketry" (Worth's report quoted in Rives 1913, 2:562). "Our people in a single day," said one American staff officer, "killed more Mexicans in the streets than fell during an entire three weeks of one of their domestic wars" (quoted in Rives 1913, 2:563). Another one wrote that "this matter of being killed was not . . . what they had been accustomed to" (quoted in Rives 1913, 2:563).

Commenting on the revolution of July, 1840, in the capital, Mathieu de Fossey wrote: "Mexicans dare not launch a bayonet assault on a fortified position, however weak it is; the smallest parapet looks to them like an impregnable bastion. Thirteen days passed in futile gunfiring against the Palace walls, and in purposeless and therefore ineffectual discharges of musketry. Among the few soldiers who were killed, more died by accident than by exposing themselves to danger" (Fossey 1857, 170).

General Winfield Scott entering the Plaza Mayor of Mexico City. Engraving by Carl Nebel, *Voyage pittoresque et archéologique dans la partie la plus intéressante du Mexique* (1836).

Fossey added in a note: "How could we, in Europe, conceive that two enemy forces remain for weeks and months within earshot, without taking the necessary measures to gain the victory? . . . How could we imagine that there are officers so naïve as to say after several days of heavy cannonades, 'Thank God, we haven't lost a man yet!' " (Fossey 1857, 517).

Americans made similar statements. Judge Robert A. Wilson, with his usual dry humor, said that during the siege of Acapulco, where the *guerrilleros* of liberal General Juan Alvarez had retreated in 1854, "the besiegers dare not risk an assault, and they had not sufficient material for conducting a regular siege." The result was that, "for some weeks, the opposing forces remained looking at each other, while almost the only blood spilled was by the clouds of musquitoes that hovered over the camp of the grand army, and by the swarms of fleas that infested the castle" (Wilson 1855, 137). And Brantz Mayer noted that during the revolution of 1841, "the work of slaughter went on; but the chief injury was inflicted on harmless non-combatants, who happened at times to pass exposed places, or to cross streets which were raked by artillery" (Mayer 1844, 81).

Little wonder that a relative of Mariana Gordoa, writing from San Luis Potosí on September 14, 1841, mentioned that the Gordoas had forsaken Mexico City for the less-comfortable but safer suburb of Tacubaya. There had just been a *pronunciamiento* in her city too, but not a shot had been fired.

Frances Calderón was in Mexico City when the rebellion of 1841 broke out. She compared it to "a game of chess, in which kings, castles, knights, and bishops, are making different moves, while the pawns are looking on or taking no part whatsoever" (Calderón de la Barca [1843] 1931, 412). The year before she had witnessed the revolution that broke out on July 15 when Gómez Farías and the banished General José Urrea pronounced for federalism. As soon as the firing began, people started running home and the Indians trotted back to their villages. The bell tolled. All the streets near the Plaza Mayor were planted with cannons. Many people stood on their balconies, looking toward the Palacio Nacional, and the *azoteas,* which were out of the line of fire were crowded with men. Woe to the passerby, the curious, the unwary! Several people, women included, who had imprudently stepped out on their balconies, were shot; many others were killed or wounded in the streets. "Both parties seem to be *fighting the city* instead of each other," wrote Frances Calderón, "and this manner of firing from behind parapets, and from the tops of houses and steeples, is decidedly safer for the soldiers than for the inhabitants" (Calderón de la Barca [1843] 1931, 231).

There was soon a scarcity of food in the center of the city, since the Indians did not bring their provisions to market. The cannons roared, and it was rumored that a party of armed *léperos* would assault the upper-class population to loot and kill. A temporary cease-fire allowed the Indians to bring fruit and vegetables from the country; they set up a market in front of the church of San Fernando. Innumerable carriages, overpacked and full of wealthy families hurrying to the country, passed along the streets while the poor made their way on foot—all taking advantage of the cease-fire.

Firing was then resumed, but it was inconclusive. Proclamations and bulletins were issued. On July 22 the archbishop invited the leaders of the *pronunciamiento* to a conference in his palace. Frances Calderón de la Barca was astonished by the calm of the population: "In what other

city in the world would they not have taken part with one or other
side? . . . Groups of people collect on the streets or stand talking before
their doors, and speculate upon probabilities, but await the decision of
their military chiefs, as if it were a judgment from heaven" (Calderón de
la Barca [1843] 1931, 246).

On the night of July 26 the articles of capitulation were signed by
both parties. On the morning of the twenty-eighth a Te Deum was sung
in the cathedral, and each party issued bulletins of victory (Calderón de
la Barca [1843] 1931, 249).

It was against the rule for winners to take advantage of the situation
to pay off old scores. The unlucky adversaries generally were pardoned.
Any punitive action harsher than exile for the leaders would have
brought about retaliation, and they were quite aware that the winner
might be the loser another day.

There is no better example of the peculiar Mexican war code than the
convention passed between the federalists and the centralists to put an
end to the civil war that had been waged in the northern states in 1840.
Joseph Milton Nance recorded, "By the terms of the Convention, the
lives, liberty, and property of all who surrendered were guaranteed; prisoners taken by both sides were to be liberated immediately; and all
officers and soldiers who formerly belonged to the regular army of Mexico were to be permitted to reenter the regular service at their former
rank, or, if they preferred, to receive their discharges" (Nance 1963,
370–71).

The centralists, moreover, agreed to honor the debt contracted by the
Provisional Government of the Republic of the Río Grande to buy military supplies, even though the vendors who had provided the rebels
with arms were often Texans or Americans. The Texans who had fought
with the federalists were to be permitted to return unmolested to their
country, and the few Europeans among the rebels were authorized to
remain in Mexico, should they wish it (Nance 1963, 371–72). Colonel
Antonio Canales, who had been one of the most persistent leaders of
federalism in northern Mexico, joined the centralist forces as a major-
general (Nance 1963, 378).

There were no hard feelings either among the population. The news
of the armistice reached Mier on November 7. On November 8, Canales
reported to Mariano Arista that, when he entered the town at night, "the
rejoicing was of such a general nature that it seems that we should never
have been divided" (Nance 1963, 372–73).

CRUELTY AND COMPASSION

Wars and revolutions were by no means simple displays of chivalry, however. At times carnage and acts of cruelty were committed. Although Waddy Thompson writes that Santa Anna, "in the various civil wars in which he has borne a conspicuous part," not only spared the lives and property of his vanquished enemies but also, if they were banished, saw that "ample provision was made for them" (Thompson 1846, 75), we have evidence of his merciless brutality on some occasions. The massacres of the garrisons of the Alamo and Goliad, in Texas; the plundering of Zacatecas in 1835; the burning of hostile towns during the war against Juan Alvarez in 1854—all cast dark shadows on the life of the Mexican dictator.

The relentless feud between Mexico and Texas also led the Mexicans to take ruthless measures against the inhabitants of their turbulent former province. Texas was admittedly a thorn in the flesh of the Mexican leaders. Hostile parties of Texans constantly ranged across the Río Grande. Gangs of dangerous Texas cattle thieves were among the banditti that roamed the northern states. And some Texas ventures, such as the Santa Fe raid in the summer of 1842 and the plunder of the Mexican town of Mier on Christmas night of the same year, were definitely warlike acts.

During their long march south the Santa Fe prisoners certainly were treated cruelly, at least in the territory of New Mexico: those unable to keep up with the column were shot and their bodies abandoned by the roadside. Yet we must remember that forced marches were imposed upon the Indian recruits as well; that most European governments, confronted with such acts of outright belligerency, would have ordered them to be shot right away; and that once they had passed El Paso, the prisoners were fairly treated. Indeed, the prisoners, 116 men, were forced to work in the streets of Tacubaya for several months, but, said Waddy Thompson, "all the work they did would have been done by two Irishmen in a week" (Thompson 1846, 93). The officers enjoyed many privileges, and the population at large showed kindness and compassion to the prisoners, visiting them, bringing them food and clothing, interceding for them. Frances Calderón went to visit the prisoners who were lodged in the convent of Santiago, about two miles from the center of Mexico City. She found the "common men" occupying the courtyard, and the officers in the large hall of the convent. "In the Mexicans generally," she wrote, "there seems very little if any vindictive feeling against them; on the contrary, a good deal of interest in their favour, mingled with some curiosity to see them" (Calderón de la Barca [1843] 1931, 520).

Santa Anna pardoned them all, and they were released on June 16, 1842. Typical of Mexican character is the ceremony that took place that day on the parade ground near the capital. Waddy Thompson was there:

> Santa Anna reviewed on that occasion a body of more than ten thousand troops, and there were not less than thirty or forty thousand other persons assembled in the field. When the order for their liberation was given, it was received with acclamation and shouts by the Mexican troops. . . . instead of jeers and insults every Mexican had a word of kindness for them, running up to them and shaking hands, and exclaiming "amigo, amigo," "my friend, my friend!" . . . Let it be remembered that these men had invaded their country, and that they had been sedulously taught to regard them as their born enemies. (Thompson 1846, 92–93)

The Mier expedition was an act of downright piracy, and the Mexican government showed its outrage by ordering the prisoners to be executed, though they had the written assurance of the Mexican general who captured them that they would be treated "with the consideration which is in accordance with the magnanimous Mexican nation" (Rives 1913, 1:491).

The unofficial intervention of Waddy Thompson probably saved the lives of most of the prisoners. After he interceded for them, a new order was sent from Mexico to kill every tenth man selected by lot. The circumstances attending the execution are shocking. From the Santiago prison, a group of survivors wrote the foreign ministers in Mexico to complain about the unfair treatment: "The victims . . . were to be determined by drawing beans from a covered mug a white bean signified exemption from execution a black bean death." After the execution of the unlucky prisoners, the others were told that "no further atonement by blood would be required"; nevertheless, Captain Ewen Cameron, a British subject, was executed also (U.S. Legation in Mexico Papers, Texas prisoners to foreign ministers in Mexico of Great Britain, the United States, France, and Germany, 27 April 1843).

Among the Mier prisoners was a boy of fifteen, John Hill, who was not confined as closely as the others because of his youth. He went to see Waddy Thompson, who suggested that he appeal directly to the president for his release. John Hill did so, and Santa Anna not only released him but adopted him. He paid for his education and "cared for him as for a son." Eventually young Hill obtained the liberation of his father and brother, who were prisoners as well (Thompson 1846, 76–77).

With the French filibusters of the Raousset-Boulbon expedition, Santa Anna likewise showed himself magnanimous. Although the French did no less than try to incite the population against the Mexican government, he commuted the death sentence of the "foreign battalion who had rebelled at Guaymas into ten years' internment in a presidio." Raousset-Boulbon was shot, but fortunately for the officers, Ernest Vigneaux and his friend Guilhot, General José María Yañez, *comandante general de Sonora*, delayed the order on the grounds that he had first to prove the identity of the two men before shooting them. Meanwhile, a French diplomat managed to obtain a pardon for them from Santa Anna (Vigneaux 1863, 287–88).

The Frenchmen were treated indulgently. To avoid the hardship of the long march to Guadalajara, Vigneaux was allowed to rent a horse, and the Mexican officers requisitioned horses for the unfit prisoners (Vigneaux 1863, 279). When they reached Tequila, a town famous for its pulque, the Mexican soldiers were confined to barracks at seven o'clock for fear they would get drunk, while the prisoners were set free for the night (Vigneaux 1863, 338). In Guadalajara they were visited "several times a day" by members of the clergy who distributed cigarettes, sugar, exhortations, and cheap pious pictures. "We were treated as spoiled children," wrote Vigneaux (Vigneaux 1863, 358).

In times of war and revolution the Mexicans indeed showed themselves at their best and at their worst.

INDIAN REVOLTS

Indians did not make war according to the rules. They fought to the finish, killed, raped, kidnapped, and burned. The two antithetic societies, the white and the red, came into open warfare during the second federal republic, and against the hostile Indians the Mexicans fought with the cruelty and determination displayed by their ancestors when they conquered Mexico. Tolerance had no place in a war of races.

Independence, as we have seen, brought with it disunity, civil war, and anarchy. During the years of chaotic warfare against Spain, Indians had been enlisted in the cause of rebellion; they were given arms, learned something of the military arts, and heard about social justice, freedom, and better days to come. Since the proclamation of independence, they had seen the Creoles break their revolutionary promises and slide comfortably back into their old ways. They had been forcibly enlisted and had died by the thousands on the battlefields. As citizens of republican Mexico they were given the vote, but they were also liable for taxes. Despite the elimination of the *encomienda*, the feudal relationship between master and servants was maintained under the republic, and the system of debt peonage was perpetuated.

The patient, long-suffering dispositions of the Indians, as well as the distinctions between groups with different languages and different interests, proved an insurmountable barrier to a general uprising. Yet discontent grew and local movements turned into genuine Indian revolutions.

El Monitor Republicano, on July 9, 1848, stated that "Events, which are our best teachers, awakened the realization in the Indians of their true value, and they felt that they could do as well as the Spaniards and the white Mexicans. What they needed was an opportunity. The war against the United States gave them that opportunity" (quoted in Salvat Editores de México, S.A. 1974, 154).

The North American invasion indeed gave an opportunity and impulse to the dissatisfied Indians. They were now ready to rebel. If we do not consider the unacculterated Yaquis of Sonora, who fought a full-scale war in the years 1845 and 1846, all the Indian revolts took place in the years after the settlement of Mexico's disastrous war with the United States in 1847. In 1848 the Maya rose in a body and fought their way across the peninsula of Yucatán, almost driving the whites into the sea; in 1848 and 1849 the Indians of the Sierra Gorda devastated northeast Mexico; in 1849 rebellions broke out in the states of Oaxaca, Tamaulipas, Veracruz, and Hidalgo; in 1850 Indians revolted in Guerrero, and in 1855 in Tlaxcala. Most of those rebellions occurred in remote areas where the presence of the whites was less felt. The populations who rose up against the whites still lived in quasitribal organizations under the authority of their *caciques*, among people of their own blood and language. Peons, as a rule, did not join forces with their rebellious brethren. Years of subservience had mollified their spirit of revolt; they had adjusted to their masters' way of life, and accepted their lot with fatalism.

Although the Caste War of Yucatán had all the characteristics of a racial war, the Maya also rebelled for the improvement of their social and economic situation, as is clearly shown in the plea the native leaders presented to the governor of Yucatán. Among their demands were the abolishment of the personal contributions of the native class; the free use of *ejidos* and uncultivated lands by the Maya, without rent or threat of seizure; the abolishment of taxes on the distillation of *aguardiente*; and forgiveness of the debts of all servants. They also demanded that Miguel Barbachano, a Ladino leader who sought the support of the Maya, be made governor of Yucatán for life (Salvat Editores de México S.A 1974, 7:156). The Ladinos were unable to settle the matter, and the conflict turned into the bloodiest of wars, reducing the population of the peninsula by more than half.

The Indians of the Sierra Gorda near Querétaro rebelled for similar motives. They demanded the creation of a national guard in lieu of the army, reform of the clergy, and distribution of lands (Salvat Editores de México S.A. 1974, 7:157). The Sierra Gorda revolution was suppressed after several months of fierce guerrilla fighting; the leader, Quiros, was shot, and several hundreds of his followers were exiled to various points on the northern border to help fight the fierce invaders there, the Apaches and the Comanches (Bancroft 1887 13:578–79).

In Coahuila, Chihuahua, and Durango, Indian depredations had been a fact of life for more than a century. During the American invasion, the Apache and Comanche attacks had been less frequent, but in 1848 the raids resumed with unprecedented boldness and frequency. To be sure, the Comanches were not motivated by the economic or social claims of the Mexican Indians. Ernest Wallace and E. Adamson Hoebel said that "the motives which led the Comanches to go to war were plunder, love of fighting, a desire for glory . . . and a determination to take and afterwards to hold free from all trespassers, both white and red men, the hunting grounds of the South Plains" (Wallace and Hoebel 1952, 245).

As a result of encroachments on their hunting grounds, the Comanches had migrated southward, attacking the Apaches on their way. The two tribes became fierce enemies, although they had a common foe; the white man. Mexican haciendas, with their huge grazing lands and their large herds of cattle and horses, were easy prey for Comanche and Apache bands. Indian raiders in Coahuila numbered in the thousands. Between 1849 and 1853, Comanches and Apaches killed 191 Coahuilans, wounded 121, and captured 63 (Harris 1964, 77). Between 1848 and August, 1853, their thefts and destruction of livestock belonging to the Sánchez Navarros totaled 7,011 horses, 1,404 mules, 14,212 sheep, 2,080 goats, and 2,567 head of cattle (Harris 1964, 92).

Whole areas had to be abandoned. The region around Santa Rosa, in

Apache warrior. Engraving by Claudio Linati, *Costumes civils, militaires el réligieux du Mexique; dessinés d'apres nature* (c. 1829)

northern Coahuila, was transformed into a wilderness. A large part of Chihuahua lay desolate. In the eastern half of Durango thousands of families were ruined. People inhabiting isolated settlements lived in terror, watching the mountains around to observe smoke signals. In the vicinity of Hermanas, a hacienda belonging to the Sánchez Navarros, Indian raids were incessant. In nearly every raid shepherds were killed or wounded, and the *mayordomo* reported that it was extremely difficult to force those "who had fled the flocks to return to their posts" (Harris 1964, 78). Hermanas, he wrote, was beginning to resemble a hospital, and "if I do not become an accomplished surgeon, it will be because of my inaptitude, not because I have not had many patients on whom to practice" (Harris 1964, 78–79). So bold did the Indians become in the course of years that the mayordomo reported to Sánchez Navarro on July 2, 1851, that during the previous week various bands of Indians, loaded with loot, had passed by the *casco* at all hours of the day and night "as if they had been in their own homes" (Harris 1964, 79).

According to John Russell Bartlett, the Sánchez Navarros made a claim on the United States for a million and a half dollars as an indemnity for cattle, mules, and horses lost to the Indians. The losses very likely were exaggerated in the claim, and understandably, Bartlett wondered why the *hacendado* did not arm his peons or hire a body of riflemen to protect his property (Bartlett [1854] 1965, 2:492). The vastness of the Sánchez Navarro latifundio may have been one reason, making the task seem impossible. Another reason, Charles H. Harris points out, is that the family may have feared the possibility of a rebellion among their herdsmen and therefore chose not to arm them (Harris 1964, 79). A third reason is that the Sánchez Navarros, being shrewd businessmen, may have thought it more profitable to seek compensation for the losses suffered by the Indians than to try to protect their domain.[1]

Both the national government and the state authorities made efforts to check Indian invasions, but they found the challenge more than they could handle. In 1849 the national guard of Saltillo was described as "being without arms or uniforms" (Harris 1964, 82). Chihuahua and Durango resorted to offering rewards; $250 for each warrior taken, $150 for boys and girls under fourteen taken alive; $100 for Indian children who were brought in dead (Bancroft 1887, 13:579, n. 5). American riflemen participated in the hunt. From southern Mexican states came a cry of indignation, and the national government annulled the decree. Scalp hunting, nevertheless, continued for many years in the northern states.

In 1851 the legislature of Coahuila raised money to launch a campaign, and 2,500 Mexicans took part in various expeditions during that year. Yet it was reported that in 1852, Indians were still in complete possession of the Bolsón of Mapimí in Coahuila and Chihuahua.

[1] The Treaty of Guadalupe Hidalgo, which had ended the Mexican War, seemed to offer the possibility of securing compensation, inasmuch as it provided that the United States should assist in checking the growing inroads of *indios bravos*, since the source of invasions lay within the American territory.

THE CASTE WAR

By far the most serious racial conflict under Santa Anna was the Caste War waged in Yucatán between 1847 and 1853. The first outbreak in 1847 had its origin in the hatred of the Maya for their rulers since the earliest years of the Spanish conquest. A native battalion had been raised by the inhabitants of Campeche, who had rebelled against Mexico. On January 15 the soldiers got out of hand, and with shouts of "kill those who have shirts," they stormed the conservative, aristocratic city of Valladolid, killing, mutilating, and raping. Oppressed mestizos in the city joined in the massacre. Nelson Reed reports that the Indians carried the bodies in the streets in a triumphal procession, then ate human flesh (Reed 1964, 34). Then, satiated with violence, they returned to their villages and waited for punishment—punishment that never came.

The rebels' seeming impunity probably stimulated their spirit of revolt. The Maya chiefs—among whom were Manuel Antonio Ay, Cecilio Chi, and Jacinto Pat—met and planned a full-scale insurrection. The tribespeople involved were chiefly the Huits, a half-acculturated Maya tribe living on the frontier. John L. Stephens, in 1841, described them thus: "Naked, armed with long guns, and with deer and wild boars slung on their backs, their aspect was the most truculent of any people we had seen" (Stephens [1843] 1963, 2:229).

Through a trusted servant, a Ladino settler learned of the conspiracy and alerted the authorities. Ay was arrested and executed. Chi and Pat saw what to expect if captured and decided to fight according to their own rules. In the wee hours of July 30, Cecilio Chi and his followers raided Tepich, south of Valladolid, slaughtering all the Ladino families of the town, sparing only a few girls for rape, "less out of lust than of hatred" (Reed 1964, 59).

Anger, fear, suspicion, and frustration led the Ladinos to retaliate harshly and blindly. Innocents paid for the atrocities of the rebels. Guiltless *caciques* were shot; petty leaders were dispatched to the fortress of San Juan de Ulúa; Indian peasants who were living peacefully in their little villages were whipped, suspended by their ears, or taken to town as slaves. Meanwhile, the rebellion spread through the south and east of the peninsula. Ladinos living in isolated settlements abandoned their homes and took refuge on the coast. Chi, who had campaigned in the revolution against Mexico, had acquired good experience in warfare. He split his forces into guerrilla groups, who roamed the country, burning, plundering, and laying waste. The booty was sent south to be traded for arms: much of the war supplies of the rebels came from nearby British Honduras.

The government proved incapable of crushing the rebellion. Through the good offices of a courageous padre, Father José Conuto Vela, a treaty was signed with Pat, but it was soon violated.

On each side men implored the True God and Divine Providence to end the conflict. To the bishop, who had sent letters to the rebels urging peace, a group of Maya leaders replied: "And now you remember that there is a True God. While you were murdering us didn't you know that there was a True God? You were always recommending the name of God to us and you never believed in His name. . . .

And now you are not prepared nor have you the courage to accept the exchange for your blows. If we are killing now, you first showed us the way" (quoted in Reed 1964, 78).

Between combat and looting, the Mayas continued to hold fiestas, calling on God, the Virgin, and various holy spirits for help, with prayers, fireworks, and *aguardiente*. Usually priests were spared: they were needed for religious ceremonies.

Refugees flocked into Mérida and Campeche, crowding into churches and convents and official buildings. In Mérida those who had not found a place to sleep camped under the arcades of the plaza. A commission was formed to feed the refugees and to collect clothes for those in rags. To make matters worse, rumors of a general slaughter of the white and mestizo population swept through the overcrowded streets of Mérida and Campeche. People had but one thing in mind: fleeing. From every port on the coast, the terrorized Yucatecans sailed on any boat available to any place it would go. The bishop left for Havana. Governor Barbachano, said Nelson Reed, "wrote out a proclamation declaring the evacuation of Mérida, then could find no paper in his deserted secretariat for the printing" (Reed 1964, 97).

The Ladino army had to learn the hard way the difference between political revolutions and racial wars. The Yucatecans organized their forces into small units, and recovery began. But it was less through military victories than because the natives, when time for planting came, returned to their *milpas*—the habits of the centuries overrode military tactics. Mérida was saved, and the population celebrated their deliverance with fireworks and a Te Deum.

And help came from abroad: Havana sent arms; Veracruz and New Orleans, corn, money, and gifts. The government of Yucatán seized church properties and converted them into cash to buy military supplies. Mexican generals and American mercenaries joined the military campaigns against the Mayas, and slowly, painfully, the Ladinos reoccupied abandoned towns and villages. When William Parish Robertson, an English traveler, visited Campeche in 1849, daily life on the coast was back to normal, but the horrors of the war were not forgotten. Among the treasures of a Spanish padre who collected Yucatecan antiquities and objects was a small box containing some of the bones of a man who had been burned alive by the Indians the preceding year—"whence," Robertson reported, "the Padre was led to give me many details of an appalling nature, touching the cruelties which had, during the course of the rising, been perpetrated by the Indians on the whites" (Robertson 1853, 1:204–5).

The Mayas were forced to retire deep into the southern and eastern forests. Their bitterness and despair grew from defeat, hunger, and the loss of the familiar land. Many surrendered; others continued the holy combat, still dreaming of a Maya kingdom.

In 1850, Governor Barbachano began selling Maya prisoners to Cuba as slaves; the money was used to pursue the war. Mexico sent subsidies and soldiers, and new tactics were adopted. After seven years the military campaigns subsided, although the Mayas had not been decisively conquered. They held control of the forests of eastern Yucatán for the rest of the century.

Near Ascension Bay, they had founded a capital, named Chan Santa Cruz. The place, known to Huit tribesmen, was said to harbor "a miraculous cross with the power of speech" (Reed 1964, 135). Thus began the cult of the Speaking Cross, a new syncretism of Spanish and Maya culture and religion, around which the Indians developed their own society.

CHAPTER EIGHT

INDIAN VILLAGES

The corn is in the sacred field
The goddess leans on her planting stick
The maguey thorn, the maguey is in my hand
In the sacred field
The goddess leans on her planting stick.

—Song of Ciuaccatl

In pre-Columbian times leading Aztec communities were governed by a body of high officials called *tlatoque* (singular, *tlatoani*), or "speakers," who exercised judicial and directive functions. To the *tlatoani* the Spaniards gave the name of *cacique*, an Arawak word they imported from the West Indies. *Caciques* were given certain rights and privileges, received salaries ranging from a few pesos a year to two hundred, and "as a badge of authority," said Lesley Byrd Simpson, "they were allowed to carry the coveted royal wand of justice" (Simpson [1941] 1966, 48). Their responsibility was to supervise labor, collect tribute, keep the Indians in line, and enforce Spanish laws.

The power of these men became great. They worked with the missionaries, and later with the secular clergy, and were accountable in their communities to a *corregidor*, the crown officer governing the district. The *cacique*, in fact, was the administrative link between the white and native societies, transmitting the foreign laws to the Indians. In Indian towns, as in Spanish towns, there was a *cabildo*, or municipal council, on which the *alcalde* and the *regidor* held the principal posts. At the beginning only a pure-blood Indian could be elected as *alcalde* or *regidor*, but eventually mestizos took the places of Indians in the major towns. In the seventeenth century a Spaniard became *gobernador* (governor) of Tenochtitlán, but in the barrios Indians retained their local government (Gibson 1964, 177).

The laws passed by the Council of the Indies in Spain during the colonial period did not end all abuses, because the legislation was often evaded, and Indian rule often was as corrupt as Spanish rule. The laws nevertheless gave the Indians some kind of protection and allowed them to keep their traditional patterns of village life. As long as Indian customs did not conflict with Spanish laws, the Spanish overlord did not interfere with them.

Settlements in pre-Columbian Mexico were, of course, of various sizes. Besides the vast city of Tenochtitlán, which was divided into four *campans,* or *barrios*, comprising several *calpulli*, or clans, there were small towns and villages.

The wandering tribes in the sierras, along the coasts, or on the northern plains lived mainly on fish and game, fruit and roots, but the Indians of the Mesa Central and Yucatán were sedentary peoples for whom the possession and use of land was a matter of the greatest importance. In his study *The Ejido: Mexico's Way Out*, Eyler N. Simpson considers a typical village formed of several *calpulli*. Each clan was assigned part of the *ejido*, or communal land, of which certain sections were for cultivation while others provided timber and firewood, or were used as hunting and fishing grounds. The agricultural lands were further divided into parcels that were distributed to the heads of households. "A third portion of the land pertaining to the *calpulli*," writes Eyler N. Simpson, "was set aside for special public purposes such as the production of supplies for the maintenance of the village chief, for the entertainment of visiting officials, for the payment of tribute to higher chieftains, for carrying on wars, and for the support of religious institutions and the priesthood" (Simpson 1937, 5).

The agrarian structures of the Aztec world were so similar to those of the conquerors that the system they imposed on the Indians fit perfectly in the existing situation. In many cases the Spanish *encomendero* simply took the place of the defeated—or dead—Indian chieftain, and the tribal system of communal and semicommunal land tenure was given a legal status after slight modifications. The Spanish crown issued laws to protect the communal property of the Indians and to prevent encroachment on their lands by the colonists. Yet in the course of a few decades the *ejido* was slowly but surely pushed back to the advantage of the hacienda.

As a result of Mexico's independence, the Indians secured legal equality with whites, but they also lost the protection of the Spanish crown, however precarious it was. In Yucatán various laws attacked and limited the *ejido*, and in 1841 the protection of tribal water rights was removed. In northern Mexico, too, greediness led the white and mestizo community to abolish certain rights and privileges that had been granted to the Indians by the crown. That was the situation of the Tlaxcalans of Coahuila (Adams 1971, 293–97). Gone was the time when the Indians could count on sympathetic viceroys, bishops, and Audiencias to champion their cause. So accustomed, however, were they to turn to the crown for support that as late as the middle of the nineteenth century a group of Indians respectfully addressed a petition to "the King"—a poignant illustration of the nonparticipation of the Indians in the national life and their ignorance of political realities (Floris Margadant 1980, 981).

Beyond the lands of the acculturated Aztecs lay a territory known as the Gran Chichimeca. There lived fierce and independent tribes who maintained no permanent villages and excelled in guerrilla warfare. In 1546 silver was discovered in the Gran Chichimeca, but the presence of the wandering tribes checked the development of Spanish settlements in the region. Franciscans and Augustinians were sent to Christianize the Chichimecas, but they succeeded in pacifying only the less-bellicose tribes.

The Spaniards then decided to send friendly Indians, such as the Tlaxcalans, as settlers. "The Tlaxcalans," writes David Bergen Adams, "were to live alongside groups of pacified northern Indians, to train them in the ways of civilized men, and to set an example of Christian conduct for them to follow" (Adams 1971, 11). In return for their services, they received privileges such as *hidalguía*, the right to bear arms and ride saddled horses, and exemption from paying tribute (Adams 1971, 35–40). At this time Tlaxcalan families founded the pueblo of San Esteban adjoining the city of Saltillo. Other Tlaxcalans settled at Parras, Monterrey, and around Monclova and San Luis Potosí. Some intermarried with the Chichimecas. They taught them the Aztec language of Nahuatl and helped Christianize them.

With the arrival of the Tlaxcalans the Valley of Saltillo became a rich agricultural region. San Esteban was a free and prosperous village, divided into four *barrios*; each family had been given a plot, which was quickly transformed into an orchard and a kitchen garden (Alessio Robles 1934, 125). A street separated San Esteban from Saltillo, and the pueblo had its own *ayuntamiento*, or town council. Through the centuries there were disputes between the Tlaxcalans of San Esteban and the white community of Saltillo over the land and water, yet the Indians managed to retain their privileges.

Events between 1820 and 1856 greatly affected the situation of the Tlaxcalans. In 1827, San Esteban was annexed by Saltillo, and during the next decade the Indians were able to retain their council three times, only to lose it afterwards. Stubbornly, the Tlaxcalans fought for their rights, applying to Mexico City to have their *cabildo* restored. In time little was left of the Indian pueblo and its land, but many aspects of the Tlaxcalan tradition remained—such as the Aztec dances on the plaza for the fiesta of San Cristo de la Capilla in Saltillo. And San Esteban, renamed Villalongín, boasts the oldest church in Saltillo.

The Tlaxcalans were farmers, ranchers, artisans, shearers. Charles H. Harris writes that among the Tlaxcalan shearers of the Saltillo area there was a trend toward professionalism (Harris [1975], 211). Negotiations with the shearers had to be made through the leader of the crew, and when offered insufficient wages or rations, they simply refused to work.

PUEBLOS AND RANCHERIAS

Spanish authority was vigorously embodied in church buildings. The church was erected in the center of the pueblo, or sometimes above it on a slope, and by its great size seemed to dominate the lives of the *poblanos*, much as the pyramids in ancient Mexico had presided over the destiny of their ancestors.

The church's portal opened onto a plaza that was the heart of the village. There stood the *cabildo*, often with the jail, the school, and the *casa de comunidad* adjacent. There market was held, and people met and gossiped. Captain Lyon, traveling in Jalisco, stayed overnight in the village of Colotlán. He was lodged in a room of the *cabildo* adjoining the "common gaol." He wrote that his windows "were constantly filled with gazers from the crowd, who in the Mexican villages are always to be seen assembled round the prison bars, where all the gossips concentrate, and all the important village questions are discussed" (Lyon 1828, 1:279–81). Lyon provides us with further details. Colotlán and its vicinity had 7,000 inhabitants. Many were from the "Tlaxcalteca nation," and some were Chichimecas. Spanish was "the language generally spoken by these people, although many still retain in their domestic circles the dialect of their ancestors." They were governed by a *jefe político*, who was a white local official, and by a pure-blood Indian *alcalde*.

Most Indian children learned their first words of Spanish at school. It was provided by law that each pueblo should have a school, but the teachers, usually the parish scribes, were hardly educated themselves and could teach nothing more than a little reading or writing. Recitation of catechism was generally the daily chore.

Visiting the small village of Ozumatlán in Michoacán, where "pigs, dogs, and people live huddled together in the utmost harmony," Captain Lyon noted that "the intellect of the rising generation is not entirely neglected, for under the sheltering eaves of a cottage I two or three times observed about half a dozen boys and one solitary girl, sitting on a log, and roaring out their respective lessons to a schoolmaster, who, at the same time, was reading aloud." And he added, "It is indeed a singular but almost universal custom in the country, that in all the schools, every child is to be heard screaming out its task at the same moment" (Lyon 1828, 2:87–88).

We possess other contemporary accounts of village schools. On his way to Palenque, John L. Stephens visited Ocosingo, an Indian village of Chiapas. In the schoolhouse "half a dozen children were sitting on a bench, and the schoolmaster, half tipsy, was educating them, i.e. teaching them to repeat by rote the formal parts of the church service" (Stephens [1841] 1969, 2:257).

Proximity to Mexico City was not a factor for good schooling. Frances Calderón's description of the school of San Juan Teotihuacán, northeast of the capital, convinces us of the poor quality of village schools all over Mexico: "The master was a poor ragged, pale, careworn looking young man, seemingly half-dinned with the noise, but very earnest in his work. The children, all speaking at once, were learning to spell out of some old bills of Congress. Several moral sentences were written on the wall in very independent orthography." One of her companions remarked that they were incorrectly spelled; the master "seemed very much astonished, and even inclined to doubt the fact" (Calderón de la Barca [1843] 1931, 154).

Hamlets, or *rancherías*, which consisted of a few huts built around an open square, had of course no school or church. In remote areas the Indians seldom came into contact with whites and did not know a word of Spanish. Their organization was tribal; the *alcalde* was the absolute ruler. Nothing could be obtained from an Indian village, in fact, except through the *alcalde*: no food, no water, no labor, no lodging, no fodder.

John L. Stephens visited many hamlets while traveling in the forests of Chiapas and in the back country of Yucatán. He left a very interesting description of one hamlet . The "rancho of Schawill," as he called it, was under the jurisdiction of the village of Nohcacab, a few leagues distant,

Indians of Yucatán at the well. Engraving by Frederick Catherwood, *Views of Ancient Monuments in Central America, Chiapas and Yucatan* (1844).

but the right to the soil was the inhabitants' inheritance. The community consisted of a hundred laborers who held and tilled the land in common. The products of the soil were shared by all, and meals prepared for all in one hut, "and every family sends for its portion, which explained a singular spectacle we had seen on our arrival; a procession of women and children, each carrying an earthen bowl containing a quantity of smoking hot broth, all coming down the same road, and dispersing among the different huts" (Stephens [1843] 1963, 2:4). No strangers were admitted in the community, and the inhabitants of Schawill practiced endogamy, although they always went to the village to attend religious festivals. "They were very strict in attendance upon the ceremonies of the Church," noted Stephens, "and had just finished the celebration of the carnival two weeks in advance of the regular time; but when we corrected their chronology, they said they could celebrate it over again" (Stephens [1843] 1963, 2:5).

The shortage of water in Yucatán was a serious problem for many Indian communities. Some hamlets were entirely destitute of water. Others, like Schawill, had water during the rainy season only; for six months of the year water had to be brought from the "rancho of Chack," three miles distant. Although throughout Yucatán the women were the drawers of water, only men were seen around the cenote of Chack, because a distance of "not quite fifteen hundred feet" had to be traversed underground "with its ladders, ascents and descents, winding and crawling passages," to reach the water (Stephens [1843] 1963, 2:16–18).

DWELLINGS AND CRAFTS

Indian dwellings had changed little since the conquest. In the *tierra caliente*, the Indians still built their huts of stakes or canes, or mud and reeds matted together, with a roof made of straw or palm leaves. The roof on one side was commonly extended into a porch supported on posts. There was no aperture other than a door, but sometimes a space of a few feet between the roof and the tops of the walls provided free circulation of air inside. Some huts were round, others square. All were small, generally only one room, and were buried in flowers and foliage.

On the Mesa Central, Indian houses were built of stones or the large, unburnt bricks called adobes, with a flat roof constructed of beams laid close together and covered with clay. Sometimes they were situated within light enclosures, and shaded with lofty trees. In the mountains the roofs were often covered with shingles, and in the plains, where maguey was abundant, maguey leaves were used for roofing.

On the earth floor inside the hut was the cooking fire, which sometimes occupied the center of the room. Near it always stood the *metate*, or grinding stone, and the *comal*, a flat dish of clay for baking the tortillas.

The poorest huts had no table, no chairs, no benches, only mats of palm leaves or rushes for seats and table and bed. The richest had an altar consisting of a table pushed against the wall, covered with a spread, with a niche where the favorite saint or saints were kept. In Yucatán the most conspicuous piece of furniture in the house was the hammock. It served for sleeping at night as well as for the afternoon siesta.

In one corner was the weaving apparatus of the women, composed of a few simple rods; in another, a few earthen pots and jars for cooking and storing. Utensils, such as hoes, strings, and nets, hung on the walls, and baskets were suspended from the roof. They contained the scanty provisions of the family—chili, salt, beans, cotton, eggs, etc. Sometimes pieces of half-dried beef, raw deerskins, or the hide of a wild animal hung from the beams in odoriferous festoons. Small Christian images were found in most Indian dwellings, but crucifixes were seldom seen. The Tarascans of Michoacán and the Zapotecs of the Isthmus of Tehuantepec lived in lovely villages made up of neat, well-kept huts, where pretty pottery was hung on the wall as ornaments.

The Indians of pre-Columbian times were skillful artisans. They had handed down from generation to generation their arts and the traditions of form and pattern. Thus the inhabitants of the village of Tonalá, four miles distant from the city of Guadalajara, were celebrated for their manufacture of all kinds of earthenware, "some of which nearly approach the Etruscan in lightness and elegance of form," remarked Captain Lyon; "their toys, masks, grotesque figures and ornaments are most deservedly admired" (Lyon 1828, 2:43). Frances Calderón spent several days among the Tarascans of Michoacán, admiring their villages, their dresses, their jewels, and their dishes "made of a specie of gourd." The fruit was cut in two, each one furnishing two dishes; "the inside is scooped out and a durable varnish given it by means of a mineral earth, of different bright colours, generally red." On the outside the Indians painted flowers, and some of them were even gilded (Calderón de la Barca [1843] 1931, 493). Other communities were famous for their figures of saints made with feathers of *colibris*, or hummingbirds, or for their pottery, their weaving, their wood carving, or their beautiful work in wax and other crafts. Indians also were celebrated for the skillfulness they showed "in counterfeiting ancient idols, which they dispose of for good pay to British antequarians," wrote Sartorius (Sartorius [1858] 1961, 79).

DAILY LIFE

Indian men and women worked hard, but the woman undoubtedly did the greater part of the work. She was up at dawn, lighted the fire, ground the maize for the morning soup and the tortillas, drew water, fetched the wood, fed the pigs and chickens, took care of the children, prepared the meals, spun cotton, wove the family clothes, sewed, washed, dyed, and manufactured the earthenware that she sold at the market.

Men spent the day in the fields, working their *milpas*. On the border of the maize field they planted beans, chilis, tomatoes, sweet potatoes, cotton, pumpkins, and onions, but only enough for their own use.

Tortilla makers. Engraving by Carl Nebel, *Voyage pittoresque et archéologique dans la partie la plus intéressante du Mexique* (1836).

Chickens and pigs rarely found their way into the family pot; they were taken instead to market in order to raise money for church fees, or for the village fiesta. Indians also planted fruit trees around their huts and sold the fruit to make a few more pesos. Some raised sheep.

Those dwelling on rivers and lakes became fishermen and ferrymen, and those living in the vicinity of cities furnished wood and food for the inhabitants. Indians were the market gardeners of Mexico City. The *chinampas* of Lakes Chalco and Xochimilco produced vegetables and flowers in large quantities.

As their forefathers had done, the Indians of the Valley of Mexico also sought a subsistence in the swamps and canals. They caught whitefish, frogs, and the *axolotl*, a kind of salamander. They collected flies' eggs, watercress, and water lilies, hunted aquatic birds, and extracted salt.

But agriculture remained the basis of Indian life, and the system of agriculture was crude. The poorest Indians did not even use a plow or harrow. The machete and the *coa*, or planting stick, were the only instruments they employed. John L. Stephens observed field work in Yucatán: "A place is selected in the woods, from which the trees are cut down and burned. In May or June, the corn is planted. This is done by making little holes in the ground with a pointed stick, putting in a few grains of corn and covering them over. Once in the ground, it is left to take care of itself, and if it will not grow, it is considered that the land is not worth having" (Stephens [1843] 1963, 1:137).

Some branches of agriculture, such as the cultivation of vanilla, cochineal, and jalap, were entirely in the hands of the Indians. Their patience and their dedication to these ancestral cultures prevented them from abandoning them for more profitable staples. The task of cleaning the leaves of the nopal cactus, on which cochineals lay their eggs, was left to the women.

Maize continued to be the main crop, and the Indians planted it in the same familiar way, in hills arranged in rows. After the harvest, the maize was set aside for the winter; large quantities of cobs were stored in the community granaries, and small amounts of the shelled kernels were kept in family jars. The maize was so important to their lives that "Indians ate well when the maize was plentiful and starved when the maize was scarce" (Gibson 1964, 311). Next in significance was the highly versatile maguey, although the plant was a mixed blessing. As Charles Gibson rightly remarked, "A major obstacle in the program for exterminating Indian drunkenness was the circumstance that the maguey had so many uses and was so important a factor in Indian life" (Gibson 1964, 318).

Overindulgence in drinking, lack of protein, intermingled family relations within the same village, and hereditary disease were enough to cause degeneracy, and most observers noted that Indian children often looked unhealthy. Yet there were healthy and vigorous Indian populations in many areas, particularly in the *tierra caliente* and Yucatán.

In every village there were a few old women or a *curandero* to tend the sick. They knew the virtues of many plants, and generally treated their patients as well as regular physicians. Aztec doctors had a remarkable knowledge of herbs, which their descendants had not entirely lost. Bleeding and bathing were their other favorite remedies. Besides bathing in the rivers, lakes, streams, and fountains, Indians still used the ancestral *temescal*, or sweathouse—a low hut made of unbaked bricks, about eight feet wide and six feet high, with such a low door that a person could enter only on his knees. Water was poured on the red-hot stones, and sweat was produced from the thick, hot vapor that filled the *temes-*

cal. Frances Calderón wrote that the *temescal* "is still to be seen in many Indian villages" (Calderón de la Barca [1843] 1931, 165), and Carl Sartorius affirmed that nearly every house had a *temescal* located next to it. Usually two people bathed together and helped each other. "When all the pores are open," he said, "cold water is thrown upon the patients, who are then rubbed and subjected to all the operations of a Russian bath" (Sartorius [1858] 1961, 72).

The *temescal* was not only considered a remedy; it was also commonly used by the Indians for bathing. Aztecs did not make soap but washed with materials such as the fruit of the *copalxocotl* and the root of the *saponaria americana* (Soustelle 1955, 157). Under Spanish rule, said Gibson, they began employing *tequisquitl* soils for the making of soap, but more for the Spanish market than for themselves (Gibson 1964, 339). Although Carl Sartorius writes that soap was found in Indian huts, it seems that the washing habits of old were not abandoned (Sartorius [1858] 1961, 69).

As the Indians retained their traditional agriculture and way of living, they also kept their traditions of commerce. Market day was an important feature of life in Indian communities. It was an occasion for making a few pesos or purchasing some badly needed goods, for socializing, and, unfortunately, for drinking.

Every pueblo and every town had a market day, to which Indians often had to travel long distances to sell their foodstuffs and their crafts. While at Bolaños, in the state of Jalisco, Captain Lyon noticed among the traders some twenty Huichol Indians selling a coarse salt that they had brought from the Pacific coast. "These and other Indians," he wrote, "make the shores of the Pacific about six days' journey from Bolaños, at their travelling rate of seven or eight leagues per day." The Huicholes lived in the village of San Sebastián, which was situated "eighteen leagues to the westward of Bolaños, and two days and a half from the spot whence the salt is procured" (Lyon 1828, 1:321–22).

Although not all Indians had to travel that far to sell their products, they commonly walked—or trotted, their usual traveling pace—for considerable distances. Sartorius said that "times without number" he had seen Indians of the Sierras "travelling twenty five or thirty miles to a market, over paths whose difficulties one can hardly conceive. . . . Tired out, and perhaps wet through by showers of rain, they arrive at their destination, and pass the night in an open porch, in order early in the morning to offer their products for sale." (Sartorius [1858] 1961, 80).

Men and women carried their products on large, light frames, or in baskets suspended at the back by a broad band tied around the fore-head. Besides the heavy burden on the back, the woman often had an infant at the breast. Their strong legs seemed never to tire; whether climbing the rugged mountains or going through deep ravines, they kept their trot, and never got out of breath.

Indian markets were, and still are, a rhapsody of color. Men and women sat behind heaps of fruit, vegetables, and pottery, among wool serapes, woven mats, shells, and jewels. The bargaining was carried on quietly, and barter, in the first half of the nineteenth century, was still a means of purchase. At suppertime merchants offered foods ranging from roasted turkeys to the omnipresent tortillas. At the fair at Jalacho, a village of Yucatán, John L. Stephens noticed that every vendor of eatables had on the table a pile of cacao grains that they were constantly counting and exchanging with the Indians. He wrote:

> There is no copper money in Yucatán, nor any coin whatever under a medio, or six and a quarter cents, and this deficiency is supplied by these grains of cacao. The medio is divided into twenty parts, generally of five grains each, but the number is increased or decreased according to the quantity of the article in the market, and its real value. As the earnings of the Indians are small . . . these grains of cacao, or fractional parts of a medio, are the coin in most common use among them. (Stephens [1843] 1963, 1:114)

The earnings of the day were unfortunately not always spent wisely. Pulque could be bought everywhere, and at night drunken men filled the paths or the streets. At times men drank so much that they could hardly stand on their feet, and the wife had to wait for the "recovery" of the husband before going home. Women also occasionally took to drinking and could be seen "returning home . . . by taking a zigzag direction through the streets" (Calderón de la Barca [1843] 1931, 261). And too often the docile Indians, whose politeness and humility were praised by all observers, became violent when intoxicated. Quarrels terminated in fights, and not infrequently in stabbings.

OUR LADY, TONANTZIN, AND IX CHEL

Maya ceremonies demanded ritualistic drinking and ritualistic purification afterwards. In the Aztec religion a cult revolved about the maguey plant. The goddess Mayauel represented the plant, and she and her 400 sons were associated with pulque and drunkenness. But except at prescribed religious ceremonies, overdrinking was prohibited. Public drunkenness was considered a serious crime. An intemperate noble suffered public disgrace, loss of office, even strangulation; a plebeian who had already been convicted for drunkenness was stoned and beaten to death. Old people, however, were, allowed to drink on certain occasions.

Aztec civilization died. The Aztec class of priests, the human sacrifices, and the temples in which those acts were performed disappeared immediately after the conquest. Long-bearded, bare-footed, white-skinned friars came to live with the Indians and began the process of converting them to Christianity. The Indians tore down their temples to build churches and monasteries in their place, though here and there the friars simply turned old pagan shrines into Christian places of worship. Most natives accepted Christianity, but they did not abandon their old cultures and traditions, and Indian Christianity was from the start strongly tinged with pagan values and beliefs.

Faced with the contradictory ideas of their old and new priests, the Indians were naturally confused. They never understood the basic Christian concepts of virtue and sin, punishment and reward in the afterworld. Although the Aztec religion had heavens and hells, they had no moral significance; they were merely thirteen overworlds and nine underworlds. The thirteen heavens were the dwelling places of the gods, according to their rank in the hierarchy.

Nonetheless, Aztec ethics forbade blasphemy, religious skepticism, incest, adultery, theft, murder, witchcraft, and slander. The relationships were similar in many ways between Aztecs and their gods and Catholics and their saints, and parallels existed between Aztec and Christian ceremonies and sacraments. Before the coming of the Spaniards the Aztecs had practiced baptism, confession, penance, and even communion. The midwife baptized the newborn baby with water while addressing prayers to the Water Goddess; Aztec confession cured sicknesses sent by angry gods; the penance imposed by priests included self-mutilation and fasting. Aztec communion consisted of eating dough images of pagan gods and the flesh of sacrificed victims (Madsen 1960, 124–25). Self-sacrifice was a way of ensuring the favor of the gods; the higher the social position of the individual, the greater the amount of suffering required.

To add to the confusion of the new converts, many Indian festivals took place at about the same time of the year as Catholic festivals. Thus the Christian Easter came very close to the Aztec festival Toxcatl, a ceremony held in honor of the god Tezcatlipoca to celebrate the rainy season. During the month of Tepeiluitl, which ended about November 1, a ceremony honoring the dead and the rain gods took place; the festival of Etzalqualiztli came close to Corpus Christi; and so on.

The parallels are not surprising if one considers that the seeds of Christianity in Europe also had been sown in pagan soil and had developed into a religion in which the pagan nature of the early converts is easy to discern. Many Christian festivals are European pagan feasts remade for Catholicism. They combined the elements of Christian observance with popular traditions. The religious feasts of old were both sacred and profane; the pagan Europeans celebrated the end of winter, the return of spring, the coming of rainy days, or the time of harvest. Christianity was implanted in the New World in a similar way.

The Spaniards forced Indian children to attend Catholic schools, taught them the new religion, and prohibited the worship of pagan gods. Gradually the Catholic saints assumed most of the functions of the Aztec gods; the symbol of the crucifixion was accepted, as was the Christian God, although not as an exclusive or omnipotent deity. Indians accepted the concept of the soul, but extended it to animals and objects. In Yucatán the Cross was an important feature in Indian villages, but less in association with the passion of Christ than as a magical object, a charm. The Indian pantheon was vast, allowing room for foreign deities. They accepted the Christian saints as they had in ancient times accepted the dieties of other tribes.

The history of the Virgin of Guadalupe is a typical example of Christo-paganism. Near Tenochtitlán was an Aztec temple dedicated to the goddess Tonantzín, the mother of the gods, to whom the Indians used to offer sacrifices. One day, on that very spot, a dark Virgin appeared to a young Indian, Cuaupatoahuac, who had recently been baptized and given the name of Juan Diego. The legendary date of the Virgin's first appearance is 1531, and "by the 1550's an incipient Indian ceremonial had come into existence surrounding the Virgin's miraculous powers and cures" (Gibson 1964, 133). The clergy tried to arrest the growth of the cult. They did not believe in the miraculous apparition and the image of the dark Virgin painted on Juan Diego's cloak, and they thought that the sudden devotion of the Indians for the Virgin was suspect. Father Bernardino de Sahagún wrote of the Lady of Guadalupe:

> In this place they had a temple dedicated to the mother of the gods, whom they called Tonantzín, which means "our mother." There were many sacrifices in her honor. . . . And so they come to visit this Tonantzín from afar, as much as before, which devotion is suspicious, because everywhere there

are many churches for Our Lady and they do not attend those; but they come from great distances here. (quoted in Thompson 1960, 15)

Another example of Christo-paganism is the cult of the Señor de Chalma, a life-sized Christ on a cross who appeared two years after the Tonantzín vision in a cave where the Aztec god Oztocteotl had been venerated (Madsen 1960, 136).

Not all of the Aztec gods had been destroyed. Many had been hidden in caves, dropped into lakes, buried in forests, and had not been forgotten. Images and statues considered antiquities were still worshipped here and there. Brantz Mayer was informed that the keepers of the University of Mexico sometimes found garlands of flowers around a "hideous" statue exhibited in the building (Mayer 1844, 109).

The Maya Lacandons of Chiapas still offered incense in the ruined temples. The lonely forests of Yucatán were still inhabited by demons and spirits. Many villages, said Nelson Reed, had books written by Chilam Balam, who had prophesied the coming of the whites (Reed 1964, 39). Stephens reports that the Indians living near the ruins of Zayi said that "on Good Friday of every year music was heard sounding among the ruins" (Stephens [1843] 1963, 2:14). Tlaloc, the Rain God, was worshipped all over Mexico. The Mixes of southern Mexico, isolated in their mountain fortress, venerated the spirits of lightning, of the earth, and of the clouds; and the Mixtecs of Oaxaca, said Mathieu de Fossey, refused to let strangers undertake diggings in the ruined cities of their ancestors (Fossey 1857, 376). Among the half-pagan Mayas, there was confusion between the Virgin and Ix Chel, the old Moon Goddess.

COFRADIAS, SANTOS, AND FIESTAS

The major concern of religion for the Meso-American Indians, particularly the Aztecs, was the cycles and rhythms of the universe. Aztec life, under their priests, had been a rhythmic pattern of rituals. As George C. Vaillant wrote, "the gods ruled; the priests interpreted and interposed, and the people obeyed, not the priest, but the rhythm of action whereby the gods lived" (Vaillant 1941, 187).

The Aztecs had an array of gods to be honored at the appropriate time by the priesthood. To be sure, the layman did not daily honor each god, but he could find out the name of the divinity to appease him or her before embarking on an undertaking, or in time of distress. The Aztecs performed eighteen major ceremonies in accordance with the solar year, and each was celebrated with fasting, dances, songs, sacrifices, dramas, and feasting. In addition, groups and villages had their own gods and fiestas. These local deities protected the community, and elaborate fiestas were dedicated to them.

It is therefore quite understandable that two Catholic institutions were eagerly adopted by Indian communities: the cult of the saints and the *cofradía*.

The *cofradías*, or lay brotherhoods, became very much a part of Indian life. They were part of the conversion program, and were for the church and the clergy a source of income, yet they were readily accepted by the Indians because they offered their members spiritual security as well as a sense of stability and collective identity, both of which were lacking in post-conquest times. "To Indians," writes Charles Gibson, "the cofradía appeared as an institution acceptable to whites, but non-white and in some measure anti-white. To the clergy, the Indian cofradía was a means of ensuring a steady church income from a reduced population" (Gibson 1964, 132).

The members of the *cofradía* supported the priests and paid for monthly masses, burials (sometimes members were guaranteed an Indian burial), masses for the souls of departed members, celebrations of holy days, and, of course, the *fiesta titular*. The more expensive the costs of membership the greater the reward.

The *fiesta titular*, or holy day of the town or village, became the high spot of Indian life, and the *santo* replaced the village deity of old. The cult of the saints did not rest on formalized doctrines, but took various forms, and the object of devotion varied from one village to another. It could be a saint's image, a religious painting, a relic of an early missionary, a stone from an ancient temple, or a cross. Yet they all had a few essential features in common: the *santo* was a supernatural being, residing in a particular place, who had miraculous powers. In the *santo* rested the strength of the pueblo. Each pueblo was very proud of its own patron, and rivalries arose between pueblos as to whose patron was the most powerful. On special occasions the *santo* of one village was lent to another village. Like the old pagan deity, he or she had to be honored in a manner most enjoyable, that is with fireworks, music, *aguardiente*, food, candles, dances, masks, incense, flowers, and processions.

In most villages a tract of land was dedicated to the *santo*, and the income from the land was devoted to fiesta expenses. The land was considered "the saint's land"; it belonged to the village *santo*. Elsewhere the *cofradía* and the community joined forces to finance the fiesta. A *mayordomo*, or manager, was responsible for its organization. The post was honorary and might be a step up the social ladder of the village hierarchy. It was by no means a sinecure. Failure to perform adequately might bring disaster to the community, and expenses always exceeded the receipts. *Mayordomos* had to make up the losses from their own pockets.

Some villages had several patron saints. Of Nohcacab, for example, John L. Stephens wrote: "Besides smaller saints, the favourites of individuals, it has nine principal ones, who have been selected as special objects of veneration: San Mateo, the patron, and Santa Bárbara, the patroness of the village; Nuestra Señora de la Concepción; Nuestra Señora del Rosario; El Señor del Transfiguración; El Señor de Misericordia; San Antonio, the patron of souls, and El Santo Cristo del Amor (Stephens [1843] 1963, 1:228).

While Stephens was working at the ruins of Kabab with Frederick Catherwood, the fiesta of Corpus Alma began. It was

> a festival of nine days' observance in honour of Santo Cristo del Amor. Its opening was announced by the ringing of church bells and firing of rockets, which, fortunately, as we were away at the ruins, we avoided hearing; but in the evening came the procession and the baile, to which we were formally invited by a committee, consisting of the padrecito, the alcalde, and a much more important person than either, styled El Patron del Santo, or the Patron of the Saint. (Stephens [1843] 1963, 1:228)

Stephens was quite surprised to discover that the Saviour was there reverenced as a saint and that as a saint He had a patron—actually a *mayordomo*:

> The procession had formed in the body of the church, and at the head of it, in the doorway, were Indians bearing the cross. . . . Next to the cross were four Indians bearing on a barrow the figure of the saint, being that of the Saviour on the cross. . . . This was followed by the patron and his mayoles, the padrecito and ourselves, the vecinos, or white people of the village, and a long train of Indian men and women, bareheaded, in white dresses, and all bearing long lighted candles. (Stephens [1843] 1963, 1:229)

They marched through the street leading to the "patron's" house. Fireworks exploded, and a "flaming ball" whizzed along, scattering fire on the heads of the worshippers. At the door of the house the "padrecito" chanted a salve. In the "single long room" of the house, an altar, adorned with flowers, had been set at one end, while at the other end, on a long table, were spread "dulces, bread, cheese and various compound mixtures both for eating and drinking." The saint was placed on the altar, and the padre and his family, followed by the *vecinos*, the mestizos, and the Indian servants and children, took places in an enclosure at the back of the house. "Preparations were immediately made for dancing, and the ball was opened by the patron of the saint. . . . At eleven o'clock, the ball broke up . . . the vecinos lighted their torches, and all went home in a body. . . . The Indians remained to take their places, and pass the night in the ball-room dancing in honour of the saint." Every evening there was a new ball honoring the saint (Stephens [1863] 1963, 1:229–31).

Many foreign observers have left interesting accounts of Indian religious customs and fiestas, whether they were shocked, attracted, or merely amused. H. G. Ward said that during the festival of the patron saint of Itzmiquilpan, in Hidalgo, the main street of the village was lighted up "with a number of large paper lanterns, covered with the figures of Saints and Angels, most brilliantly coloured" (Ward 1828, 2:368). Frances Calderón de la Barca, who was in Pátzcuaro, in the state of Michoacán, at the time of the fiesta of San Andrés, wrote that the Indians "carried the saint in very fine robes, the women bearing coloured flags and lighted tapers, and the men playing on violins, flutes, and drums. All had garlands of flowers to hang on the altars" (Calderón de la Barca [1843] 1931, 492).

While he was in Michoacán, Captain Lyon passed an immense group of people "bearing a large covered picture of our Lady of Guadalupe across the plains to its proper church, whence it had been lent to hallow a mass in a distant village. Four horsemen preceded this holy painting, and all the Indian women bore large bunches of flowers in honour of this their favourite saint" (Lyon 1828, 2:92). Mathieu de Fossey, who was in Oaxaca at the time of Corpus Christi, reports that a "delegation of Indians from near-by villages marched through the streets, bearing the images of their patron saints, preceded by a tamborin and a chirimie, a kind of clarinet with a wild and piercing sound" (Fossey 1857, 356). And Robert A. Wilson saw "fantastic dances performed by Indians under the supervision of priests and bishops" during the fiesta of Our Lady of Guadalupe (Wilson 1855, 231).

Like the image of the *santo*, the village cross occupied an important place in the devotions of Indian communities, particularly among the Mayas of Chiapas and Yucatán. At the time of planting the farmer made offerings to the four spirits guarding his field, one at each corner, for without their help the corn would never grow. The village was likewise protected by four spirits, "one to each of the crosses erected at the edge of the village," according to Nelson Reed (Reed 1964, 39). The Maya recognized five directions; the fifth was the center, and was in every village marked with a cross and usually a ceiba, the sacred tree of the Maya, which was thought by the Ancient Ones to occupy the center of the sky. "The fifth direction was under the care of the village patron saint, who controlled the well-being of the entire community" (Reed 1964, 39).

Besides the guardian of the village, every family had its own individual guardian, generally a cross, which was an object of worship. Sometimes the cross was dressed in a huipil, thereby indicating its personification (Thompson 1960, 24).

Indians could kneel for hours before an altar with unique stillness, or they could express themselves in excess by breaking their normal rules of behavior and committing violent acts in an orgy of release. The fiesta undoubtedly was a communal release as well as a propitiation of supernatural forces. During a fiesta, wrote Octavio Paz, the Mexican "*descarga su alma,*" or "unburdens his soul" (Paz [1950] 1959, 43).

The more isolated the community, the more pagan the ceremony. Although every pueblo had a church, not all had a resident priest. Mass was held very irregularly, and religious instruction was totally inadequate. Even when priests took their duties to heart, their curacy was often so vast and their parishioners so scattered that they were unable to give them proper attention. John L. Stephens, who accompanied the *cura* of Tekoh in one of his tours, writes that the good priest was everywhere welcomed. When they arrived at the village of Telchaquillo, "immediately the bell of the church tolled, to give notice of his arrival, that all who wished to confess or get married, who had sick to be visited, children to be baptized, or dead to be buried, might apply to him, and have their wants attended to" (Stephens [1843] 1963, 1:70). When they reached the hacienda of Xcanchakan, which was within the priest's curacy, "again immediately upon our arrival the bell of the church tolled to announce his arrival to the sick, those who wished to confess, marry, or be baptized. This over, it struck the solemn note of the *oración*, or vesper prayers. All rose, and, with uncovered heads, stood silent till that last note died away" (Stephens [1843] 1963, 1:81). When they left, the Indians came over to the *cura*, and respectfully kissed his hand.

The scarcity of priests was not peculiar to Yucatán. Frances Calderón writes of the small pueblo of Tziracuaratino, in Michoacán: "There was nothing to be seen in the village . . . but a good-looking old church, which two old women were sweeping out; but they told us they rarely had mass there, as the padre lived a long way off" (Calderón de la Barca [1843] 1931, 498).

What did the Catholic Church finally accomplish? We should let a Mexican, Octavio Paz, answer the question: "Through the Catholic faith, the Indians, orphans since the link with their ancient culture had been severed and their gods and cities destroyed, found once more a place in the world. . . . The flight of their gods and the death of their chieftains had left the natives in a solitude as complete as it is difficult for modern man to conceive" (Paz [1950] 1959, 92).

CHAPTER NINE

DEATH IN THE LIFE
OF THE MEXICAN

*Death is a mirror which reflects the vain
gesticulation of life.... Our death illumines our
life. If our death is lacking in meaning, so is
our life.*—Octavio Paz

Dead, naked, rotten, and stinking, so will we be—
thus the populations of fifteenth-century Europe were reminded of the
precariousness of life when the Cult of Death reached its peak. Never
before was so much said and written about the need for salvation, the
pain of hell, and the physical details of death (Huizinga [1919] 1967,
141–55; Chaunu 1975, 186–91). In the next century, while most
Europeans reveled in the pleasures and license of the Renaissance, the
Spaniards continued to delight in the thought of dust and worms. In
Mexico they encountered a population whose concern with death was
as deep as their own.

For the Christian, the dominant idea concerning death is the spiritual
journey of the soul to the hereafter. As Octavio Paz puts it, death is "a
passage, a mortal jump between two lives, the temporal and the eternal"
(Paz [1950] 1959, 51). For the Aztec, death was the noblest manner of
participating in the perpetual regeneration of the creative forces of the
universe. "Life, death and resurrection were stages in an insatiably repeated cosmic process," writes Paz. "Life had no higher function than to
flow into death, which is its opposite and its complement; and death, in
turn, was not an end in itself. With his death, man nourished the ever
voracious appetite of life" (Paz [1950] 1959, 49).

The fatalism of both the Indians and the Spanish, who agreed in the
belief that life is only a fleeting passage, is deeply rooted in the Mexican
soul. Mexicans talk and write about death, even their own, as a natural

thing. They approach it without fear as part of their fate; furthermore, death exerts on them a ghoulish fascination. It is a daily concern, an organic part of their thought, a familiar motif in their art. Death pleases their fancy.

Life with all its vanities "is a cadaver, it is dust, it is shadow, it is nothing." So wrote Sor Juana Inés de la Cruz (1651–95), one of the great Mexican poets of all time, in her Sonnet I (Cruz [1938] 1941, 47). Everywhere in Mexico you are reminded that power, honor, and riches are nothing, that death carries off the bravest, the prettiest, the richest, the youngest. The subject of death was preponderant in Aztec art. Death masks were made of jade, shell, and obsidian mosaics. Skulls adorned pyramids and temples, or they were carved in stone, lava, jade, and obsidian. In Spanish Mexico skulls were woven in garments, painted on coffins and frescoes, embroidered in spreads and draperies. They decorated altars and were carved on walls. Skulls and bones were piled up in churchyards as proof of the ultimate leveling; or made of candy and bread, they were eaten with glee on November 2, the Day of the Dead. Skulls were also made into toys, as were skeletons and coffins. P. Banchard reports that near the cathedral of Mexico City, in a shop where children's toys were sold, he saw little cadavers dressed in monk's robes laid in coffins. They were for commemorating the dead (Blanchard and Dauzats 1839, 167–68).

Death was portrayed in popular dances, and on Good Friday penitents carried skulls and images of death. Representations of death as a skeleton with a scythe were found in some churches, as in the European *danses macabres* of the fifteenth century.

Church art followed the lugubrious tendency of the conquistadors: Christs were made to bleed; they writhed in agony; the crown of thorns was an instrument of torture that draws blood. Blood poured from the broken knees, from the torn feet and hands, from the wound in the side.

On the Day of the Dead churches "present a gloomy spectacle," wrote Frances Calderón, "darkened and hung with black cloth, while in the middle aisle is a coffin, covered also with black, and painted with skulls and other emblems of mortality" (Calderón de la Barca [1843] 1931, 279).

But the Mexicans laughed back and challenged death. In villages and hamlets, November 2 was by no means a sad day. The celebration of All Souls' Day paralleled an ancient Aztec feast in which the dead were believed to come to earth to visit their friends and relatives. The Day of the Dead was a perfect opportunity for the dead and the living to meet

"Death Attacks Even the Young Woman." Engraving in Joaquín Bolaños, *La portentosa vida de la muerte, emperatriz de los sepulcros, vengadora de los agravios, y muy señora de la humana naturaleza, cuya célebre historia encomienda a los hombres de buen gusto Fray Joaquín Bolaños* (1792).

again, and the arrival of the dead was announced at midnight with fire-crackers. Indian women took flowers, candles, and food to the cemetery and talked to the dead. In some villages fires burned in the houses and streets to warm the dead on the night preceding their arrival; in others, altars were set up in front of the huts, and food, drink, and flowers were spread on the altars. The families actually ate the food, but the dead were fed in spirit. God would punish living persons who did not give proper food to the dead, by killing them within a week and by sending them to hell and eternal torture.

In Yucatán the customs differed slightly from those of the Valley of Mexico. On the Day of the Dead, said John L. Stephens, a ceremony called Mukbipoyo was rigidly observed by the Maya. Every Indian burned consecrated candles in honor of his deceased relatives, and in memory of those who had died within the year. Besides, Indians baked in the earth "a pie consisting of a paste of Indian corn, stuffed with pork and fowls, and seasoned with chili, and during the day, every good Yucateco eats nothing but this." In the back country, where the Indian remained half pagan, people placed a portion of the same pie under a tree, or in some retired place, "for their deceased friends to eat" (Stephens [1843] 1963, 1:21).

A DAY OF REJOICING

The perfect faith of the Indian, which made him believe in miracles, also made him accept death as one of the accidents of life. "'Voy a descansar,' 'I am going to rest,' 'Mis trabajos son acabados,' 'My labours are ended,' are the words of the Indian as he lies down to die," noted Stephens, "but to the stranger in that country death is the king of terrors" (Stephens [1843] 1963, 1:263).

While at Ticul, in Yucatán, Stephens visited the cemetery, the *campo santo*: "[It] had been opened but five years, and already it presented a ghastly spectacle. There were many new-made graves, and on several of the vaults were a skull and small collection of bones in a box or tied up in a napkin, being the remains of one buried within and taken out to make room for another corpse" (Stephens [1843] 1963, 1:169).

At one corner was a walled enclosure within which was the charnel house of the cemetery. A flight of steps led to the top of the wall. On the platform of the steps, as well as along the wall, were skulls and bones, all labeled to make known to whom they had once belonged: "Within the enclosure, the earth was covered several feet deep with the promiscuous and undistinguishable bones of rich and poor, high and low, men, women, and children, Spaniards, Mestizoes and Indians, all mingled together as they happened to fall. Among them were fragments of bright coloured dresses, and the long hair of women still clinging to the skull" (Stephens [1843] 1963, 1:170).

In the church, one of the altars was decorated with human skulls and crossbones, and in one place, in a niche, was a funeral urn containing the ashes of a lady of Ticul, under which was an inscription that struck the American traveler:

¡Hombres!
He aqui el termino de nuestros afanes;
La muerte, tierra, nada.

[O Man!
Behold the end of our troubles—
Death, Earth, Nothing]
(Stephens [1843] 1963, 1:155)

John L. Stephens next visited Nohcacab. Adjoining the church was a charnel house "along the wall of which was a row of skulls." Within the enclosure, as in Ticul, was a collection of skulls and bones scattered pell-mell; and along the wall, "hanging by cords, were the bones and skulls of individuals in boxes and baskets, or tied up in cloths, with names written upon them." In the church, near one of the altars, was also a box containing the bones of a woman, "the wife of a lively old gentleman" whom Stephens used to see everyday. "They were clean and bright as if polished, with the skull and cross-bones in front, the legs and arms laid on the bottom, and the ribs disposed regularly in order, one above the other, as in life, having been so arranged by the husband himself" (Stephens [1843] 1963, 1:259–60). In the choir of the church, in the embrasure of a large window, were rows of skulls, "all labelled on the forehead." Stephens read a few inscriptions: "Soy Pedro Moreno: un Ave María y un Padre Nuesto por Dios, hermano"; "I am Apolono Balche: a Paternoster and an Ave María for God's sake, brother." Every skull bore the name of its owner, and all begged a prayer, except one, that of Richard Joseph de la Merced Truxeque and Arana. "I am enjoying the kingdom of God forever," read the inscription on his forehead. Said Stephens: "This was the skull of a child, which, dying without sin, had ascended to heaven, and needed not the prayers of man" (Stephens [1843] 1963, 1:261–62).

The death of a child under seven was considered a source of rejoicing, at least among the poorer classes. The effect, however, was distressing for foreign observers. Captain Hall was upset by the merrymaking surrounding the burial of a little girl in San Blas. His respect for the family and his curiosity to see the ceremony "were barely sufficient motives," he wrote, "to induce me to accompany the procession where fiddles, drums, and fifes played merry tunes round the bier; while the priests chanted hymns of rejoicing at the accession which had been made to the host of little angels" (Hall 1824, 2:266–67).

Such a joyful attitude was affirmed by all. Captain Lyon, who encountered in Tula "a crowd of people with a young woman who was bearing on her head a little dead child, dressed in coloured papers," wrote that a fiddler and a man playing the guitar accompanied the procession, and that on the way to the burial ground, a man threw up rockets, "of which he bore a large bundle under his arm." The whole ceremony was one of cheerful gaiety, and Lyon was informed that the burial would be followed by a *fandango* (Lyon 1828, 1:143–44).

There were flowers and merry music, too, for a dead little girl of the village of Santa María de Tule, near Oaxaca. An old man seated before the door of a hut begged Mathieu de Fossey to come in. Inside, reports the Frenchman, were a score of young men; some were singing, others playing the guitar or clapping their hands to beat out the rhythm. In a corner, "the body of a three year-old girl was lying in a basket adorned with flowers and foliage, and surrounded by lighted candles. A crown of bright metal encircled her head, and her body, save the face, was covered with petals of flowers" (Fossey 1857, 364).

The ceremony of the *velorio* was observed whenever there was a death in the family. The padre of Nohcacab told John L. Stephens that the *velorio* was intended to distract the family and keep them from going to sleep. But the ceremony, he explained, was different at the death of a grown person. Because the death of a child was a subject of rejoicing, the night was passed in card playing, jesting, and storytelling. "But in the case of grown persons . . . as they are not so sure what becomes of the spirit, they have no jesting or storytelling, and only play cards" (Stephens [1843] 1963, 1:218–19).

Jewels replaced paper flowers on the cadavers of rich children, but the spirit of the ceremony remained the same. When the last scion of a "noble house" died, reported Frances Calderón, the child was not only enveloped in rich lace, but "the diamonds of three condesas and four marquesas" were put on him, "necklaces, bracelets, rings, brooches, and tiaras, to the value of several hundred thousand dollars." The street was hung with draperies, and a band played music while "he was visited by all titled relatives of the family in his dead spendour" (Calderón de la Barca [1843] 1931, 89).

We should mention that the Gordoas did not seem to conform in accepting death as a part of life where their children were concerned. The death of a baby at birth was mourned by its mother for a year, and there was no celebration of any kind at the time of its death (Dolores Rubio to Mariana Gordoa, June 18, 1841, Gordoa Family Papers).

Child burials could be ghastly. At the village of Tekoh, in Yucatán, Stephens saw the body of a child, laid on a bier and "wrapped in a tinsel dress of paper of different colours, in which red and gold were predominant, and amid this finery worms several inches long were issuing from its nostrils, curling and twisting over its face" (Stephens [1843] 1963, 1:68). And in Chiapas, Stephens happened to be in the church of the village of Las Playas when a cheerful procession entered, led by the sexton, who was carrying in his arms the body of a child "dressed in white, with a wreath of flowers around its head." The floor of the church was earthen, and the grave was dug inside. The sexton placed the little body in the grave and covered it with a few inches of earth. He "got into the grave, and stamped it down with his feet. He then got out and threw in more, and, going outside the church, brought back a pounder . . . and again taking his place in the grave, threw up the pounder at the full swing of his arm, and brought it down with all his strength over the head of the child," and adding to the horror of the spectacle, the father himself went into the grave, took the pounder from the sexton's hands, and struck until the floor of the church was made even (Stephens [1841] 1969, 2:371–72).

RITES OF DEATH

Death was a familiar guest. The tolling of the bells for the dying and the dead, as well as the tinkling of the little bells announcing the approach of the Host, were heard day and night in large cities.

When the little bell chimed, people frequently exclaimed, "¡Dios viene! ¡Dios viene! [God is coming! God is coming!]" and they took their hats off and dropped to their knees, crossing themselves devotedly. A coach with glass windows on all sides, drawn by mules, passed slowly. A priest in his vestment would be seated inside. He would be preceded by a man ringing the small bell, and followed by a dozen friars with lighted candles, or by a band of boys chanting a hymn. And as the coach made its way through the streets, a deathlike silence succeeded the hubbub. But the carriage would no sooner turn the corner than the street would come alive again. Death was forgotten, momentarily. "Until very recently," wrote Waddy Thompson, "everyone was required to kneel, and a very few years since an American shoemaker was murdered in his shop for refusing to do it. But now they are satisfied if you pull off your hat, and stop until the Host passes" (Thompson 1846, 102).

The procession would be more or less numerous, and the person carrying the viaticum more or less important, according to the social rank of the dying. Sometimes the procession was accompanied by one or two large bands of musicians, or by a guard of honor, sandaled monks, and officers in full uniforms; and occasionally a band played at the doors of dying persons until they drew their last breaths. According to eyewitnesses, the viaticum for Santa Anna's first wife, Doña Inés García, was a ceremony of considerable pomp.

Brantz Mayer was there as the secretary of the United States delegation. Early in the morning it was rumored in Mexico City that the wife of Santa Anna was dangerously ill; then, at about noon, notes of invitation were sent to all members of the diplomatic corps, "requesting their presence at the ceremony of the *Viaticum*; and at seven o'clock," said Brantz Mayer, "we repaired, in uniform, to the Palace." There, the diplomats, as well as prominent citizens, strangers, and friends of the "suffering lady," were given wax torches and ranged around the walls of the audience chamber.

The large bell of the cathedral began to toll. From the window overlooking the Plaza Mayor, Mayer saw the procession coming out of the cathedral, preceded by the military band: "Slowly it advanced to the Palace gates—the jeweled robes of the Archbishop and attendant priests, flashing in the blaze of a thousand lights, as they approached the portals. . . . The Cabinet Ministers and Chiefs of the army then accompanied the priests into the chamber of the lady, where the required functions were performed." When the ceremony was over, the procession returned to the cathedral. "The effect of this procession—with its torches blazing in the night like so many diamonds—its solemn military music, and its melancholy hymn—was solemn and picturesque" (Mayer 1844, 228).

There was a similar display at the death of General José Morán, hero of the wars of independence, and at that of General Valentín Canalizo's wife, who passed away while her husband was president ad interim during an absence of Santa Anna. Both were embalmed, both were placed in open biers and lay in state for several days; both had glass eyes inserted. The wife of General Canalizo was "gorgeously dressed and glittering in jewels" (Thompson 1846, 215), while General Morán was dressed in the "full uniform of a Major-general, with boots, spurs, plumed hat, sword, and even the cane by his side, as is usual with Spanish officers." Brantz Mayer said that he would never forget the "stony gaze of the *glass eyes*, as the dead body of the General issued from his gate-way." The procession moved along the streets to the sound of solemn music. The service was performed with all ecclesiastical splendor, "and a multitude of priests . . . immediately commenced their masses for the repose of the hero's soul" (Mayer 1844, 228–29).

Among the wealthy Mexicans, the *honras,* the celebration of mass for the repose of the soul, was also an occasion for ostentatious splendor. When Frances Calderón attended the *honras* for the daughter of the Marquis of Salvatierra, the walls and pillars of the church of San Agustín, she wrote, "were covered with draperies of rich crimson velvet. Innumerable wax candles were lighted, and an invisible band of music played during the intervals of the deep-rolling organ. All the monks of San Augustin, with their white hoods, and sandalled feet, and carrying lighted tapers, were ranged near the altar" (Calderón de la Barca [1843] 1931, 100).

Even the executions of banditti displayed a solemnity that contrasted with the gaiety usually surrounding such a ceremony in other countries. Thus we are told that, in Guanajuato on the eve of the execution of a highwayman, the bells of the churches began tolling at sunset and "kept up for nearly two hours"; then a procession proceeded to the prison. First came a company of soldiers with a military band, followed by the bishop of Guanajuato "bearing the Host, under a canopy of white and silver borne by priests, who also carried lanterns of blue glass." Then came another company of soldiers, followed by a double line of citizens, "each of whom held an immense burning taper in his hand." After the viaticum was administered to the criminal, the procession returned to the cathedral, which was brilliantly lighted and filled with a dense crowd. The military band was stationed in the center and accompanied by the organ. The people constantly repeated their paternosters, and it seemed to Bayard Taylor, who witnessed the scene, that they felt "a deep sympathy with the convicted" (Taylor [1850] 1949, 292).

"The most curious feature of the scene," he adds, "was a company of small boys carrying bundles of leaves on which was printed the 'Last Dying Speech and Confession', in poetry, the burden being '*Adios, Guanajuato amado!*'" These boys scattered about through the crowd crying

"'Here you have my sentence, my confession, my death, my farewell to Guanajuato!'—all for a *cuartilla*" (Taylor [1850] 1949, 293).

SELF-PENANCE

The application of human sacrifices in Indian ceremonies had revolted the Spaniards. Bernal Díaz wrote at length about the walls of the shrines "clotted with blood" and the soil "bathed with it" (Díaz del Castillo 1956, 220). The Aztecs, on the other hand, were repelled at the cruelty shown by the conquistadors on numerous occasions. Both behaviors shock our twentieth-century sensibilities.

For the Meso-American Indian self-sacrifice was a sure way to ensure the favor of the gods. Among the Aztecs self-penance was the affair of everyone, while in Mayaland the priests and the royalty engaged in the practice more often than the common people. In addition, food taboos and sexual abstinence were rigidly observed by Maya priests before and during rituals (Coe [1966] 1980, 155). Aztecs and Mayas mutilated themselves with knives, or drew a string threaded with maguey thorns through their tongues; or passed a sharp reed through the ears, tongues, lips, and penis; or simply fasted.

Self-penance through bloodletting was also common among the Christians as a means of achieving God's mercy, or to express remorse and to expiate the sins of all. Thus emerged the cult of the flagellants, which had appeared in Europe in the fourteenth century. The movement was quickly suppressed, but flagellation as a means of penitence remained.

Among cloistered nuns self-penance was practiced through the centuries. Although nuns, as a rule, lived an easy life in Mexico, Spanish mysticism, exemplified by Teresa de Avila, found a few adherents. Frances Calderón, accompanied by a bishop glittering with jewels, visited the convent of the sisters of Santa Teresa, in Mexico City, where twenty nuns, among them three novices, were "buried alive." The nuns showed the visitors a crown of thorns that some of them wore on certain days by way of penance. "It is made of iron," wrote Frances Calderón, "so that the nails entering inwards, run into the head, and make it bleed. While she wears this on her head, a sort of wooden bit is put into her mouth, and she lies prostrate on her face till dinner is ended." Frances visited the cells. She was horror-struck at the self-inflicted tortures. "Each bed consists of a wooden plank raised in the middle, and on days of penitence crossed by wooden bars. The pillow is wooden, with a cross lying on it, which they hold in their hands when they lie down." Occasionally around her waist the nun also wears a band with iron points turned inwards, Fanny said; and on her breast "a cross with nails, of which the points enter the flesh, of the truth of which I had melancholy ocular demonstration. Then, after having scourged herself with a whip covered with iron nails, she lies down for a few hours on the wooden bars, and rises at 4 o'clock" (Calderón de la Barca [1843] 1931, 273–75).

Desagravios, or public penance, was part of the Mexican heritage from both the Aztec and Spanish civilizations. It was performed once a year by all Mexicans. The women attended church in the morning, the men in the evening. Although women were not admitted to the men's penance, Frances Calderón managed to enter a small side door and, "passing through long vaulted passages, and up steep winding stairs," she reached a gallery "looking down directly upon the church" (Calderón de la Barca [1843] 1931, 264).

The scene described by Fanny seems to be taken from a medieval book. About 150 men, wrapped in cloaks and serapes, were assembled in the dimly lighted church, and from the pulpit a monk was describing with terrifying details the torments prepared in hell for the unrepentant sinner. "When the discourse was finished, they all joined in prayer with much fervour and enthusiasm, beating their breasts, and falling upon their faces." The monk then read several passages from the Bible relating the suffering of Christ. Soon afterwards the organ struck up the Miserere, and suddenly all was darkness except for a huge crucifix. A voice cried, "My brothers, when Christ was fastened to the pillar by the Jews, he was *scourged!*" And the next sound Frances Calderón heard was that of hundreds of scourges "descending upon the bare flesh," and the sound "became *splashing* from the blood that was flowing. . . . At the end of half an hour a little bell was rung, and the voice of the monk was heard, calling upon them to desist; but such was their enthusiasm, that the horrible lashing continued louder and fiercer than ever" (Calderón de la Barca [1843] 1931, 264–65).

Waddy Thompson, who watched a *desagravios* in the church of San Agustín in Mexico City, confirms Frances Calderón's description: "It was a real *bona fide* castigation," he wrote. "Of this I have no doubt, for I picked up one of the *disciplinas*, the instrument used, and it was wet and soaked with blood." The participants were not masochists or sadists, or an association of ascetics of excessive piety who sought spirituality by mortifying the flesh. "I stood at the door as the penitents came out," said Waddy Thompson, "and recognized amongst them some of the most respectable people in Mexico" (Thompson 1846, 114). By re-enacting the scourging of Christ upon their own bodies, they simply intended to express remorse and expiate their sins.

NO SALVATION OUTSIDE THE CHURCH

The church did not bring virtue to the western hemisphere, but a creed. From the very beginning, the clergy directed their flocks to a scrupulous observance of the forms of the Catholic Church, rather than its moral or spiritual values. The church provided a single answer to life's questions: *Extra ecclesiam nulla salus*, "No salvation outside the church." Salvation could be reached only through rituals, offerings, penance, and prayers. The alternative to salvation was Hell. Heaven was permanently closed to heretics and Jews, but not to Catholic sinners, since they could atone for their faults by penitence and absolution. Hence the terrible impact of anathema and excommunication, the most powerful weapons in the arsenal of the church. The unfortunate persons who were excommunicated would feel the heat of eternal fire. It is no wonder, against such a background, that so many Mexicans sank into superstition and intolerance.

Purity of religion was one of the Three Guarantees proclaimed by Iturbide and the army at Iguala in 1821. The Mexican Congress of 1824, as a concession to popular prejudice, also adopted an article forbidding freedom of religion in the republic. To the disgrace of Mexico, the right of burial had to be secured for non-Catholic foreigners through treaties.

The first country to acquire the right was Great Britain. H. G. Ward reports that in many states "the prohibitory clause in the religious article of the Federal Act, has been omitted" and that the "right of sepulture, according to the forms of the Protestant church, which is secured to His Majesty's subjects by treaty, has not only been universally conceded, but burying grounds have been voluntarily assigned for the purpose by the local Authorities, wherever a resident foreign Consul is established" (Ward 1828, 1:354). Yet non-Catholics were not allowed to be buried in the regular cemeteries, and when they were buried elsewhere, their graves were sometimes violated by fanatics. It also happened that local priests refused to bury in "Christian ground" any Protestant foreigner who had the misfortune to meet death in Mexico. Waddy Thompson recounts the story of a Lieutenant Sevey, a "very gallant and fine young man," whose friends could obtain burial for him only after having given the priest a hundred and fifty dollars" (Thompson 1846, 215–16).

The lovely burial ground of Santa María in Mexico City, with its

niches just large enough to receive a coffin, its gravel walks, its flowers and shrubberies, and its splendid marble tombs, was not for the
Protestants.

For good or ill, priests were the directors of the people's conscience.
The padre was venerated and feared because he might have the key to
salvation. A person stricken by disease always called for a priest, even
before calling for a doctor; and when the sick recovered, votive offerings
were the usual way of thanking the Virgin or the saints for intervening.
When earth tremors were felt, there was no terror or confusion in the
streets; people simply dropped on their knees, wherever they were,
whatever they were doing, and prayed, "the half-naked Indian beside
the veiled *dama*, and the loathsome leper beside the gaudily dressed
official. The rider kneeled beside his horse, and the arriero among his
mules; the carriages had halted, and their gay contents bent in clusters
in the centre of the pavement." When the shock was over, "each went
about his business" (Latrobe 1836, 104).

Superstition was at the core of religion. Scapularies, medals, bits of
clothes, and bags of relics hung around the necks of many officers going
to war. During the war with the United States, the Polkos, a company
of idle youths who raised the standard of revolt against the liberals when
the latter endeavored to seize church property, exhibited on their chests
so many pious tokens that, according to José Fernando Ramírez, the
minister of foreign affairs in 1847, "anyone unacquainted with our customs" would have thought that he was "in a camp of martyrs of the
Faith" (Ramírez 1950, 106).

Mexicans wore them less as a shield against an enemy bullet than as
a ticket to enter heaven. The fear of burning in hell forever, or at the
very least, of being exiled in a gloomy purgatory for so long a time that
the human mind could not even imagine it, prompted individuals to
place themselves under the protection of the Virgin and the blissful
saints; sources of comfort and compassion, they were ever ready to in-
tercede with God Almighty on their behalf.

An easy way to get a foothold in heaven was through charitable
works, alms, and donations. Mexicans, and more specifically Mexican
women, were celebrated for their kindness and their generosity. Yet the
fact that so many persons bequeathed large amounts of money to the
church on their deathbeds seems to indicate that a last-minute donation
could set ajar the gates of heaven, and unscrupulous priests too often
took advantage of the situation in urging the dying to invest heavily in
salvation. As Ernest Gruening observed, "Abuse of death-bed confes-

sions to the destitution of legitimate heirs was notorious both in Spain and in New Spain" (Gruening 1928, 183).

HOLY WEEK

The double influence, Spanish and Indian, was felt in the rituals and fiestas that stood as milestones in the life of the Mexican. The Mexican church was a church of emotion where the unflagging faith of the Indian mingled with the tormented mysticism of the Spaniard; during a fiesta, the Mexican expressed himself as freely and emotionally as possible. Just as there was no fixed boundary between Christianity and paganism in Mexican ceremonies, so too, there was no clear line between joy and sorrow. "The night of a fiesta is also a night of mourning," observed Octavio Paz (Paz [1950] 1959, 47). In the tumult of a night of fiesta, life and death merged into one another.

It was probably during Holy Week that the syncretism of the Christian and Aztec religions and cultures achieved the most interesting results. The festivities marked the swing from life to death, then from death to life with prayers, dances, rattles, fireworks, processions, and folk dramas. There was often rivalry between villages in the splendor of the festivities, for the preparation of which Indians devoted much of their time and money. Palm Sunday was usually celebrated with a procession in which a wooden image of Christ seated on an ass was borne through the village to the church. In the *tierra caliente*, said Carl Sartorius, the Indians called this image San Ramos. The village streets were decorated with flowers and palm branches, and "the most lugubrious music" was heard. At sunset on Holy Thursday the villagers carried in a procession a large image of Christ dressed in violet-colored silk or velvet, and incense was burned around the church, just as the Aztecs had burned copal around the temples of their gods. The apostles made their appearance, either as statues or played by Indians dressed in character (Sartorius [1858] 1961, 155–56).

On Good Friday, the culminating point of the whole festival was the crucifixion procession. To the music of drums and fifes, penitents led the way. Some were in shrouds; others wore the crown of thorns, skulls in hand; still others marched with their hands tied behind them and a rope around their necks, or carrying crosses of human bones. They were followed by the image of the Saviour, surrounded by Roman guards and the Pharisees. Then came the faithful, carrying an image of the Holy Virgin. In the great square, in front of the church, the padre described in vivid terms the treachery of the Pharisees, the condemnation and the suffering of the innocent God, and the grief of the Virgin, while sighs and groans were heard in the crowd. Women sobbed openly, and men stroked their faces to show their contrition.

But on Sábado de Gloria all rejoiced. Judas, the archtraitor, had to be punished; he had to expire in fire and smoke. Early in the morning, effigies of Judas filled with firecrackers were exploded, and everyone started dancing and singing around the huge bonfire (Sartorius [1858] 1961, 157–59).

In many villages Good Friday was marked by a folk drama. In Patos, headquarters of the Sánchez Navarros' latifundio, a sham battle between Christians and Indians was part of the festivities. The Christians had rifles; the Indians, who wore masks and headdresses capped with feathers, were armed with bows and arrows (Harris 1964, 37).

The festivities of Passion Week in the capital were also a blend of the sacred and the profane, the religious and the burlesque. Preparations were made for several days before Palm Sunday, and often Indians flocked to Mexico City from great distances to bring palm branches and flowers to decorate shrines and altars, as well as to adorn the houses, streets, plazas, and even the innumerable *pulquerías*. On the morning of Palm Sunday everyone went to church. "The whole cathedral presented the appearance of a forest of palm-trees, . . ." reports Frances Calderón. "Each palm was about seven feet high, so as far to overshadow the head of the Indian who carried it; and whenever they are blessed, they are carried home to adorn the walls of their huts" (Calderón de la Barca [1843] 1931, 129).

From Palm Sunday on, and for a whole week, all business stopped; shops were closed, and a large proportion of the inhabitants of the Valley of Mexico repaired to the city. "About the evening of Wednesday," said Charles J. Latrobe, "the scene on the Plaza Mayor, in front of the cathedral, baffles all description" (Latrobe 1836, 119). The plaza was crowded with people of all classes and all ages, and before the palace, and in front of the *portales*, bamboo frameworks were erected, thatched by matting and shut by palm leaves and other foliages. In these booths were sold "refreshments, and liquors of various kinds—lemonade, pinade, a liquor called *chea*, and *pulque*," as well as dulces, "for which the city is celebrated." Some booths were large enough to offer seats and tables to the consumer. All were tastefully ornamented with flowers, and at night illuminated with lamps, tapers, and torches.

"The trade of the fair—for fair it was—seemed to be chiefly in the hands of Indians, or those in whom the Indian blood predominated"

(Latrobe 1836, 120). The crowd thickened hour after hour, day after day. On Holy Thursday the bells stopped tolling, carriages disappeared from the streets, and "the richest ladies being on foot," writes Frances Calderón, "take the opportunity of displaying all the riches of their toilet." In the words of the witty Scottish wife of the Spanish minister, "Diamonds and pearls walk the streets" (Calderón de la Barca [1843] 1931, 130).

They mingled on the plaza with half-naked Indians with babies on their backs, wealthy *rancheros* in bright costumes, and pretty *poblanas* in their holiday dresses. Shrouded in their mantillas, the rich ladies went on foot from church to church, in accordance with the ritual that enjoined them to visit as many churches as possible during forty-eight hours. Frances Calderón noted that among the "lower classes" the worship was emphatically the worship of the Virgin. "Before her shrines, and at all hours, thousands are kneeling," she wrote. "With faces expressive of the most intense love and devotion, they address the mild image of the Mother of God. To the Son their feelings seem composed of respectful pity, of humble but more distant adoration" (Calderón de la Barca [1843] 1931, 129). The priests blazed in gold and jewels, and the churches, illuminated by thousands of candles, were decorated with orange trees, shrubberies, and flowers.

At night there was a procession. The Virgin, the saints, the Holy Trinity, the Savior bearing the cross, the Savior crucified, angels, and apostles were carried past in succession.

Good Friday was a day of sorrow and humiliation, and the scene in the city dramatically changed. The ladies attended church in black, and the churches presented their most gloomy aspect: the altars were despoiled of their rich ornaments and veiled with black draperies; the organs were as mute as the bells. But in the streets, the hubbub was extraordinary. The vendors still plied their trade, a military band could be heard, and the noise of the innumerable *matracas*, or rattles, with which everyone in Mexico was armed during the last days of Holy Week, filled the air from morning till night.

In the afternoon the scenes of the Passion were enacted in churches and, according to Charles J. Latrobe, "turned into comedy; while waltzes and contradances were played over the bier, on which the effigy of our Saviour was laid out in state" (Latrobe 1936, 123). Latrobe, being a Protestant, may have been somewhat prejudiced, but José Fernando Ramírez, watching a procession on Good Friday, wrote, "It becomes obvious that Christianity has degenerated into gross idolatry, and that out-

and-out ugly polytheism is the only religion of the priesthood and of the people" (Ramírez 1950, 114).

In the evening the booths commenced the sale of fireworks in the form of the archtraitor Judas Iscariot, which were to be let off on Saturday morning. Hundreds of these figures, varying in size and monstrosity, were seen tied together by the neck, dangling and bobbing from long poles over the heads of the multitude. Some were a foot long, others were the size of a human figure; all were painted in bright colors. And there were more processions in the streets, more Virgins in glory or in grief, more saints and angels and dragons and glittering figures, and more sale of pulque and other refreshments for the faithful.

At an early hour on Saturday the deep bell of the cathedral tolled; the trumpet and organ struck up; the dark veils disappeared from the altars. As the artillery thundered on the Plaza Mayor, the bells of every church in the city echoed the cathedral chiming, and the Judases exploded by the thousand.

In less than an hour the streets resounded again with the roll of carriages and the clapping of hoofs on the pavement; the reopening of the opera was publicly announced; people talked about bullfights and balls and parties. The time of humiliation and sorrow was over. Life had won over death. "On Easter Sunday," wrote Carl Sartorius, "every-day life recommences with dancing and jollity" (Sartorius [1858] 1961, 159).

CHAPTER TEN

EDUCATION AND CULTURE

In the midst of so many causes of backwardness, the country has nevertheless made notable progress, not so much owing to the impetus of government as to the overcoming of obstacles which institutions and political difficulties have imposed.—Lucas Alamán

The conservative historian Lucas Alamán in making that appraisal of Mexico as he saw it in 1852 was speaking generally of cultural attainments from education to the arts. The optimism for the new republic shared by the intellectuals in 1821 was by then tempered by the reality of years of turmoil and unrest. Alamán lamented the lack of a national plan for education and the resulting poor distribution of schools, the insufficient number of qualified teachers, and the tendency to stress training in law, as if more lawyers were needed, instead of training in the arts or agriculture. And yet "great effort had been expended in public instruction," he asserted, "and no country even the most advanced of Europe dispensed free education in all its forms more abundantly than did Mexico" (Alamán [1849–52] 1942, 5:842). Certain achievements were apparent. People in general knew how to write better. The quality of newspapers and of printed works was much improved since the early years of independence.

Mexico had always recognized the importance of education. The first law governing public education in Mexico, the General Regulations for Public Instruction, was passed in 1821. Its framers were strongly influenced by the liberal 1813 laws of the Cortes of Spain, which had abolished the guilds, including those for primary teachers. Now anyone who wished could open a school with a minimum of regulation from the Mexican government. The number of schools increased, but in effect, quantity took precedence over quality. And we have seen in chapter 8 how bad the quality could be in Indian villages.

The Constitution of 1824, reflecting a federalist philosophy, designated a few schools of higher learning for the teaching of natural sciences, arts, and languages, but left responsibility for public education to state legislatures. This mandate was discharged in as many ways as there were states. In general, it came to be that city governments maintained free elementary schools and examined public school teachers and, at times, private school teachers as well. With the new Constitution of 1836 the central government was empowered to regulate education throughout the republic (Salvat Editores de México, S.A. 1974, 7: 238–39), but uniformity of regulation was never achieved.

An interesting, albeit incomplete, chart of statistics for 1845 from the Ministry of Justice and Public Education shows the number of primary students and schools throughout the country. Most schools were public; only a fifth of them were private. The chart shows that 2,200 students in Zacatecas attended 56 schools; 3,260 students in Puebla attended 38 schools; while in the state of Mexico a whopping 46,698 students attended 960 schools (Salvat Editores de México, S.A. 1974, 7:252). The effort at least to provide education for all is evident.

PRIMARY EDUCATION

Numerous types of schooling existed: private tutoring at home for the very rich; private schools for boys and girls, together or separately; private and free church schools for both sexes; the schools called Amigas; and the popular monitorial, or Lancasterian, schools. Elementary education seldom encompassed more than the teaching of reading, writing, arithmetic, Christian doctrine, civics, and sometimes, drawing. Girls were taught the fine arts of sewing and embroidery as well as the core curriculum (Salvat Editores de México, S.A. 1974, 7:239). At that point formal training ended for most girls. Frances Calderón surprised a lady one day by asking if her daughter went to school. "Good Heavens!" she replied in shock, "she is past eleven years old!" (Calderón de la Barca [1843] 1931, 221–22).

Thinking back to his childhood days, the Mexican writer Antonio García Cubas wrote of his experiences in the Amiga that he attended with an older sister. His teacher, typical of her kind, was a somewhat elderly lady with white hair piled high on her head in a knot. She made her living by holding classes in her home for young girls, including a few, very young boys. Her living room served as the classroom.

The method of instruction, as in all Amigas, was individual. One by one, beginning with the slowest, each pupil approached the teacher and opened the *Silabario del Niño Jesús*, the "Speller of the Baby Jesus," on her lap. As the teacher indicated the first page with a pointer, the child would begin "Jesus and the Cross, and the one that follows is A" (García Cubas 1904, 401–2). Then on to the letter B, pointing and pronouncing. The alphabet was completed in this way. Next came the syllables, then whole words, until little by little, day by day, the entire monotonous reader was completed. That achievement was an occasion for celebration, which the family of the fortunate pupil, according to its means, observed with candy and cakes for all the children.

The pupils were also exposed daily to the precepts of Christian doctrine, as set forth in the catechism of Father Gerónimo Ripalda. They learned the words if not the meaning by listening to the teacher and repeating her singsong in chorus, with the same stress on the last syllable of each verse.

On Saturdays the teacher rested from her labors, but nevertheless received her pupils, who presented her with their weekly tuition. This was usually one peseta, accompanied perhaps by some small gift. She in turn rewarded the most diligent with such trifles as colored paper lanterns (García Cubas 1904, 402).

One day the audacious Antonio dared plant a kiss on the cheek of one of the little girls, within sight of the horrified teacher. She obliged the offender to kneel on the floor and to remain with arms extended in a cross. Not satisfied with this punishment, she advised the boy's sister not to return to the Amiga with her brother. And so young Antonio next found himself in Father Zapata's school for boys (García Cubas 1904, 403).

Small private boys' schools were common. If the school was large enough, the school master had one or two assistants. Pupils were divided into two groups: one for those just learning to read, and the other for more advanced readers who were perfecting their writing. Large charts hung on the walls illustrating the styles of writing. The boys sat at tables with paper they had previously lined with a ruler. Their pens were bird feathers which had been carefully sharpened by the teacher. Only the most advanced pupils used pen and ink; beginners practiced on slates. Lessons were recited aloud, sometimes in a low voice, sometimes in a scream (Salvat Editores de México, S.A. 1974, 240). Joel Poinsett commented on a school he visited where on a "half dozen low benches, were ten or twelve little urchins, all repeating their lessons at the same time, as loud as they could bawl" (Poinsett 1824, 190). The school master stalked about the room, rod in hand, and though he had never traveled beyond his place of birth, he was held in great respect by the villagers.

Such small schools were completely inadequate for educating masses of children. A new method was needed and was found: the Lancasterian system of monitorial education, a system originally devised by Joseph Lancaster of England.

LANCASTERIAN SCHOOLS

If anything could be called a unifying force in nineteenth-century Mexico, it was surely devotion to the Lancasterian ideal. The Lancasterian Company counted among its members such diverse figures as Antonio López de Santa Anna, conservative Lucas Alamán, liberal José Luis Mora, the bishops of both Puebla and Michoacán, and the Conde de la Cortina. They looked upon this system, in which one head teacher, with the aid of numerous advanced students, could supervise the studies of several hundred pupils at once, as the great hope for extending free public education across Mexico. Early fears that the company was too closely identified with Masons and anti-Catholics soon melted when it became clear that there was no intention of eliminating the teaching of the Catholic religion from the curriculum (Salvat Editores de México, S.A. 1974, 7:243).

In 1822 the company with contributions of its members established the first Lancasterian school in the former quarters of the Inquisition in Mexico City. A year later a second school for over 600 students was opened in the old Bethlehemite convent (Wilson [1941] 1974, 134–38). More Lancasterian schools for both boys and girls sprang up not only in the capital but in other parts of the country, especially Guadalajara and Guanajuato (Wilson [1941] 1974, 139). They gained such popularity that in 1842 the Lancasterian Company was placed in complete charge of public instruction, and it continued so until nearly the end of the century. Not until May, 1890, was the system officially abandoned (Wilson [1941] 1974, 143).

Antonio García Cubas, who also attended a Lancasterian school for a short time, wrote of the intricacies of a typical day's schedule, where discipline, conformity, and the rule of the bell prevailed: "At eight in the morning we gathered at the school, and before entering the classroom we lined up in a long, narrow corridor. An inspector, armed with a little bell which indicated all the various activities of the school, made the cleanliness inspection" (García Cubas 1904, 403–4). All hands were extended and the inspector gave a sharp blow with the bell to any hands he found dirty or with long nails.

The slow sound of the bell then directed the boys in military formation to the classroom, which was filled with row upon row of long tables with attached benches. The instructors, called *monitores* or *decuriones*, were already standing there at the right of their respective benches, near signs on poles, called *telégrafos*, that displayed the letters to be copied. These instructors had arrived earlier to receive coaching from the teacher on the lessons of the day. His desk faced the benches on an elevated platform at the front. At the command of the inspector, all students faced their tables, removed their hats, knelt and prayed together that the Almighty would bless their studies. Then they rose to begin work. "Simultaneously they moved their right leg between the bench and table, then the left, and immediately sat down. Lastly they placed their hands first on their knees and then on the tables" (García Cubas 1904, 404). Classes could now commence.

The first lesson, writing, was taught at eight levels. The youngest pupils did not have the regular, slightly inclined wooden tables, but long, low, horizontal boxes that were filled from one end to the other with fine sand. Seated on one side of the box, the ten children assigned to one instructor watched as he drew a letter in the sand, then they traced over it. When the letter was learned, they drew it without his help. In later lessons the instructor would call attention to letters written on the *telégrafo*. In a very special high, slow voice he would say, "First class. Attention. Capital A" (García Cubas 1904, 404). And the children would draw the indicated letter with their finger or pointer for his approval. Capital letters were practiced in the morning, small letters in the afternoon.

In the next five, more-advanced sections of writing, students used slates to take down dictation of whole words of from one to five syllables (Salvat Editores de México, S.A. 1974, 7:242). Always the lesson was preceded by the commands "hands on knees, hands on table, present slates and chalk, clean slates" (García Cubas, 1904, 404). To avoid confusion and to preserve order, the instructor of the first class dictated his word first, and each instructor in turn, down the line, waited until the preceding instructor's orders were concluded before giving his. After three words, a call to "examine" was issued by the teacher, and appropriate inspection was made. Only at the seventh and eighth levels were students permitted to use pen and ink. They improved their penmanship and learned something of morality and manners by copying great works and sayings (Salvat Editores de México, S.A. 1974, 242).

Reading followed writing, and at the sound of the bell all students rose from their tables and walked to the aisles where they grouped themselves in semicircles—in a procedure called "evolution," executed in three minutes in complete silence. *Telégrafos* designated the various levels, with the number of the class on one side and the letters *EX* for exam on the other. With bamboo pointers the instructors indicated letters, words, or readings written on large posters hung on the wall, and the students responded aloud (Salvat Editores de México, S.A. 1974, 7:242). Advanced classes read such works as *The Historical Catechism of Abbot Fleury* (García Cubas 1904, 405).

Arithmetic followed. Beginners used blackboards, while the higher classes used slates and extended their mathematical studies to include fractions and the rule of three (García Cubas 1904, 405). A half hour was spent at the benches and a quarter hour in semicircles reciting the multiplication tables (Salvat Editores de México, S.A. 1974, 7:243).

Semicircles were likewise employed in teaching the lesson in Christian doctrine, where the catechism was memorized. The best-prepared child occupied the place of honor in his semicircle, but if he failed to respond correctly, the honor went to the child who could (Salvat Editores de México 1974, 7:242).

Two hours were allowed for lunch, and school was dismissed shortly before five o'clock. But first, all slates were collected and the children were ordered to kneel for a closing prayer. Again the bell was rung, and at successive peals the boys donned their hats, put their hands straight down their trousers seams, and as their names were called, formed a line against the wall closest to the teacher's platform. Here they listened to the punishments to be imposed that day, and then, in order according to the eight classes, they followed their instructors out of the school into the street, free and rejoicing (García Cubas 1904, 406).

Rewards and punishments were keys in the Lancasterian system. A disobedient child might have a sign placed around his neck that said "Pig" or "Naughty" or "Gossiper" or "Unruly", or he might be made to kneel extending his arms in a cross, as was young Antonio in the Amiga. If the offense was more serious, he might receive a whipping. But along with such disciplinary actions, an effort was made to keep the child constantly so busy learning new things in his small group that he would not be bored. To that end each child was examined individually every month by the teacher, and those who mastered one level in a particular subject advanced to the next, with the promotion noted in the register. In this way a child could be in an advanced reading group, an intermediate writing group, and an elementary arithmetic group simultaneously. Ability, not age, determined placement (Salvat Editores de México, S.A. 1974, 243).

For all its merits the Lancasterian system was not without its opponents, who complained about the regimentation and the punishments. More basic defects were the lack of qualified teachers and the lack of uniformity in books and methods (Wilson [1941] 1974, 142). At least one Lancasterian school, the Filantropía of Mexico City, was organized with an entire division dedicated to teaching the theory and practice of monitorial instruction. This normal school for over 400 students was conducted at night at a cost of two pesos, a fee that could be waived by the municipal government (Wilson [1941] 1974, 138–39).

A further division of the Filantropía was on a secondary level, with instruction for 300 people in lineal drawing, geography, history, mythology, French, Latin, and mathematics—all for three pesos (Wilson [1941] 1974, 138). García Cubas could recall four Lancasterian schools in Mexico City for boys, five for girls, one mixed, and a night school for adults (García Cubas 1904, 407). The Lancasterian system seemed to have no limits.

SECONDARY EDUCATION AND BEYOND

Instruction beyond the elementary level did not often follow the Lancasterian path. *Colegios* for secondary education—including four in the capital and eight in the provinces, as well as ten seminaries—had survived from the colonial period. Those were gradually augmented by new literary and scientific institutes throughout the country. Their curriculums were expanded to include courses such as modern languages, drawing, and more emphasis on science (Salvat Editores de México, S.A. 1974, 7:244).

Any student pursuing a regular course of study could enter a *colegio* or institute; the Colegio de San Ildefonso, for example, which Luis Gonzaga Gordoa attended, or the Colegio de San Gregorio, attended by Antonio García Cubas. For the first two years he would study Latin grammar, struggling from the lowest level of the *mínimos* up through the *menores* and then the *medianos*. At last he might arrive at the level of the *mayores*, in what García Cubas called the *colegio chico* (García Cubas 1904, 414). There he was confronted with three years of elementary philosophy and classes in logic, math and physics, and perhaps history, political economy, or geography. After completion of the five years of preparatory classes, he was ready to begin his professional studies in one of four fields: law, theology, medicine, or science. The length of professional study depended on the school, but varied from three to six years. In San Gregorio four years were required for the study of law, in what García Cubas termed the *colegio grande* (García Cubas 1904, 415). The happy conclusion of professional studies entitled the student to the benefits of a bachelor's degree.

That pinnacle of learning was not easily attained, as may be perceived in García Cubas's memoirs. If the old adage of the time was true that "education enters with blood" (García Cubas 1904, 413), García Cubas felt assured that the Colegio de San Gregorio excelled. A new resident student at the school had first to arrange his possessions in one of the six dormitories of the *colegio chico*, assigned to him by the teacher in charge of housing, the *maestro de aposentos*. He had to mark all his books on page fifty with his designated number. He had to brave the sneers and tricks of his classmates and adjust to the nickname that they were sure to bestow on him according to his characteristics or defects. A student with an insipient beard was the "Goat"; one with bright eyes, the "Rat"; one who was overweight, the "Hippopotamus." And he had to accustom himself to the formal black dress and top hat required of all San Gregorians no matter how small, which caused them to be known as the "Buzzards" (García Cubas 1904, 421).

As in a Lancasterian school, a student's every move was ordered by bells. At dawn they summoned him to forsake his bed and go out into the patio to wash. He then performed whatever housekeeping chore he had been assigned, before attending mass. Only then were he and his companions served breakfast in the refectory—a cup of chocolate, a piece of bread, and a dish of white corn-flour *atole*. Four bells at nine o'clock announced Latin lessons, which had to be recited from memory with no stuttering or fluster. For those who failed—twenty blows on the palm with a ruler. García Cubas in one class witnessed fifty such blows administered to the bottom of the feet of one student whose hands were too toughened to be sensitive. Speaking from experience, he added, blows to the hands ceased to hurt after the first eight or ten; the hand simply went to sleep. He hastened to add that these punishments were not owing to his bad memory in Latin but rather to the natural distractions of boys (García Cubas 1904, 414). The rigorous discipline of the *colegio chico* was more relaxed in the *colegio grande*, and the reliance on memory alone was supplemented with appropriate explanations by learned professors.

Until that stage in his education, the beginning student in the *colegio chico* learned to conform to the bells. He relaxed after Latin in a period of rough-and-tumble play with his classmates in the patio. He prepared afternoon classes until midday, when he was served his meal of soup, stew, beans, bread, tortilla, a piece of fruit, and occasionally some pastry—but only after the older students of the *colegio grande* had eaten. The afternoon brought a choice between drawing and music, then more vigorous games, more study, a recitation of the rosary, the evening meal, and still more study, until nine o'clock, when the bells called all students back to their dimly lit rooms for the night (García Cubas 1904, 416–17).

Throughout their years at San Gregorio all students were required to perform assigned duties, whether ringing the bells, helping in the library, or singing in the choir at mass. And they were subject to severe, even cruel, punishments for misconduct (García Cubas 1904, 418). Whippings, confinement in the damp basement, denial of food, these were the measures employed by the rector to maintain order. On the other hand, those students who excelled in their classes received public recognition. The same general conditions prevailed in all Mexican *colegios* of the time.

Efforts to educate the Indians were, as has been discussed in chapter 8, inadequate. Much was said, but little was accomplished. It is interesting to note that Luis Gonzaga Gordoa, as a deputy in 1824, put himself on record as opposing any policy that would isolate Indians. He believed that they should be educated in regular *colegios*, where they could benefit from example, from better teaching, and from useful friendships (*El Sol*, no. 484, October 10, 1824, 470). With that view in mind, Gordoa opposed a law that awarded the assets of the defunct Royal Hospital to the Colegio de San Gregorio, which was to provide free education to two or more Indians from each state. He preferred that the funds go to his alma mater, San Ildefonso. San Gregorio indeed had been founded in the sixteenth century by the Jesuits as a school for Indians, but Antonio García Cubas in writing about his school days there failed to mention the presence of any Indians.

THE UNIVERSITY OF MEXICO

Above and apart from the *colegios* was the venerable National and Pontifical University of Mexico. Founded in 1554, it had fallen into a decline by the time of the republic and was even closed briefly during the 1833 reforms of Gómez Farías.

The purpose of the university was to complete or to improve upon the studies at the *colegios* (García Cubas 1904, 399). A student with a bachelor's degree did not necessarily take any classes at the university. It served more an honorary than a teaching function. The classes it occasionally offered merely duplicated those at the professional level in the *colegios*. However, the degree of *licenciado* was awarded by the university to those who had practiced their professions for some years or had expanded their knowledge through private study or teaching and had sucessfully presented themselves for examination at the university (Salvat Editores de México, S.A. 1974, 7:248). Similarly, the degree of doctor could be conferred upon those holding the *licenciatura*.

Before receiving any degree, a candidate would customarily be subjected to a period of taunting and ridicule, including idiotic and stupid, even humiliating, questions in ceremonies called *vejámenes*. He would afterwards be properly honored. These ceremonies became so abusive that they were eliminated completely, and then the various *colegios* competed with one another in the pomp and lavishness with which awards were presented (García Cubas 1904, 399).

Graduates of the School of Mining, which required practical experience at Pachuca, could obtain higher degrees in science at the university, which thus produced excellent engineers, geologists, and assayers, according to García Cubas (García Cubas 1904, 401). However, Lucas Alamán, himself a mining engineer, deplored the difficulty of finding men capable of directing the operations of a mine. The School of Medicine, on the other hand, he said, had no lack of bright, industrious students (Alamán [1849–52] 1942, 5:842). Away from Mexico City complete professional courses in both medicine and law were offered at the universities of Guadalajara, Mérida, and Chiapas (Salvat Editores de México, S.A. 1974, 7:248).

Training in the fine arts was the mission of the prestigious Academy of San Carlos in Mexico City, which had been founded in 1785 and was supported by the crown. Drawing, painting, sculpture, architecture, and mathematics were taught by European masters in the prevailing neo-classical style. One at once recalls the indestructible equestrian bronze statue of Carlos IV, the masterpiece of Manuel Tolsá, who was the Spanish director of sculpture and architecture at San Carlos.

Prestigious as San Carlos was during the viceroyalty, it was forced to close its doors after independence for lack of money. In 1822, Joel Poinsett remarked sadly as he looked around the academy, "We saw a long line of benches and desks, with designs and models for the pupils, as if they had left them yesterday, whereas no lessons have been given here for more than twelve months past" (Poinsett 1824, 72). The academy opened again in 1824 and limped along in pathetic penury, all but bankrupt, for nearly twenty years. Brantz Mayer in 1842 lamented the "miserable condition" (Mayer 1844, 271) of the institution, which had been enthusiastically praised by Humboldt earlier in the century. Fanny Calderón, referring to "the abandoned state of the building" and the absence of the formerly "excellent classes of sculpture and painting," concluded that "the low state of the fine arts in Mexico, at the present day, are amongst the sad proofs . . . of the melancholy effect produced by years of civil war and unsettled government" (Calderón de la Barca [1843] 1931, 128). Yet those "dark ages" (Charlot 1962, 69) of the academy between 1824 and 1843 may well have contributed more to the art of the new nation than anyone then imagined.

ART

At its inception the Academy of San Carlos had been subject to the cultural dictates and orthodoxy of Spain. After its reorganization in 1843 it was governed by German aesthetics transmitted by way of Rome and Barcelona. Only in the intervening twenty years was the academy free to develop its own concept of Mexican art (Charlot 1962, 69–70). It is significant that the first general director of the academy chosen after independence was the sculptor Pedro Patiño Ixtolinque, a full-blooded Indian and a hero in the wars for independence. His nationalism may be discerned in his choice of themes, if not his aesthetics. In honoring the revolutionary hero José María Morelos, for example, he carved the figure of an Indian woman. That she was depicted in the Greco-Roman style reveals his neoclassical training; however, he was able to impart more freedom of expression to his students, such as Vicente Montiel, in whose works "the first stirrings of a national art" are evident (Charlot 1962, 72).

Later, young students of painting, who had been born citizens of the new republic, worked under the direction of Miguel Mata, whose influence pointed toward romanticism and away from neoclassism. Primitivo Miranda was one such student, and Juan Cordero was another. Both were nurtured at San Carlos during the academy's lean years. Both managed on their own at different times to study at the Academy of San Lucas in Rome. After the Academy of San Carlos was reorganized, both received pensions to continue their studies in Rome, where they won prizes and gained recognition. Both returned triumphant to Mexico City to find the academy so completely restructured and restaffed that they were little more than intruders. For Miranda this spelled obscurity, for Cordero challenge.

The changes at the academy were due in no small part to Santa Anna, who in 1843 signed the presidential decree that outlined the provisions of the reorganization. Directors of painting, sculpture, and engraving, with yearly salaries of 3,000 pesos, were to be selected from among the leading artists of Europe—there was to be no more room for Mexican nationals. Support for the new academy was to come from the proceeds of the national lottery, which proved to be more than sufficient. With this funding the building was repaired and later purchased, gas was installed, live models and mannequins were made available, scholarships were offered, annual competitions were held, and the most promising students were awarded study abroad (Charlot 1962, 108; Fernández 1983, 41–42). The latter provision maintained Miranda and Cordero in Italy.

Assuming the new position of director of painting was the Spaniard Pelegrín Clavé, a Catalan influenced strongly by the French painter Jean Auguste Dominique Ingres and the German painter Johann Friedrich Overbeck. Clavé in turn influenced a generation of Mexican painters who flourished in the second half of the century. He favored religious and historical subjects, but excelled primarily as a portraitist of the upper class in Mexico City (Salvat Editores de México, S.A. 1974, 7:229). Portrait painting was much in vogue. Pelegrín Clavé is credited with a fine portrait of Antonio Eugenio Gordoa, brother of the deputy, now in a private collection in Zacatecas. A major portion of Clavé's works were produced, and remained, in Mexico.

Rivalry between Clavé and Juan Cordero was inevitable. It was hotly disputed which was the better painter. At the time opinions were drawn along political lines: the liberals favored the Mexican Cordero, while the conservatives preferred the Spanish Clavé. It is clear that Cordero was

Don Antonio Eugenio Gordoa. Painting attributed to Pelegrín Clavé. Courtesy Federico Sescosse.

the more versatile of the two. His fame rested not only on his considerable ability as a portraitist, as seen in his painting of Doña Dolores Tosta
de Santa Anna, called the "most Mexican painting which the XIX century produced" (Fernández 1983, 69). His *Colón ante los Reyes Católicos,*
or "Columbus before Ferdinand and Isabella," was the first historical
painting with an American theme exhibited in the capital, preceding
Clavé's *Isabel de Portugal* by four years (Fernández 1983, 67). Cordero
also led the way in the painting of murals, with *Jesús entre los doctores*
for the church of Jesús María. He and his supporters staunchly believed
he should replace Clavé as director of painting at San Carlos, and he
even convinced Santa Anna of his error in excluding nationals from the
academy faculty. However, before any appointment could be implemented, Santa Anna was in his final exile, and the officers of the
academy who favored Clavé prevailed.

A vast array of art was produced outside the sphere of influence of
the academy by a succession of foreigners who were irresistibly attracted
to Mexico by the writings of Humboldt. Topping the list perhaps was
the Italian Claudio Linati, who arrived in 1825 and set up Mexico's first
lithographic studio, which was later acquired by the academy when
Linati returned to Europe. From the studio he published a set of hand-
illuminated lithographs, *Costumes de Mexique,* which with great charm
and accuracy depict the complete range of Mexican types from priest to
soldier.

Other European artists came after Linati. Frederic Waldeck, from
Prague, found inspiration for his drawings in the antiquities of pre-
Columbian Mexico. Others such as Daniel Thomas Egerton, of England,
Carl Nebel, of Germany, Jean Moritz Rugendas, of Germany, and Frederick Catherwood, who accompanied John Stephens, recorded the
beauty of the Mexican landscape, Mexican characters and customs, and
the archaeological ruins.

Away from the capital and throughout the provinces the popular art
of anonymous painters was thriving. Oblivious to the standards of aca-
demic art, they painted *retablos* and the heroes and events of the wars
of independence to their own liking. A few artists made names for themselves. José María Estrada became known for his portraits, and Agustín
Arrieta for his faithful portrayal of scenes of daily life, scenes of the
market, the kitchen, and the tavern. These popular painters may have
succeeded even more than the academics in creating truly Mexican art
(Salvat Editores de México, S.A. 1974, 7:230).

MUSIC

Mexican music evolved in the same manner as the fine arts. During the first half of the nineteenth century popular music flourished while classical music remained in the doldrums (Campos 1928, 159–60). Anonymous musicians who did not even put their songs on paper left melodies destined to become a part of Mexican life: "Las mañanitas," "El durazno," "La pasadita," "El tapatío," and many, many more (Campos 1928, 160). These songs were indeed a reflexion of the times that produced them, telling of love, losses, death, war, and humor; they became part of the everyday life of the people at fiestas, or wherever there was music and dancing. This spontaneous and melodic music may have received some inspiration from the arias of the Italian operas that were widely admired across the land at the time (Campos 1928, 160).

Foreign influences were more apparent at cultivated levels of society where foreign composers, foreign operas, foreign artists, and foreign teachers ruled the day. This was not so surprising, since with independence came the first opportunities for foreign musicians to make appearances in Mexico. It was taken for granted that every young lady of the upper classes would have lessons in singing or on an instrument. Her teacher more likely than not was a foreigner, who probably had advertised his services in the newspaper (Salvat Editores de México, S.A. 1974, 7:224). In the concert hall the works of Mozart, Beethoven, and Handel were well known, and the perennial favorite operas were Italian. Traveling opera companies from France and Italy made Mexico City one of their regular stops. Frances Calderón, who during her two-year stay in Mexico attended nearly every opera presented, mentioned specifically seeing *Lucia de Lammermoor*, by Donizetti, *Giulietta e Romeo*, by Vaccai, and *La Sonnambula*, by Bellini (Calderón de la Barca [1843] 1931, 390, 391, 407, 444). Among the foreign artists who entertained on the concert stage, a great favorite was the luckless Spanish tenor Manuel García, who arrived in 1827. Even more widely acclaimed was the beautiful German opera singer Henriette Sontag, whose fate it was while on tour in North America in 1854 to contract cholera and die in Mexico.

The love of the Mexicans for good music was as obvious as were their natural musical talents. Antonio García Cubas put it quite poetically when he observed to his readers that Mexicans had always adored the muse Euterpe and therefore it was not at all strange that so many distinguished Mexican musicians had been favored by that divine muse (García Cubas 1904, 518). Though it would not be until later in the century that Mexican composers achieved fame and a Mexican opera was performed, Mexicans were gradually taking their rightful place in the world of music. Professional and amateur musicians regularly participated in religious and civic celebrations (Salvat Editores de México, S.A. 1974, 7:226). In 1825 the Sociedad Filarmónica was founded by composer and music educator Mariano Elízaga, and in 1839 the Gran Sociedad was founded by José Antonio Gómez. These two organizations, and later the Sociedad Filarmónica Mexicana, would eventually lead to the founding of the National Conservatory in 1866 (Campos 1928, 168). Mariano Elízaga deserves particular recognition also for his contribution in the founding in 1826 of the first music press in Mexico capable of reproducing the conventional staff. His "Valse with Variations" was the first work printed (Stevenson [1952] 1971, 188–89).

The first Mexican pianist to appear on stage with visiting foreign artists was Tomás León in the mid-1850s. García Cubas recalled the many musical evenings he spent at the home of Tomás León, and one occasion remained fixed in his memory. León and a fellow musician were playing as a piano duet Beethoven's Pastoral Symphony, in which the pleasures of an idyllic country scene are interrupted by an oncoming storm. At the peak of the musical tempest, executed with all the required vigor by the two pianists, the heavens opened and torrents of rain beat down upon the window panes. A tremendous bolt of lightning struck nearby, shaking the gathering and adding to their appreciation of the composer's phrases. Little by little the real and the imitation rainstorms subsided until complete tranquility was again restored and a tender and melancholic hymn of thanksgiving closed the presentation (García Cubas 1904, 519–20).

At about this same time, in 1854, Henriette Sontag on her final tour in Mexico City met and applauded the nine-year-old Angela Peralta, whose prodigious voice and talent were later to triumph on the operatic stages of Europe and to capture the hearts of her adoring fellow Mexicans (Campos 1928, 216–18). An angel in name and voice, Angela Peralta was the first Mexican musician to gain international renown.

The year 1854, as we have mentioned, also saw the culmination of a prolonged search for a national hymn. Frustrated attempts had been made since 1849 to put together the magic combination of poetry and music that would gain public approval. Finally, on September 16, 1854, the words of poet Francisco González Bocanegra and the music of Jaime

Nunó, both chosen in open competition, were heard for the first time in concert at the National Theater (Baqueiro Foster 1964, 1:567). And Santa Anna was there to make it all official.

LITERATURE

Nowhere was the freedom achieved with independence more obvious than in literature. As in art and music, the constraints of colonialism gave way to the expression of new feelings and ideas, which would attain full flower only later in the century. Few truly great writers were produced during the initial years of the republic, but writers were all learning what it means to be Mexican.

In the field of poetry three principal figures bridged the transition between the old and the new. All had been trained in the forms of neoclassicism. Two of them went on to excel in a genre not previously cultivated, that of patriotic poetry, and the other ushered in the beginning of romanticism. Andrés Quintana Roo, whom Fanny Calderón knew and judged to be "the best modern poet in Mexico" (Calderón de la Barca [1843] 1931, 348) had suffered much for the cause of independence and was the first to celebrate that independence in his "Ode to the 16th of September" (Jiménez Rueda 1944, 71). Francisco Ortega, a deputy and a historian as well as a poet, denounced the imperialism of Iturbide (Jiménez Rueda 1944, 70). And Francisco Manuel Sánchez de Tagle, a learned aristocrat and patriot, became a full exponent of romanticism in his poems of love and sorrow, religion, and country (García Rivas 1972, 2:27).

In 1826, during the short time that Claudio Linati was in Mexico City, he associated with the Cuban poet José María Heredia in the publication of El Iris, the first literary periodical of independent Mexico. Much of the poetry and criticism in El Iris was by Heredia, who also introduced his readers to English literature and romanticism. Heredia, because of his long residence and his contribution in Mexico, enjoys a unique place of honor in Mexican letters (García Rivas 1972, 2:19–20).

Romanticism drew on European models and gave expression to the revolutionary spirit. It became the predominant literary style, but was adapted to individual tastes. Harking back to the past, José Joaquín Pesado sought to interpret religious dogma and theology and to create an indigenous poetry by reviving the setting and customs of pre-Columbian legends. Religion too was the concern of his physician friend Manuel Carpio, whose first poem, published in 1832, was "Ode to the Virgin of Guadalupe." Other religious poems by Carpio were classic in form but romantic in his imaginative depiction of the mysterious Orient (Jiménez Rueda 1944, 96–98).

Almost by chance, the notable literary Academy of Letrán was founded in 1836 by the poet brothers José María and Juan Nepomuceno Lacunza, Manuel Tossiat Ferrer, and Guillermo Prieto. The four met regularly in a room of the Colegio de San Juan de Letrán to discuss literature and to critique each other's work. When Andrés Quintana Roo, the acknowledged dean of Mexican poetry, happened one day to join the gathering, he was declared the perpetual president. Membership grew to include a diversity of writers of all persuasions—the only requisite being the presentation of an original piece of poetry or prose unanimously accepted by the group (Prieto 1906, 1:165–66). The discussions that took place stimulated the members to study grammarians in order to perfect their powers of expression. At the same time literature was both democratized and Mexicanized, since merit alone was recognized, without regard to age, position, social class, or wealth (Wilson 1941, 173). For twenty years, until 1856, the Academy of Letrán exerted a strong influence as a cultural center (García Rivas 1972, 2:87).

Two of the regular associates at the Letrán Academy were the poet dramatists Fernando Calderón and Ignacio Rodríguez Galván (García Rivas 1972, 27–28). Their short and ill-fated lives were as romantic as the works they created. Calderón drew inspiration for his verse dramas from English history, with which he was none too familiar. His best work was the dramatic comedy *A ninguna de las tres,* or "None of the Three," which continues to be popular in Mexico (Salvat Editores de México, S.A. 1974, 7:224). Rodríguez Galván wrote about legends and episodes from the colonial past, which he interpreted freely. His finest achievement as a lyric poet was "Profecía," about Cuauhtémoc, the last Aztec emperor. And the poet Francisco González Bocanegra, who wrote the words to the national hymn, was another romantic poet who was also a dramatist.

On the other hand, the man recognized as the greatest Mexican dramatist of the nineteenth century, Manuel Eduardo de Gorostiza, who lived a romantic life as a liberal, soldier, and diplomat on both sides of the Atlantic, chose to write in classic style with a strict observance of the unities (Jiménez Rueda 1944, 100). Of his numerous plays which faithfully reflected manners and customs, his best known and most popular with the Mexican audiences was *Contigo pan y cebolla,* or "With You, Bread and Onion," a comedy that Fanny Calderón declared was "delightful" (Calderón de la Barca [1843] 1931, 347). Sartorius expressed little praise for the Mexican theater in general, but he considered the works of Gorostiza to be "about the best," and he mentioned that they had been "honourably received in Spain" (Sartorius [1858] 1961, 126). Another important dramatist was Fernando Orozco y Berra, who happened also to be a doctor, a journalist, and a novelist of some repute (García Rivas 1972, 2:114–15).

To consider the Mexican novel, we must revert briefly outside the time limits of the Santa Anna era to the years immediately preceding independence. The novel was without antecedents in colonial Mexico (García Rivas 1972, 2:129); nevertheless, before the period ended, one of the most completely Mexican novels was produced by one of Mexico's most representative writers, José Joaquín Fernández de Lizardi, who was born in 1776 and died in 1827. He was a journalist, poet, dramatist, and novelist. As a journalist writing under the pseudonym of El Pensador Mexicano, he espoused the cause of independence and freedom of the press, and for a time suffered imprisonment. As a novelist he published in installments in 1816 the first and finest of his four novels, *El periquillo sarniento*, or "The Itching Parrot." The time was ripe for such a book, which portrayed the characteristics of the mestizo middle class. Inspired by Spanish picaresque novels, Fernández de Lizardi narrated the adventures of Pedro Sarniento, a mestizo in the service of many masters (Jiménez Rueda 1944, 103–104). In doing so, he revealed the life and customs of Mexico's multilayered society. Romantic tendencies are perceived in Fernández de Lizardi, as well as realism, naturalism, a touch of satire, and a markedly moralistic tone (Jiménez Rueda 1944, 102).

The door was now open for the writers of romantic and historical novels, but few would be truly distinguished until later in the century. We can, however, mention again Fernando Orozco y Berra, whose *La guerra de treinte años*, or "The Thirty Years' War," portrayed no historical war, but the protagonist's thirty years of experience as a Don Juan—this from an author whose own years totaled only twenty-nine. Popular too were novels published serially, each chapter crafted to keep readers in suspense and oblige them to buy the next weekly installment. The most successful writer of this genre was Manuel Payno. His *Fistol del diablo*, or "The Devil's Scarf Pin," written in 1845 and 1846, took its readers on a circuitous journey through all strata of Mexican society, scrutinizing every corner with minute detail and good humor. Current history found its way into the pages of this novel, and Payno censured the role of Santa Anna in the dismal events surrounding the fall of Mexico to the American troops. At one point the character Manuel "tried to organize some kind of defense, to save at least the heavy artillery, the store of munitions in the Citadel; but his efforts were in vain, no one obeyed and nothing but curses and recriminations against General Santa Anna were to be heard. He had compromised the city only to abandon it afterwards" (Payno [1845–46] 1967, 879). Payno was to continue writing until the end of his long life, dedicating equal energy to endeavors as poet, dramatist, professor of history, deputy, senator, and journalist (García Rivas 1972, 2:138).

As the new republic worked its way through those early years, seeking to bring order and identity out of chaos, it was inevitable that the intelligentsia should become embroiled in the quest for solutions. Men of letters were at the same time political activists using the pen, if not the sword, to defend their ideas. Very typical of this period was the proliferation of *hojas sueltas*, or handbills, published by almost every intellectual in an effort to attack or promote or explain something (Salvat Editores de México, S.A. 1974, 7:220). *Hojas sueltas* were the radio and the TV of the day, along with the newspapers.

With independence newspapers became more numerous and gained in importance. They served various purposes. Besides the local and, sometimes, foreign news, there were literary sections that introduced the public to new authors and foreign translations. There were sections on science and art and, of course, the inevitable advertisements. But most important were the editorials (Salvat Editores de México, S.A. 1974, 7:221). Every issue was discussed, every political persuasion aired. And every intellectual, whether federalist or centralist, conservative or liberal, either contributed to a newspaper or published his own. Journalism could at times be hazardous, as Guillermo Prieto once discovered. After a sarcastic and impudent article of his on the occasion of Santa Anna's birthday, Prieto found himself suddenly escorted into the presence of the angry dictator. After hearing more disrespectful words, Santa Anna advanced threateningly with a raised walking stick, and Prieto made a fast exit out a side door (Prieto 1906, 2:407–9).

Novelist-journalist Fernández de Lizardi, in his final years, 1826 and 1827, advanced the liberal cause in yet one more newspaper, *Correo Semanario de México*. In the 1830s José María Luis Mora, another liberal, especially in education, contributed to *El Observador de la República Mexicana* and *El Indicador de la Federación Mexicana* in support of the reforms of Gómez Farías (Salvat Editores de México, S.A. 1974, 7:222). Of more lasting influence for the liberal cause during the century was *El Siglo XIX,* published by Ignacio Cumplido. As *El Siglo XIX* was the

D. SIMPLICIO.

Periódico Burlesco, Crítico y Filosófico, por unos Simples.

TOMO II. SEGUNDA EPOCA. NUM. 24.

Este periódico se publica los miércoles y sábados de cada semana: consta de un pliego. Si el número de suscritores lo permite, se dará cada mes dos litografias, mientras se dispongan los grabados en madera.

Los números sueltos valen un real, y la suscricion es de 6 reales adelantados por 8 números para la capital, y 7 reales para fuera, franco de porte. Las suscriciones se reciben en los mismos lugares que la Revista de México.

VARIEDADES.

ESTUDIOS LITERARIOS DE DON SIMPLICIO.

No hay duda; ahora que estoy tan descansado como ministro del esterior, leamos, amigos; estudiemos, para ejercer la sublime magistratura de escritores públicos; lo mismo hará en sus ratos perdidos algun redactor *in partibus* del Diario, que puede llevar un púlpito en cada dedo; pero no quiero preceptos, quiero quisicosas, á las cuales mutatis mutandis. ¡Zas! allá va eso, y si me salen con que no sé lo que escribo, les enseño un Juvenal ó un Quebedo, ó alguno de esos, como pudiera hacer algun barbilampiño del *Tiempo*, cuando le echan en cara que no sabe lo que se dice.

Esto de escribir satírico es peliagudo, y hacerse el gracioso suele tener el leve defecto de no caer en gracia; pero si fueran graciosos todos los que caen en gracia, no tendriamos el ministerio que tenemos, y sabe Dios dónde estaria el que firmó la circular de imprenta.

Léamos.

Nigromante.—Desdeñando valerse de artificio,
La sátira maligna en la apariencia,
Sana de corazon, persigue al vicio,
"Por vengar la virtud y la inocencia."

D. Simplicio.—Como en México lo hace D. Simplicio. ¡Bravo! Clarito me brotó un remache endecasílabo, que me vie-

ne tan á pelo como á un monarquista un consulado en la Habana.

Pero con eso solo no soy literato; no seamos como dice el Tiempo: literato de Diccionario y Enciclopedias; eso no casa; pero siendo cierto lo que se diga, ¡qué mas dá! A propósito, yo para cierto vichos no quiero ser oportuno, sino importuno, y dé donde diere. Va de cuento.

Divertianse en un camino dos gabachos en componer versos; pero tan bribones los tales versos, tan truncos y disparatados, como artículos de plan de monarquía, ó como contrato de hacienda de los nuestros. Esmerábanse los copleros, y entre consonante y consonante se decian sendas injurias.

Uno dijo por fin:

Yo me llamo Juan Arana,
Que me gusto mucho tu hermana.

Indignóse el contrario, y colérico se retiró á caza de conceptos, no ya para aparecer poeta, sino en despique.—Silencio.—Oye:

Yo me llamo D. José Antonio,
Que enamoro y me corresponde tu madre.

—¡Hé, no pega! no sirve, necio, no es verso.
—No es verso, pero es cierto; esclamó triunfante el poetastro improvisado.

Así pues, yo D. Simplicio, quiero plantar una banderilla á ciertos vichos, aunque no sea con gracia, y.... no puedo, porque tengo la mollera dura como ley de proscripcion, ¡y luego, vea

bulwark for liberals, so was *La Cruz* for conservatives such as José Joaquín Pesado, who steadfastly defended the church (Jiménez Rueda 1944, 135). The newspaper *El Tiempo* and its continuation *El Universal* were largely the work of Lucas Alamán (Salvat Editores de México, S.A. 1974, 7:223), one of the most respected of conservatives.

In 1845 two life-long friends and liberals, Guillermo Prieto and Ignacio Ramírez, joined with Manuel Payno and Vicente Segura in the publication of the satirical literary-political periodical *Don Simplicio.* Here were two of the most brilliant and influential minds of Mexico: Prieto, a journalist, poet, dramatist, writer on customs and manners, senator, deputy, and minister; and Ramírez, also a journalist, poet, deputy, and minister, but also an educator and philosopher, orator, and scientist. Their association reached back to their days at the Academy of Letrán, when Ramírez, seeking membership into that select group, had created pandemonium with his speech which began "There is no God." All present were so astonished at his erudition and the beauty of his style that he gained unanimous approval even from those who opposed his viewpoint (Maciel 1980, 28).

With the publication of *Don Simplicio,* Ignacio Ramírez assumed the pseudonym El Nigromante, by which he was henceforth known, and Guillermo Prieto became "D. Simplicio." There was no institution or national problem that did not attract the attention of "the simpletons" (Maciel 1980, 32–33). The church was one object of their attacks. Prieto, in his *Memorias,* recalled some of the satirical verse he and Ramírez had composed which popularized the paper:

> With bonnet walks the soldier
> And with helmet goes the priest.
> The cross and the sword together
> Rule over the Nation,
> ¡Long live the beautiful union![1]
> (Prieto 1906, 2:184)

In addition, economic problems, the unstable political condition and the great inequalities in the social system were the objects of *Don Sim-*

---

[1]   Con bonete anda el soldado,
Y el clérigo con morrión.
La cruz y la espada unidas
Gobiernan á la Nación,
   ¡Que viva la bella unión!

plicio's principal thrusts (Maciel 1980, 33–34). Ramírez, who was more radical than liberal, believed that the country did not need reforms alone, but a profound change in the socioeconomic structure that had not been achieved with independence. *Don Simplicio* survived until 1847. The problems continued.

Guillermo Prieto and Ignacio Ramírez, as well as Manuel Payno, were destined once again to collaborate at a later date in another newspaper, *El Nigromante* (Merrifield de Castro n.d., 51). But in the meantime, in 1855, Antonio López de Santa Anna was ignominiously exiled for the last time, and in compliance with the Plan of Ayutla a special congress convened to draw up a new constitution. Both Ignacio Ramírez and Guillermo Prieto participated in that effort, but the Constitution of 1857 is part of another story. The era of Santa Anna had ended.

CONCLUSIONS

What was it then, the era of Santa Anna from 1822 till 1855? What have we seen as we have attempted to revisit the days and lives of the Mexican people during those tumultuous years?

We have witnessed a country longing for the rewards of independence, but torn by internal dissension, in which the precedent of the *pronunciamientos* was firmly set. Mexico was a country desperately in need of wise and honest statesmen, and to be sure, there were a few, such as Valentín Gómez Farías or Lucas Alamán, but for the most part Mexico was saddled with a series of weak, ambitious, or misguided leaders. Outstanding among the latter was Antonio López de Santa Anna. His influence for good or ill was felt in the lives of all. In and out of the presidency eleven times, he was never able to fulfill the expectations that his fellow citizens held for him. Instead, when his days of power had ended, he left a country impoverished and reduced in size by half. Mexico had been ravaged by wars and overwhelmed by economic woes and profiteering.

How did these adversities affect society? Curiously, life in Mexico was hardly disturbed. Calamities brought about by the revolutions and wars were never ubiquitous, but sporadic in time and place. In between battles life in the capital was as gay and frivolous as if the firing and killing had never taken place. In spite of the bleak background, gaiety and festivities prevailed. The population in remote parts of Mexico was

241

not even aware of what was going on elsewhere in their country, and quite often did not care.

Independence from Spain did not improve the lot of the Indians. Their way of life and their status in society deteriorated as they were stripped of the protection of the Spanish crown. They lost lands and were often displaced. The mestizos began now to take advantage of new opportunities and at times to rise on the social scale. The white man, however, was still the master in Mexico as he had been in New Spain, although Creoles now took the place of Spaniards in positions of power. The Gordoa family, with their mines and haciendas, were never in a more advantageous situation.

Although Mexico City was the center of wealth and political authority, as well as the favorite battleground for factions, every town throughout the country had a social and political life of its own. A city like Puebla, for example, rivaled and even surpassed the capital in many ways. While life in towns, large and small, preserved its unique blend of history and customs, both European and Indian, the pleasures and pastimes of the capital—the theater, bullfights, the calendar of holidays, and gambling—were enjoyed by people the country over.

Much of the fabric of life of colonial days continued unchanged in the early years of the republic and underwent only a gradual evolution. The various means of transportation—the horse, the mule, porters and mule trains, carriages and stagecoaches, the *litera* and even the exotic sedan chair—were still in use. They only became more difficult to employ as the system of roads was allowed to fall into disrepair. The advent of modern improvements such as the railroad was still in the future.

Unchanged too was the feeling permeating all society, whether inherited from the Aztecs or from the medieval church, that death was a part of life. Death walked as a not unwelcome companion among the Mexicans.

But fresh winds were blowing. With the new openness of independence, Mexico was exposed to foreign influences as never before, and no country was more admired than France. There was real progress in certain areas of life. No one could deny the advances made, even in minute degrees, in the lives of some of the workers. Working conditions in the textile mills and in the mines were becoming less oppressive. Foreign investments brought new opportunities, and Mexican entrepreneurs such as Esteban Antuñano began to promote innovative ideas for the welfare of common people.

Although the need far exceeded the resources, a valiant effort was launched during the first years of the republic to provide education for all. The Lancasterian schools were the finest examples of the attempt. The benefits of independence may be more readily seen in the fields of arts and letters, where there was a newfound freedom of expression, a loosening of restrictions. Artists and writers were free to examine themselves, to question, to disagree, and to begin to understand themselves as citizens of the nation of Mexico. The examples of painter Juan Cordero, dramatists Fernando Calderón and Ignacio Rodríguez Galván, and journalists Guillermo Prieto and Ignacio Ramírez come readily to mind.

The transition from colony to independent country may have been characterized by political and economic chaos, but Mexico endured and was sustained by its patient and long-suffering citizenry, who changed but slowly. The Santa Anna era was little more than the first step on the long road toward self-realization and nationhood.

REFERENCES

Adams, David Bergen. 1971. "The Tlaxcalan Colonies of Spanish Coahuila and Nuevo León: An Aspect of the Settlement of Northern Mexico." Ph.D. diss., University of Texas. Ann Arbor, Mich.: University Microfilms International, 1974.

Alamán, Lucas. 1849–52. *Historia de Méjico*. Vol. 5. México: Editorial Jus, 1942.

Alessio Robles, Vito. 1934. *Saltillo en la historia y la leyenda*. México: A. del Bosque.

Altman, Ida, and James Lockhart, eds. 1976. *Provinces of Early Mexico: Variants of Spanish American Regional Evolution*. Los Angeles: University of California, Los Angeles, Latin American Center.

Alvarez y Alvarez de la Cadena, Luis, ed. 1945. *México: leyendas, costumbres, trajes y danzas*. 2d. ed. México: Jesús Medina, 1970.

Arizpe, Raphael R. 1900. *El alumbrado público en la ciudad de México*. México: Tip. y lit. "La Europea."

Bancroft, Hubert Howe. 1883–90. *The Works of Hubert Howe Bancroft*. Vols. 1–5, *The Native Races of the Pacific States of North America*, 1886. Vols. 9–14, *The History of Mexico*, 1885 and 1887. Vols. 15–16, *History of the North Mexican States and Texas*, 1889. San Francisco: A. L. Bancroft.

Baqueiro Foster, Gerónimo. 1964. *Historia de la música en México*. Vol. 3, *La música en el período independiente*. México: Secretaría de Educación Pública.

Barinetti, Carlo. 1841. *A Voyage to Mexico and Havana*. New York: C. Vinten.

Bartlett, John Russell. 1854. *Personal Narrative of Explorations and Incidents in Texas, New Mexico, California, Sonora, and Chihuahua*. 2 vols. Chicago: Rio Grande Press, 1965.

Beaufoy, Mark. 1828. *Mexican Illustrations, Founded upon Facts*. London: Carpenter and Son.

Bellemare, Louis de [pseud., Gabriel Ferry]. 1856. *Vagabond Life in Mexico*. New York: Harper and Brothers.

Berlandier, Jean-Louis. [1980]. *Journey to Mexico During the Years 1826–1834*. Translated from the French by Sheila M. Ohlendorf. Austin: Texas State Historical Association.

Blanchard, P., and A. Dauzats. 1839. *San Juan de Ulúa; ou relation de l'expédition française au Mexique*. Paris: Fide.

Borah, Woodrow, and Sherburne F. Cook. 1960. *The Population of Central Mexico in 1548: An Analysis of the Suma de vistas de pueblos*. Berkeley: University of California Press.

Boyer, Richard E., and Keith A. Davis. 1973. *Urbanization in 19th Century Latin America: Statistics and Sources*. Los Angeles: Latin American Center, University of California Press.

Brading, D. A. 1971. *Miners and Merchants in Bourbon Mexico 1763–1810*. Cambridge: Cambridge University Press.

———. 1978. *Haciendas and Ranchos in the Mexican Bajío*. New York: Cambridge University Press.

Brenner, Anita. 1929. *Idols Behind Altars*. New York: Harcourt, Brace.

Bullock, W. 1824. *Six Months' Residence and Travel in Mexico*. London: John Murray.

Cabrera Ipiña, Octaviano. 1970. *El Real de Catorce*. 2d. ed. México: Sociedad Potosina de Estudios Históricos, 1975.

Calderón de la Barca, Frances Erskine Inglis. 1843. *Life in Mexico During a Residence of Two Years in That Country*. New York: E. P. Dutton, 1931.

———. *Life in Mexico: The Letters of Fanny Calderón de la Barca*. Edited and annotated by Howard T. and Marion Hall Fisher. Garden City, N.Y.: Doubleday and Company, Inc. 1966.

Callcott, Wilfrid Hardy. 1936. *Santa Anna: The Story of an Enigma Who Once was Mexico*. Norman: University of Oklahoma Press.

Campos, Rubén M. 1928. *El folklore y la música mexicana. Investigación acerca de la cultura musical en México (1525–1925)*. México: Talleres Gráficos de la Nación.

Carpenter, William W. 1851. *Travels and Adventure in Mexico*. New York: Harper and Brothers.

Charlot, Jean. 1962. *Mexican Art and the Academy of San Carlos, 1785–1915*. Austin: University of Texas Press.

Chaunu, Pierre. 1975. *Le Temps des reformes*. Paris: Fayard.

Chevalier, François. 1952. *La Formation des grands domaines au Mexique; terre et société aux XVIe–XVIIe siècles*. Paris: Institut de l'ethnologie.

Coe, Michael D. 1966. *The Maya*. London: Thames and Hudson, 1980.

Covarrubias, Miguel. 1946. *Mexico South: The Isthmus of Tehuantepec*. New York: Alfred Knopf.

Crawford, Ann Fears, ed. 1967. *The Eagle: The Autobiography of Santa Anna.* Austin, Pemberton Press.

Cross, Harry Edward. 1976. "The Mining Economy of Zacatecas: Mexico in the 19th Century." Ph.D. diss., University of California, Berkeley. Ann Arbor, Mich.: University Microforms International, 1980.

Cruz, Juana Inés de la. 1938. *Obras escogidas.* 3d. ed. Buenos Aires: Espasa Calpe, 1941.

Cué Cánovas, Agustín. 1947. *Historia social y económica de México.* México: Editorial América.

Dahlgren, Charles B. 1887. *Minas históricas de la república Mexicana.* México: Oficina Tipográfica de la Secretaría de Fomento.

Díaz-Berrio Fernández, Salvador. 1976. *Zona de monumentos históricos de Real de Catorce, SLP, estudio para su rehabilitación.* San Luis Potosí, México: Instituto Nacional de Antropología e Historia.

Díaz del Castillo, Bernal. 1956. *The Discovery and Conquest of Mexico.* Translated from the Spanish by A. P. Maudslay. New York: Farrar, Straus, and Cudahy.

Diccionario Porrúa de historia, biografía y geografía de México. 1964. México: Editorial Porrúa, 1970.

Enciclopedia de México. 1966–77. 12 vols. México: Instituto de la Enciclopedia de México.

Fernández, Justino. 1983. *El arte del siglo XIX en México.* 1983. México: U.N.A.M.

Floris Margadant, Guillermo. 1980. "Official Mexican Attitudes Toward the Indians: An Historical Essay." *Tulane Law Review* 54:964–86.

[Forbes]. 1851. *A Trip to Mexico or Recollections on a Ten-Month's Ramble in 1849–50.* London: Smith, Elder.

Fossey, Mathieu de. 1857. *Le Mexique.* Paris: Plon.

García Cubas, Antonio. 1904. *El libro de mis recuerdos; narraciones históricas, anecdóticas y de costumbres mexicanas anteriores al actual estado social.* México: Impr. de A. García Cubas, Hermanos sucesores.

García Rivas, Heriberto. 1971–72. *Historia de la literatura mexicana.* 2 vols. México: Textos Universitarios.

Gibson, Charles. 1964. *The Aztecs Under Spanish Rule.* Stanford, Calif.: Stanford University Press.

Gilliam, Albert M. 1847. *Travels in Mexico During the Years 1843 and 44.* Aberdeen: George Clark and Son.

González, Luis. 1981. "Naissance de l'état mexicain." In *Petite Histoire du Mexique.* Paris: Armand Colin.

Gordoa Family Papers, 1822–46. Latin American Library, Tulane University, New Orleans, La.

Gregg, Josiah. 1844. *Commerce of the Prairies by Josiah Gregg.* Edited by Milo Milton Quaife. Chicago: R. R. Donnelley and Sons. 1926.

Gruening, Ernest Henry. 1928. *Mexico, and Its Heritage.* New York: Century Co.

Hall, Basil. 1824. *Extracts from a Journal Written on the Coasts of Chili, Peru, and*

Mexico in the Years 1820, 1821, 1822. 2 vols. Edinburgh: Archibald Constable.

Hardy, Robert William Hale. 1829. *Travel in the Interior of Mexico in 1825, 1826, 1827 and 1828.* London: H. Coburn and R. Berilly.

Harris, Charles H. III. 1964. *The Sánchez Navarros: A Socioeconomic Study of a Coahuilan Latifundio, 1846–1853.* Chicago: Loyola University Press.

————. [1975]. *A Mexican Family Empire: The Latifundio of the Sanchez Navarros, 1765–1867.* Austin: University of Texas Press.

Hoyo, Eugenio del. 1960. "Vignette of the City." *Artes de México* 194–95: 133–44.

Historia general de México. 1976. 4 vols. México: Colegio de México.

Huizinga, J. 1919. *Le Déclin du Moyen Age.* Translated from the Dutch by J. Bastin. Paris: Petite Bibiothèque Payot, 1967.

Humboldt, Alexander von. 1822. *Ensayo político sobre el reino de la Nueva-España.* 4 vols. Translated from the French by Vicente González Arnao. Paris: Rosa.

Jiménez Rueda, Julio. 1944. *Letras mexicanas.* México: Fondo de Cultura Económica.

Jones, Oakah L., Jr. 1968. *Santa Anna.* New York: Twayne Publishers.

Koppe, Carl Wilhelm. 1835. *Cartas a la patria: dos cartas alemanas sobre el México de 1830.* Edited and translated by Juan A. Ortega. México: Imprenta Universitaria, 1955.

Lasserre, Guy. 1974. *Les Amériques du Centre.* Paris: Presses Universitaire de France.

Latrobe, Charles Joseph. 1836. *The Rambler in Mexico.* New York: Harper and Brothers.

Lewis, Oscar. 1949. *Sea Routes to the Gold Fields: The Migration by Water to California in 1849–1852.* New York: Alfred A. Knopf.

Lyon, G. F. 1828. *Journal of a Residence and Tour in the Republic of Mexico in the Year 1826; with Some Account of the Mines of That Country.* 2 vols. London: John Murray.

McBride, George McCutchen. 1923. *The Land System of Mexico.* New York: American Geographical Society.

Maciel, David R. 1980. *Ignacio Ramírez ideólogo del liberalismo social en México.* México: U.N.A.M.

MacLachlan, Colin M., and Jaime E. Rodríguez O. 1980. *The Forging of the Cosmic Race: A Reinterpretation of Colonial Mexico.* Berkeley: University of California Press.

Madsen, William. 1960. "Christo-paganism: A Study of Mexican Religious Syncretism." *Nativism and Syncretism.* Publication 19, pp. 105–80. New Orleans: Middle American Research Institute, Tulane University.

Marcy, Randolph Barnes. 1854. *Exploration of the Red River of Louisiana in the Year 1852.* Washington, D.C.: A. C. P. Nicholson, Public Printer.

Mason, R. H. 1852. *Pictures of Life in Mexico.* 2 vols. London: Smith Elder.

Mayer, Brantz. 1844. *Mexico as It Was and as It Is*. New York: J. Winchester.

Merrifield de Castro, Ellen Elvira. N.d. *Guillermo Prieto y su visión sobre la historia de México*. México: U.N.A.M. Facultad de Filosofía y Letras.

Meyer, Michael C., and William L. Sherman. 1979. *The Course of Mexican History*. 3d. ed. New York: Oxford University Press, 1987.

Miller, Robert Ryal. 1985. *Mexico: A History*. Norman: University of Oklahoma Press.

Nance, Joseph Milton. 1963. *After San Jacinto*. Austin: University of Texas Press.

Norman, Benjamin Moore. 1845. *Rambles by Land and Water, or Notes of Travel in Cuba and Mexico*. New York: Paine and Burgess.

Orbigny, Alcide d'. 1836. *Voyage pittoresque dans les deux Amériques*. Paris: Chez L. Tendré.

Parkes, Henry Bamford. 1938. *A History of Mexico*. Boston: Houghton Mifflin, 1950.

Pasquel, Leonardo. 1969. *Biografía integral de la ciudad de Veracruz, 1519–1969*. México: Editorial Citlaltépetl.

Paynes, Robert. 1968. *Mexico*. New York: Harcourt, Brace and World.

Payno, Manuel. 1845–46. *El fistol del diablo*. México: Editorial Porrúa, 1967.

———. 1889–91. *Los bandidos de Río Frío*. 2d. ed. México: Editorial Porrúa, 1964.

Paz, Octavio. 1950. *El laberinto de la soledad*. 2d. ed. México: Fondo de Cultura Económica, 1959.

Peña, José Enrique de la. 1975. *With Santa Anna in Texas: A Personal Narrative of the Revolution*. Translated by Carmen Perry. College Station: Texas A&M University Press.

Poinsett, Joel Robert. 1824. *Notes on Mexico Made in the Autumn of 1822 Accompanied by an Historical Sketch of the Revolution, and Translations of Official Reports on the Present State of That Country . . . By a Citizen of the United States*. Philadelphia: H. C. Caley and I. Lea.

Potash, Robert A. 1983. *Mexican Government and Industrial Development in the Early Republic*. Amherst: University of Massachusetts Press.

Priestley, Herbert Imgram. 1923. *The Mexican Nation: A History*. New York: Macmillan, 1926.

Prieto, Guillermo. 1906. *Memorias de mis tiempos*. 2 vols. Paris: Vda. de C. Bouret.

Ramírez, José Fernando. 1950. *Mexico During the War with the United States*. Edited by Walter V. Scholes. Translated by Elliot B. Scherr. Columbia: University of Missouri Press.

Ramos, Samuel. 1962. *Profile of Man and Culture in Mexico*. Translated by Peter G. Earle. Austin: University of Texas Press.

Reed, Nelson. 1964. *The Caste War of Yucatan*. Stanford, Calif.: Stanford University Press.

Reyes de la Maza, Luis. 1969. *El teatro mexicano durante la independencia (1810–1839)*. México: U.N.A.M

————. 1972. *Cien años de teatro en México 1810–1910*. México: Secretaría de Educación Pública.

Rives, George Lockart. 1913. *The United States and Mexico, 1821–1848*. 2 vols. New York: Charles Scribner's Sons.

Robertson, William Parish. 1853. *A Visit to Mexico, by the West Indies, Yucatan, and United States*. 2 vols. London: Simpkin, Marshall.

Roeder, Ralph. 1947. *Juárez and His Mexico: A Biographical History*. 2 vols. New York: Viking Press.

Romero, Matías. 1898. *Geographical and Statistical Notes on Mexico*. New York: G. P. Putnam's Sons.

Salvat Editores de México,S.A. 1974. *Historia de México*. 11 vols. México: Salvat Editores de México, S.A.

Sartorius, Christian. 1858. *Mexico About 1850*. Stuttgart: Brockhaus, 1961.

Simpson, Eyler N. 1937. *The Ejido: Mexico's Way Out*. Chapel Hill: University of North Carolina Press.

Simpson, Lesley Byrd. 1941. *Many Mexicos*. 4th ed. rev. Berkeley: University of California Press, 1966.

El Sol. 1824. México. (Newspaper.)

Soustelle, Jacques. 1955. *La Vie quotidienne des Aztèques à la veille de la Conquête*. Paris: Hachette.

Spencer, Robert F., Jesse D. Jennings, et al. 1965. *The Native Americans*. New York: Harper and Row.

Stephens, John L. 1841. *Incidents of Travel in Central America, Chiapas, and Yucatan*. 2 vols. New York: Harper and Brothers, 1969.

————. 1843. *Incidents of Travel in Yucatan*. 2 vols. New York: Dover Publications, 1963.

Stevenson, Robert. 1952. *Music in Mexico: A Historical Survey*. New York: Thomas Y. Crowell Company.

Tayloe, Edward Thornton. 1959. *Mexico, 1825–1828: The Journal and Correspondence of E. T. T*. Chapel Hill: University of North Carolina Press.

Taylor, Bayard. 1850. *Eldorado or Adventures in the Path of Empire*. New York: Alfred A. Knopf, 1949.

Thompson, Donald E. 1960. "Maya Paganism and Christianity." *Nativism and Syncretism*. Publication 19, pp. 1–35. New Orleans: Middle American Research Institute, Tulane University.

Thompson, Waddy. 1846. *Recollections of Mexico*. New York: Wiley and Putnam.

United States Legation in Mexico Papers, 1824–43. Latin American Library, Tulane University, New Orleans, La.

Vaillant, George C. 1941. *Aztecs of Mexico: Origin, Rise, and Fall of the Aztec Nation*. Garden City, N.Y.: Doubleday, Doran.

Valadés, José C. 1936. *Mexico, Santa Anna y la guerra de Texas*. México: Editorial Diana, 1979.

Vargas Martínez, Ubaldo. 1961. *La Ciudad de México (1325–1960)*. México: Departamento del Distrito Federal.

Varona, Esteban Antonio de. 1956. *Acapulco.* Translated from the Spanish by Leonard Cooper. México: Unión Gráfica.

―――. 1957. *Oaxaca.* Translated from the Spanish by Leonard Cooper. México: Unión Gráfica.

Vigneaux, Ernest. 1863. *Souvenirs d'un prisonnier de guerre français au Méxique.* Paris: Hachette.

Wallace, Ernest, and E. Adamson Hoebel. 1954. *The Comanches: Lords of the South Plains.* Norman: University of Oklahoma Press.

Ward, H. G. 1828. *Mexico in 1827.* 2 vols. London: Henry Colburn.

Wilson, Irma. 1941. *Mexico: A Century of Educational Thought.* Reprint, Westport, Conn.: Greenwood Press, 1974.

Wilson, Robert Anderson. 1855. *Mexico: Its Peasants and Its Priests.* New York: Harper and Brothers.

INDEX

253